FROM PRIMITIVE TO INDIGENOUS

The academic study of Indigenous Religions developed historically from missiological and anthropological sources, but little analysis has been devoted to this classification within departments of religious studies. Evaluating this assumption in the light of case studies drawn from Zimbabwe, Alaska and shamanic traditions, and in view of current debates over 'primitivism', James Cox mounts a defence for the scholarly use of the category 'Indigenous Religions'.

VITALITY OF INDIGENOUS RELIGIONS

Series Editors
Graham Harvey, Open University, UK
Lawrence Martin, University of Wisconsin, Eau Claire, USA
Tabona Shoko, University of Zimbabwe, Zimbabwe
Ines Talamantez, University of California, USA

Ashgate's *Vitality of Indigenous Religions* series offers an exciting new cluster of research monographs, drawing together volumes from leading international scholars across a wide range of disciplinary perspectives. Indigenous religions are vital and empowering for many thousands of indigenous peoples globally, and dialogue with, and consideration of, these diverse religious life-ways promises to challenge and refine the methodologies of a number of academic disciplines, whilst greatly enhancing understandings of the world.

This series explores the development of contemporary indigenous religions from traditional, ancestral precursors, but the characteristic contribution of the series is its focus on their living and current manifestations. Devoted to the contemporary expression, experience and understanding of particular indigenous peoples and their religions, books address key issues which include: the sacredness of land, exile from lands, diasporic survival and diversification, the indigenization of Christianity and other missionary religions, sacred language, and re-vitalization movements. Proving of particular value to academics, graduates, postgraduates and higher level undergraduate readers worldwide, this series holds obvious attraction to scholars of Native American studies, Maori studies, African studies and offers invaluable contributions to religious studies, sociology, anthropology, geography and other related subject areas.

OTHER TITLES IN THE SERIES

Karanga Indigenous Religion in Zimbabwe
Health and Well-Being
Tabona Shoko
ISBN 978–0–7546–5881–8

Indigenous Peoples' Wisdom and Power
Affirming Our Knowledge Through Narratives
Edited by Nomalungelo I. Goduka and Julian E. Kunnie
ISBN 978–0–7546–1597–2

Indigenous Diasporas and Dislocations
Edited by Graham Harvey and Charles D. Thompson Jr.
ISBN 978–0–7546–3906–0

The Vitality of Karamojong Religion
Dying Tradition or Living Faith?
Ben Knighton
ISBN 978–0–7546–0383–2

201.42 COX

15 MAY 2025

WITHDRAWN

York St John

3 8025 00525008 2

From Primitive to Indigenous

The Academic Study of Indigenous Religions

JAMES L. COX
University of Edinburgh, UK

YORK ST. JOHN
COLLEGE LIBRARY

ASHGATE

© James L. Cox 2007

.All rights reserved. No part of this publication may be reproduced, stored in a retrieval system or transmitted in any form or by any means, electronic, mechanical, photocopying, recording or otherwise without the prior permission of the publisher.

James L. Cox has asserted his moral right under the Copyright, Designs and Patents Act, 1988, to be identified as the author of this work.

Published by
Ashgate Publishing Limited
Gower House
Croft Road
Aldershot
Hampshire GU11 3HR
England

Ashgate Publishing Company
Suite 420
101 Cherry Street
Burlington, VT 05401–4405
USA

Ashgate website: http://www.ashgate.com

British Library Cataloguing in Publication Data
Cox, James L. (James Leland)
    From primitive to indigenous : the academic study of indigenous religions. –
    (Vitality of indigenous religions series)
    1. Religions – Study and teaching 2. Indigenous peoples – Religion
    I. Title
    200.7'1

    ISBN 978–0–7546–5569–5

Library of Congress Cataloging-in-Publication Data
Cox, James L. (James Leland)
    From primitive to indigenous : the academic study of indigenous religions / James L. Cox.
        p. cm. – (Vitality of indigenous religions series)
    Includes bibliographical references and index.
    ISBN 978–0–7546–5569–5 (hardcover : alk. paper)
    1. Indigenous peoples – Religion.
    I. Title.

    BL380.C69 2007
    201'.4–dc22   2006029305

This book is printed on acid free paper

Printed and bound in Great Britain by MPG Books Ltd, Bodmin, Cornwall

To Andrew F. Walls

A mentor, example and friend

Contents

List of Maps

Acknowledgements

When I first took up my appointment in the University of Edinburgh in 1993, I was asked to devise lectures for a section on 'Primal Religions' in the pre-Honours 'World Religions' course. I was confronted immediately by a series of problems: How should I define 'primal religions'? What characteristics could I employ to describe adequately the immense variety of religious practices of peoples living in diverse locations around the globe? How could I compress into a five-week slot sufficient material to make my lectures meaningful to students? These questions challenged me to consider the viability of such a topic in a religious studies curriculum. I became convinced that the advantages of teaching the subject outweighed its theoretical and practical difficulties, particularly since students were being taught the so-called major religious traditions, each within a similar time frame. I concluded, nonetheless, that the entire approach to teaching primal religions alongside the world religions needed radical re-thinking. This book represents my reflections on this topic over the past decade, during which time the University of Edinburgh has introduced into its Religious Studies Honours degree a specialization in what is now called 'Indigenous Religions'. This has been accompanied during the same period by a growth of academic interest internationally in the study of Indigenous Religions.

I am indebted to many people who in numerous ways have encouraged me to undertake this project and have engaged in discussions with me during its development. I am particularly grateful to Professor Andrew Walls, who for more than thirty years has been my mentor, example and inspiration. Although I eventually have taken the study of Indigenous Religions in a different direction from what I think would be his own preferred course, I am aware that I have built my thinking on the groundbreaking work of a giant in this field. I also want to acknowledge Professor Alistair Kee, who suggested to me after I became convener of the Religious Studies Subject Group in 1999, that we should develop the specialization in Indigenous Religions in a way that would make Edinburgh's religious studies programme distinctive from any other in the United Kingdom. As I pursued this aim, I obtained consistent support from my colleagues in the School of Divinity, who have incorporated this subject into the overall academic profile of the School. I have also received repeated encouragement from my colleagues in Religious Studies, particularly Dr Jeanne Openshaw, who initially expressed reservations about the term 'indigenous' as a category for the study of religion, but subsequently has become a lynchpin in the programme, first by teaching with me an introductory course on Indigenous Religions and then by expanding her own expertise in India to consider 'religion from below' as part of her Indigenous Religions remit. Dr Jack Thompson, who now directs the Centre for the Study of Christianity in the Non-Western World (CSCNWW), has also provided invaluable teaching support in the programme, based on his many years of work in Malawi and on his extensive research on new religious movements generally. Dr Elizabeth Koepping has made important contributions from her own in-depth field studies conducted in Borneo. Before he accepted a major appointment in the University of Lund in 2005, Professor David Kerr participated in the teaching programme by offering a course on Islam in Africa, a section of which focused on Islamic influences within Indigenous Religions. Dr Afe Adogame, who joined the School of Divinity as Lecturer in World Christianity in 2005, has already made substantial contributions to the curriculum by offering courses in Indigenous Religions in West Africa and by examining the interaction between the new wave of charismatic Christian churches in Africa and traditional worldviews. I want also to express my thanks to Dr Steven Sutcliffe and to Dr Hannah Holtschneider, who have taken up many of my teaching and administrative responsibilities during my sabbatical year.

At the outset, I want to give particular recognition to Dr Graham Harvey of the Open University, who has played such an important role in recent years in promoting the study of Indigenous Religions. Although it will become clear to readers of this book that I differ markedly in many respects from his position, I want to underscore my high regard for his excellence as an academic researcher and writer. I have benefited from discussions with Dr Harvey over the years and I am extremely grateful for his input into the issues I discuss in this text. Despite the fact that I align myself generally with a methodology he rejects as being too closely based on Western dichotomies and Cartesian dualisms, I affirm his commitment to engaging with indigenous peoples in a humane and deeply respectful manner.

This project has been made possible by a grant from the Arts and Humanities Research Council (AHRC) under its very important and generous Research Leave Scheme. As a recipient of one these awards, I want to express my appreciation to the AHRC for reviewing my proposal so carefully and for deeming it worthy of support. The AHRC grant was matched by another semester's leave provided by the School of Divinity. Taken together, these awards have made it possible for me to complete the manuscript in a timely fashion. Throughout the year I have been relieved of my teaching and administrative duties with the full support of Professor David Fergusson, head of the School of Divinity, to whom I express my warmest appreciation. Finally, I would like to thank Ashgate for agreeing to publish this manuscript and especially to the Religion Editor, Sarah Lloyd, for her guidance during its preparation.

James L Cox
Edinburgh, July 2006

Introduction

Problems, Research Context
and Overview

The primary aim of this book is to analyse critically the history of and the assumptions underlying the use of the category 'Indigenous Religions' as a distinct tradition alongside 'world religions'.[1] I have been motivated to write such a book for many years as a direct result of my involvement in planning academic programmes in religious studies in numerous teaching and research contexts. I have found in general (although there are notable exceptions) that in most university departments of religion and in the textbooks they employ, religions continue to be taught and written about according to long-established divisions defined along lines dictated by the 'major traditions', usually consisting of Hinduism, Buddhism, Christianity, Islam and Judaism along with other combinations, sometimes including Confucianism, Taoism, Jainism or Sikhism. Typically, little attention is given to the study of traditions falling outside these main divisions. This omission has been noted recently by Jacob Olupona, who complains in the preface to his important edited book, *Beyond Primitivism*, that 'while the "world" religious traditions of Buddhism, Judaism, Hinduism, Islam, and Christianity are amply studied and represented in the academy, the study of "indigenous" religions is speciously cut off from religious studies' (2004: xiv). Olupona's observation underscores the point that if indigenous religious perspectives continue to be ignored, or at least marginalized in academic circles, a highly significant portion of the world's religious adherents will be excluded from scholarly research and teaching in religious studies.

This problem is not resolved simply by introducing courses into university curricula on Indigenous Religions. After some consideration, it soon becomes evident that to speak of Indigenous Religions as a single category is highly problematic, particularly since there are as many indigenous religious traditions as there are indigenous peoples, and because indigenous views often have been adapted into the world religions themselves. It would be impossible to cover adequately the religions of peoples who fit within such an all-encompassing classification. For this reason, where courses have been developed in universities in this field, they usually restrict their scope to the religions of peoples living within particular regions, such as African Indigenous Religions, or the beliefs and practices of Australian aboriginal peoples, or Native American religious traditions. In my own course on this topic in the University of Edinburgh, I focus on case examples, as I do in this book, based on my own research in Alaska and in Zimbabwe. Even this approach does not solve the

---

[1]   I am following the convention throughout this book of employing the upper case whenever the category Indigenous Religions is used in a comparable way to references to any world religion, such as Hinduism, Buddhism or Christianity. I am also using Indigenous Religions in the plural as opposed to the singular, which I explain at the conclusion of Chapter 4.

problem, since in restricted local studies, numerous variations occur in the traditions of the people, as soon becomes evident when comparing, for example, death practices of the Inupiat of northern Alaska with the Yup'ik speaking peoples of the southwest region of the state. In Zimbabwe, important variations in ritual practice can be observed even amongst neighbouring communities, while seemingly contradictory explanations of events have been recounted to me by those I have interviewed within the same village. If local differences of such magnitude exist within the same region, the problems for teaching Indigenous Religions are exacerbated when university lecturers offer courses on African Indigenous Religions or Native American religious traditions, and even appear insurmountable when lumped under the generic category, 'Indigenous Religions'.

Identifying which group is indigenous and which is not defines a further difficulty for researchers. In places like India, with an ancient history of engagement between various civilizations, the problem is so difficult that to speak of indigenous peoples tends to confuse issues of identity rather than to clarify them. Even in southern Africa, where encounters with European and Islamic traders and settlers are relatively recent, determining who is indigenous and who is not becomes a highly contentious issue, often loaded with political and ethnic overtones. In Zimbabwe, for example, as we will see in more detail later, the Ndebele occupation of the western and south western part of the country occurred in the early nineteenth century, when largely Shona-speaking peoples were absorbed into a new Zulu state (Bourdillon, 1987: 14). The Shona, on the other hand, do not represent the indigenous people of the region, if by indigenous we mean original to the land, since they form part of general Bantu migrations from the central regions of Africa arriving in what is now Zimbabwe perhaps as early as the first century CE (Beach, 1980: 7–9). As Alan Barnhard and Justin Kendrik (2001: viii) point out: 'Those known as Bushmen, San Basarwa, Ju/'hoan, Kua, Khoe or N/oakhoe, have, according to some specialists, a cultural continuity in those lands of perhaps 400 centuries'. Yet, for political reasons in Zimbabwe, indigenous rights to the land are asserted for such 'non-indigenous peoples' as the Shona and the Ndebele in opposition to the colonial settlers who appropriated much of the best farmland for themselves throughout the first half of the twentieth century.

The political connotations to the term 'indigenous' extend to global contexts, since it is meaningless to speak of 'indigenous' without implying its counterpart 'non-indigenous', and the colonial history that produced both categories. This point has been made forcefully by Charles Long (2004: 89), who notes that 'although the notion of the indigenous implies the identity and reality of a people prior to the impingement of the worlds of modernity, in point of fact the "indigenous" has little meaning apart from the colonial and imperial cultures in the modern period'. This demands that students of Indigenous Religions not only become aware of the historical contexts associated with the term, but it moves the discussion towards issues of power generated by the typically exotic construction of the 'Other' embedded within late nineteenth- and early twentieth- century studies of 'primitive' peoples conducted by early anthropologists, colonial administrators, missionaries and others working within the hegemonic institutions of European and American expansion. The seemingly humanistic and egalitarian motives implied in Olupona's comment that I quoted above thus may veil instead a longstanding Western philosophical and theological assumption, called 'primitivism' by Armin Geertz (2004: 50), which he characterizes as the longing 'for another time or another place, a distant paradise, or a future utopia' and which he aligns with nineteenth-century assumptions about social and cultural evolution.

Although the term 'indigenous' provides the primary focus for my discussion in this book, its connection to the equally contentious category 'religion' cannot be avoided. Scholars often argue that amongst indigenous societies religion cannot be separated from other aspects of life. Every act, from eating to sexual intercourse, has religious implications. To follow a Western dualistic model, where religion is dissected from the secular, on this line of thinking only muddies the water when this is used to analyse indigenous societies. And yet, it is perfectly clear that an indigenous person knows the difference, for example, between a sacred mountain that is subject to strict prohibitions and a mountain that bears no such significance for the community. Or, indigenous people know that certain behaviours pertain within ritual contexts that do not apply in other parts of life. The argument put forward by those like John Mbiti, and many others who generalize about Indigenous Religions, that the practitioners are (in Mbiti's case with reference to Africa) 'notoriously religious' (Mbiti, 1969: 1) begins to look patronizing when examined very closely. The most critical problem may result, however, not so much from the efforts amongst scholars of Indigenous Religions to stress the ubiquity of religion within indigenous societies as it does from the concept 'religion' itself, which clearly has been created out of a Western discourse about certain types of practices, beliefs and actions that have strong theological antecedents. An important consideration in this book, therefore, will be to analyse the term religion, particularly as it is used in connection with the study of indigenous societies.

The Research Context

A lively debate contesting the relationship between Indigenous Religions and so-called Western primitivism has occurred recently, which I consider to be so important that I have made it the principal topic in the final chapter of this book. As we will see, a pivotal contribution to the debate has been made by Armin Geertz who asks in the title to his paper in Olupona's *Beyond Primitivism*, 'Can we move beyond primitivism?' (2004: 37–70). Geertz's paper prompted J.G. Platvoet (2004: 52), to criticize Graham Harvey's recent spate of edited volumes on Indigenous Religions as an example of 'neo-primitivism'. Harvey, who is recognized as one of the key international scholars on Indigenous Religions, responded robustly to this criticism by defending his work as fully academic and empathetic, primarily because the methods he advocates are self-reflexive and dialogical (2004: 38–9). A great deal of the current international attention being directed towards Indigenous Religions can be attributed to Harvey, who now has edited or co-edited four volumes on this topic (2000, 2002a; Harvey and Thompson, 2005; Ralls-MacLeod and Harvey, 2000), written two books of related interest (1997, 2005a) and also has edited a useful reader on shamanism (2002b). In his introduction to many of these volumes, Harvey draws attention to the ways indigenous peoples have been classified in prior literature, and notes that many of the terms employed, such as primitive, primal, tribal, preliterate, non-literate and stone-age, had the effect of denigrating the cultures they were intended to describe (Ralls-MacLeod and Harvey, 2000: 6).

Harvey is not alone in pioneering this field, of course. He follows a long line of scholars who have given attention to the impact of nomenclature on attitudes, some of whom worked in missionary contexts (see Ludwig and Adogame, 2004).

As early as the 1940s, for example, E Geoffrey Parrinder (1949: 2), who at the time was a Methodist missionary working in west Africa, drew attention to the power of language by exposing the pejorative and degrading connotations of the widely applied term, fetishism. Mircea Eliade at the University of Chicago, who by the mid-1960s was acknowledged as one of the leading figures in the academic study of religions, discussed 'primitive religions' in many of his books (often under the category, 'archaic'), and even edited an anthology of those writing about the world's religions under the intriguing title, *From Primitives to Zen* (1967). As I will outline in Chapter 1 of the present volume, the teaching of 'Primal Religions' was initiated in the 1970s in the University of Aberdeen by Andrew Walls and Harold Turner. Prior to that, Turner (1971) had written at Leicester about 'tribal religions', which he and Walls translated at Aberdeen into 'primal', arguing that it was a better descriptive category than any other under which to consolidate similar phenomena found around the globe. When the Aberdeen programme moved to Edinburgh in 1987, 'Primal Religions' as a distinct topic was taught in the postgraduate Centre for the Study of Christianity in the Non-Western World and was introduced into the undergraduate programme by John Parratt. In my own article, 'The Classification "Primal Religions" as a Non-Empirical Christian Theological Construct', first published in 1995 and revised for a chapter of my book, *Rational Ancestors: Scientific Rationality and African Indigenous Religions* (1998), I argue that the term 'primal' not only is unwarranted on scientific grounds, but even more tellingly, proves useful for theologians looking for a pseudo-scientific justification for the missionary theory that the 'primal' worldview provides a base on which all world religions are built and thus, in the case of Christianity, anticipates the fullness of the message of Jesus Christ. At the conclusion, I suggest that the term 'indigenous' should replace 'primal' as a category in religious studies, and I call for local and specific applications of the term, but making a case for employing 'indigenous', as opposed to other categories, was not the reason I wrote the article. I have postponed this task until I could subject the term to a sustained critical analysis, as I am attempting to do throughout the chapters of this book.

Although the primary research context to which I am responding in this volume focuses on the category 'Indigenous Religions', it is important to acknowledge that much has been written recently on the general term 'indigenous' within other academic contexts, largely by anthropologists, sociologists, political scientists and by scholars in the fields of ethnic and cultural studies. For example, a recent book edited by Alan Barnhard and Justin Kenrick, both anthropologists, carries the title *Africa's Indigenous Peoples: "First Peoples" or "Marginalized Minorities"?* After discussing various political uses of the term indigenous, the papers which follow focus largely on the two groups the editors regard as authentically indigenous in Africa: the San or bushmen of south western Africa and the central African Pygmies, sometimes called 'forest dwellers' (Barhnard and Kendrik, 2001: 11–12). An important contribution to the 'primitivism' debate has been provided by Aidan Campbell, who, in his book *Western Primitivism: African Ethnicity*, describes from a cultural studies perspective the romantic, but inherently racist notions found within many perceptions of so-called primitives, whom Campbell (1997: 15) claims are depicted popularly 'as comparatively self-effacing and modest, almost childish in their dependence on others'. Earlier, in a ground-breaking essay, the historian Terence Ranger (1992: 211–62) challenged the notion that Africans traditionally identified themselves according to strictly delineated cultural and ethnic labels, which, Ranger argued, became conceived rigidly only after the codification of traditional law under colonial rule. In a similar vein, the intercultural philosopher and anthropologist, Wim van Binsbergen (2003: 491), has challenged the widespread notion about Africa that the population of the continent must be 'classified into a large number of "tribes" ... characterised by its own "culture", art, language, somatic features, political organisation, including "tribal Chief", and its own "tribal homeland" or "tribal territory"'. These assumptions, which, according to van Binsbergen, originated under the rule of colonial governments, are used to confirm contemporary descriptions of Africans as intrinsically inclined to engage in 'tribal wars', since these 'are postulated to go back to remote antiquity'.

Beyond such strictly academic writings, a great deal of attention has been given around the world to the rights of indigenous peoples, particularly in relation to land claims, some coming from indigenous organizations such as the Inuit Circumpolar Conference, and others from international organizations associated with the United Nations, such as the Permanent Forum on Indigenous Peoples and the International Labour Organization (Thornberry, 2000: 79). Such movements have necessarily been required to wrestle with the difficult problem of defining what they mean by indigenous and who qualifies, for example, for protection under the United Nations Declaration on the Rights of Indigenous Peoples. The wide range of literature on this topic emanating from the United Nations has been reviewed by Emma Ginnelly, one of my postgraduate students, in an as yet unpublished MSc dissertation presented to the University of Edinburgh in 2005. Despite this general academic and activist interest in the term indigenous and the more recent publications in this area generated from within Religious Studies, none addresses specifically the category 'Indigenous Religions' as a legitimate topic for study in academic institutions.

Organization of the Chapters

It is clear from this very preliminary survey of problems surrounding the aims of this book and the research milieu in which they are set that a critical analysis of the definitions, contexts and meanings of the classification 'indigenous' and its correlation with 'religion' must occur before departments of religious studies can justify introducing Indigenous Religions as a discrete subject of study alongside other acknowledged religious traditions. I will attempt to do just this in various ways throughout the seven chapters of this book. In the first chapter, I explore the history and development of the study of Indigenous Religions in academic institutions and note how scholarly publications on indigenous peoples have influenced widespread popular perceptions. I then address in detail in Chapter 2 the problems entailed by making 'indigenous' a comparable category to terms used in other environments to classify 'world religions'. In the third chapter I outline a scientifically testable definition of 'indigenous', which I follow in Chapter 4 by developing a new definition of religion as embedded in socio-cultural contexts. I then move in Chapters 5 and 6 to examine two case studies drawn from entirely different geographical settings in order to highlight the problems associated with generalizing about specific social and cultural contexts and as a means of testing the definitions I have put forward in Chapters 3 and 4. In the concluding chapter I dissociate my own position from 'modern primitivism' by analysing a case study in 'neo-shamanism', and by rejecting finally all confessional approaches to Indigenous Religions as inherently theological.

I have chosen the case studies described in Chapters 4 and 5 for quite practical reasons, drawing on my own background and interests. Chapter 4 examines traditional ritual practices and oral traditions of the Yupiit peoples of the south western regions of Alaska. From 1981 to 1986, I worked in Anchorage, from which I made research trips to various parts of the state. I have returned to Alaska regularly in the years that have followed, have continued to read widely on the indigenous peoples in the region, have used cases from Alaskan Native peoples in my teaching in university settings, and have continued to write and publish on this subject. For the case study in this book, I have drawn largely on three sources: (1) the accounts of early ethnographers and missionaries; (2) the recent studies provided by contemporary anthropologists working in Alaska; (3) the accounts of Alaskan Native peoples concerning their key myths and rituals, both as remembered oral history and now as reconstituted practices in an era of modernization and christianization. In 1989, I went to the University of Zimbabwe as lecturer in the phenomenology of religion. Although, at the time, I knew almost nothing about pre-colonial religion in Zimbabwe, I began almost immediately to engage in seminars and tutorials with both undergraduate and postgraduate students concerning the religious beliefs, rituals and myths as the students had experienced them in their home regions. Eventually, I was invited to some of my students' home areas and participated in traditional rituals, which still are practised throughout Zimbabwe and, in the process, I interviewed numerous ritual specialists and healers. After I came to Edinburgh in 1993 to head the African Christianity Project in the Centre for the Study of Christianity in the Non-Western World, I continued to work closely with colleagues in the University of Zimbabwe and returned periodically for extended visits. In the case study I present in Chapter 5, I analyse the religious dimensions intrinsic to the socio-political structure of the Korekore people of northern Zimbabwe, which I then discuss in relation to research I conducted in 2004 in Zimbabwe on the government's current land re-settlement project.

Although I have selected the case studies based on my own experience and interests, each represents an entirely different social and cultural milieu and thus, when considered alongside one another, each works very well as a hands-on example of the inherent problem created by constructing an all-embracing category called 'Indigenous Religions'. The further problem of identifying who is authentically indigenous also surfaces in these examples, particularly since the question of authenticity can be applied to the Shona and Ndebele in Zimbabwe, and certainly becomes confused in the modern state of Alaska, which has been under American control since 1867, but for over one hundred years before had been subject to the economic and cultural modifications to traditional ways of life that had resulted from extensive contact with Russian traders and Orthodox missionaries. The constructed 'Other' also emerges in each case study, although in different contexts and with contrasting histories, and thus sets the context for my later discussion of Western 'primitivism', which emerges both in theory and practice as central to my entire project. At the end of this book, I hope to have made a strong argument in favour of employing the term 'Indigenous Religions' as a tenable academic category, which both overcomes the inherent problems I have acknowledged and at the same time transcends the primitivism debate. The practical outcome of this book, if my argument prevails, should encourage the development of taught courses and research programmes on Indigenous Religions within university departments of religious studies and in other related academic settings, with inevitable consequences for the way the terms 'indigenous' and 'religion' are understood and perceived in society at large. To address the practical issues, I have written an 'Afterword' in which I provide some concrete suggestions as to how undergraduate and postgraduate programmes in Indigenous Religions might be shaped.

Chapter 1

The Academic Study of Indigenous Religions: Underlying Assumptions and Historical Developments

The nineteenth-century preoccupation with the origin of religion led to a view that was widely accepted throughout the first part of the twentieth century that contemporary 'primitives' living in Africa, Australia, the Americas and other 'non-literate' societies provided significant insight into how religion was practised at the dawn of human history. It was from this attempt to understand how religion had come to its present phase in Western culture that the motive for much early academic interest in the religions of primitive societies was derived. The reasons for seeking such an understanding varied according to whether scholars studied primitive religions to demonstrate the value and superiority of Christianity by locating it at the apex of religious development or whether they traced the roots of Christianity to primitive thinking and thus to superstition. Nonetheless, both Christian and anti-Christian approaches within early studies of indigenous societies were conducted broadly under the same assumptions, which in turn became embedded as cardinal principles in later academic programmes in Indigenous Religions.

In this chapter, I demonstrate how these assumptions were translated into university courses, beginning with the teaching of African Traditional Religion in the first Religious Studies department of its kind at the University of Ibadan in Nigeria to the full course in Indigenous Religions currently operating in the University of Edinburgh. I will also draw attention briefly to recent developments in teaching and research that lend support to my contention that the term 'indigenous' has now become widely accepted amongst scholars of religion as a preferred term to 'primal', which was used commonly amongst scholars of religion well into the 1990s. In the process of describing this history, I will set the stage for my discussion of problems associated with the term 'indigenous' that I address in Chapters 2, 3 and 4, such as the hegemonic power of the world religions paradigm, difficulties in defining and distinguishing the indigenous from the non-indigenous, the persistent dominance of Western interests in the academic study of indigenous peoples and the critical issue of relating what we mean by 'indigenous' to the equally contentious term 'religion'. I begin by examining two quite divergent case studies, one based on a 'pro-religion' missionary interpretation and the other on an 'anti-religion' scientific platform. The first is found in a virtually unknown article appearing in a mid-nineteenth-century journal of the Church Missionary Society, and the other in the writings of James G. Frazer, who was a seminal figure not only in the development of contemporary anthropology but also in the related fields of mythology and religious studies.

The 'Natural History of Man' in Africa

The Church Missionary Society (CMS) was founded in 1799 as The Society for Missions to Africa and the East to enable the Church of England to expand its evangelistic mission in lands which had not yet been christianized. Its intention was to work within the Anglican tradition, but with a distinct emphasis on lay participation in the mission enterprise (Ward, 2000: 1). It followed the creation of the Baptist Missionary Society in 1792 and the London Missionary Society in 1795 and thus formed part of the rapid growth of Protestant missionary societies that occurred during the first half of the nineteenth century when missionaries were sent from Europe to remote locations throughout Africa, Oceania and the Americas. This phase of the missionary movement coincided with nineteenth-century attitudes prevalent in Europe that regarded indigenous societies as the least developed form of human civilization. By engaging in efforts to convert those living as 'savages' within 'primitive' societies, missionaries affirmed, oftentimes against prevailing opinion, that the native populations were capable of being uplifted from their depraved social and moral conditions.

A journal affiliated to the Church Missionary Society, called the *Church Missionary Intelligencer*, was begun in 1849 and was published regularly until 1906. The first issue of the new journal states that it had been launched to fill a need within the Society for a publication on the missionary cause that would commend itself 'to the attention of intelligent and thinking minds' (Yale University, Missionary Periodicals Base).[1] Clearly, this was intended to supplement the more popular *Missionary Gleaner*, which began in 1839, and the *Quarterly Paper*, which provided a record of the Society's proceedings (Keen, 2005). The 1869 issue of the *Church Missionary Intelligencer* contains an article entitled 'The Natural History of Man – Africa', written by William Henry Ridgeway, Rector of Sternfield, Suffolk and author of a popular fourteen page booklet entitled *Striving Together for the Faith of the Gospel* (1868).[2] Ridgeway's article provides rich insight into the attitudes towards indigenous peoples and their religions that were held widely during the middle part of the nineteenth century. It also contains a summary of the main beliefs of the Zulu and Xhosa speaking peoples of South Africa, derived from a book written by the Rev. J.G. Wood entitled *The Natural History of Man: Africa*, first published as a separate volume in 1868 in London by Routledge and Sons and later as a two volume study of the 'natural history of man' around the world.[3]

The first issue addressed by Ridgeway sounds remarkable to the modern reader: Is the African a human or an ape? It soon becomes clear that the author has raised this question in order to place the missionary point of view squarely in opposition to a widely promulgated academic argument maintained at the time that the African shares much more in common with primates than with human beings. Ridgeway begins his article by asserting that Africans must be regarded as fully human despite the fact that the continent in which they live is immersed in 'the blackness of her moral degradation' (1869: 53). If the African were not human, no missionary effort

---

[1]   http://research.yale.edu:8084/missionperiodicals.

[2]   As was the custom at the time, many articles appear in the journal without indicating the name of the author. 'The Natural History of Man – Africa' is attributed simply to 'W.H.R'.

[3]   The volume on Africa was re-printed in 1874, and accompanied the second volume on the 'uncivilized races' of Australia, New Zealand, Polynesia, America, Asia and Ancient Europe', which appeared in 1880.

could be justified, since intellectually Africans would be 'incapable of receiving Christian education'. Ridgeway notes that Europe also at one time was 'steeped in barbarism', just like much of Africa is today (1869: 53). In fact, the barbarism of many European 'aborigines' was far greater than that of 'many African tribes' (1869: 53). The author queries why 'the African should have been thus singled out for the outpourings of prejudice and detraction' (1869: 53). For those who have lived among them, just the contrary opinion is merited. Consider, for example, the industrious behaviour displayed by 'the liberated Africans at Sierra Leone'. Under the power of 'civilizing influences', it is not unusual to see a 'negro' transformed into 'a prosperous merchant, taking part in the government of the colony of which he is a citizen and supporting, nay, often originating schemes for the benefit of his degraded countrymen' (1869: 53).

Ridgeway then considers in detail the position maintained by many anthropologists and philosophers that the African bears a closer resemblance in physical structure, mental capacity and moral aptitude to 'the anthropoid ape' than to human beings. He cites an 'eminent' anthropologist of his day, Carl Vogt, who describes the 'negro' as reminding us '"irresistibly of the ape; the short neck, the long, lean limbs, the projecting, pendulous belly"', characteristics which led Vogt to conclude that the negro '"affords a glimmer of the ape beneath the human envelope"' (Ridgeway, 1869: 54).[4] Ridgeway argues against this by suggesting that there is far more similarity in physical structure between negroes and 'the white man' than between negroes and the ape. The author admits that the negro's features, large hands, broad feet, thick lips and distended nostrils, are not 'consonant with our European ideas of beauty', but after all these are mere conventions (1869: 54). A closer look at the negro leads to a far different conclusion than that drawn by Vogt: 'His arms may be ungracefully long, his neck short, and his shoulders narrow, yet may these peculiarities, which the negro shares with the gorilla, be met with in exceptional cases, though in a less degree, by any white man in the circle of his own acquaintances' (1869: 54). Further studies show convincingly that the brain of the negro 'is as large as an European', that 'his skull is not generally smaller than that of other races' and that its internal material 'is composed of the same substance' (1869: 55). Indeed, Ridgeway concludes, the negro has the power to walk in an erect position, is 'bimanous and biped' and possesses the 'faculty of articulate speech' (1869: 55). No other explanation, he asserts, can be found for the prevailing 'negrophobia' amongst contemporary academics than skin colour. 'It is the hue of the negro's skin which, in the eyes of modern anthropologists, forms an insuperable obstacle to his admission within the pale of our species' (1869: 55). In other words, simple prejudice has replaced scientific evidence for many scholars: 'A black skin is to these philosophers as a red rag to a savage bull' (1869: 55).

In the remainder of the article, Ridgeway reviews the contents of the book by the Rev. J.G. Wood, from which he obtained the title for his article. The major part of Wood's volume, which extends to nearly 800 pages, deals with African groups living south of the equator and nearly a third is devoted to a discussion of what Wood calls the Kaffirs 'which inhabit the extreme south of the continent' (Ridgeway, 1869:

---

4   Carl Vogt (1817–1895) was Professor of Natural History in the University of Geneva. His two-volumed study of the place of the human in natural history was first published in German in 1863 and translated the following year into English under the title, *Lectures on Man: His Place in Creation, and the History of the Earth* (1864).

58), what now would constitute Zulu and Xhosa groups living in South Africa.[5] Ridgeway indicates that these are not the aboriginal people of the land, since most likely 'they descended from the northern parts of the continent upon Southern Africa, and dispossessed the Hottentots, who had, in their turn, thrust out the true aborigines of the soil' (1869: 58). The term 'Hottentots' refers to a classification, now deemed derogatory, used by the white settlers to designate the Khoikhoi people, a division of the Khoisan ethnic group, closely related to the San or bushmen, a group which, as I noted in the Introduction to this book, is regarded by the contemporary anthropologists Alan Barnhard and Justin Kenrick (2001: vii–xv) as having the most legitimate claim to being 'indigenous' within southwest Africa. Although this is not the main point of Ridgeway's article, it is worth noting that we find addressed in a missionary journal at a quite early stage the persistent problem of defining which group of pre-colonial peoples can be identified as genuinely indigenous and which are better regarded as invaders.

Ridgeway then proceeds in the remainder of the article to describe the customs attributed by Wood to the 'Kaffirs'. Childbirth, both male and female, he notes, is celebrated, and only in the case of twins, is an infant sacrificed, 'as the existence of both is considered to bring ill luck to the parents' (Ridgeway, 1869: 59). A baby girl is welcomed because when the child eventually marries, the family of the man must pay the girl's family 'at least eight cows' (1869: 59). At puberty, boys undergo the rite of circumcision. Ridgeway notes that until he reaches manhood, a boy does not wear clothes, but simply paints himself and wears a belt from which a number of thongs hang. As an adult, the male puts on an 'apron' that falls behind him and sometimes adds a 'small cloak' (1869: 59). The 'Kaffir' also is fond of wearing ornaments, such as beads, buttons and strings that are highly colourful. The male adult accumulates ox tails, with rank noted by the number of tails he obtains. The principal architectural style employed in the villages is circular, and huts are built up in groups 'like an exaggerated bee-hive' (1869: 59). The 'Kaffir's' fences are also circular in a style similar to the organization of his huts. The primary unit of exchange is the cow, which is used to procure a wife. Polygamy is practised widely, since to have many wives makes work easier. This is because 'all manual work falls upon the women', who even cultivate the soil 'while their husbands sit at home' (1869: 59). The primary activities of men are warfare and hunting. The fundamental food consumed is maize, which is made into porridge (1869: 60).

Ridgeway concludes his article by considering the religion of the 'Kaffirs'. He agrees with Wood's judgement that the 'Kaffirs' do not 'have any religion at all, so far as the word conveys any idea of moral responsibility' (1869: 60).[6] They possess a vague notion of a Creator who is the originator of things, 'but they neither worship nor pray to Him'. They recite a myth about the creation of man, 'whom they suppose to have been made by splitting a reed, from which our first parents proceeded' (1869: 60). They also tell the story that death came to the world when 'the Great-great' sent two messengers to earth. The first, a chameleon, proclaimed: 'Let not the people

---

[5]   Ridgeway notes that, although in popular conception, the term Kaffir is thought to refer generally to all groups living in South Africa, in fact, 'the true Kaffirs are only to be found in a narrow slip of land which intervenes between the Draakensberg mountains and the sea which washes the south-eastern coast of the continent'. Ridgeway suggests that Wood was referring particularly of the Zulu, 'whose head-quarters are to the north of Natal' (1869: 58-9).

[6]   For a discussion of the widespread notion that the 'Kaffirs' do not have a religion, see Chidester, 1996: 24–7.

die'. The second was a salamander who conveyed just the opposite instruction. Unfortunately, the salamander arrived first amongst humans 'and since then men have been subject to death' (1869: 60). There is a general belief in 'the immortality of the soul' amongst the 'Kaffirs', since the spirits of the dead 'revisit the earth'. Ridgeway indicates that 'prophets' define the 'chief part of his religious system' acting as mediums for communication with the spirits of the dead and for uncovering witchcraft. The most important function of the prophet, however, is to make rain (1869: 60).

This article is highly significant because in the first instance it demonstrates that the sympathetic attitude maintained by missionaries towards Africans stands in sharp contrast to the debate amongst scholars of the day about the postulated human or animal nature of peoples indigenous to Africa. The conviction that the African was human, of course, was necessary for missionary work to proceed, but it was also based on the principle that human beings everywhere were the same and could be civilized and christianized. The second important characteristic of this article is its attempt to summarize the main traditions, beliefs and practices of the Zulu people into a coherent picture to aid understanding of the pre-Christian 'religious system'. Such an understanding provided the rudimentary knowledge necessary for Christian missionaries who sought to replace traditional African practices with adherence to Christian beliefs and moral attitudes. That Ridgeway underscored the lack of a moral basis to this system confirmed the idea that the African was living in darkness, but it also affirmed that this was true of all pre-Christian systems that had operated throughout history, including those of Europe. If this assertion is true, then people in every society, no matter how basic or simple, are capable of receiving, understanding and accepting Christian faith and of experiencing the social and moral benefits which follow in its wake. This could not occur unless, in some elementary sense, all humans are the same, sharing fundamentally similar religious impulses. We thus find in the case of Ridgeway's article on 'The Natural History of Man – Africa' clearly articulated two fundamental principles that we will see re-formulated into later academic studies of Indigenous Religions: (1) Africans have been marginalized by scholarly opinion due to an inherent racial prejudice; and (2) humanity, including the downtrodden peoples of Africa, share in common with the rest of humanity an innate ability to respond to a higher standard of moral teaching than they had known previously and to organize their societies in conformity with the values of the Christian religion.

The Anti-Religionist Study of Religion by James G. Frazer

The idea that the nature of humanity is everywhere the same, voiced so clearly by Ridgeway, became a central tenet amongst anthropological studies of primitive peoples towards the end of the nineteenth century under the influence of E.B. Tylor, and was developed into an anti-religionist theory by James G. Frazer (1854–1951). As I indicated in my Introduction to this book, many scholars have noted the vast significance Frazer holds for numerous disciplines, but he is chiefly known for his anthropological work outlining primitive customs and beliefs published in his multi-volumed study *The Golden Bough*, which underwent numerous editing processes between 1890 and 1915. Frazer trained in Classics and Law at Cambridge, but, as Daniel Pals (2006: 31) notes, when by chance he read E.B. Tylor's *Primitive Culture* (1871), he 'found his eyes suddenly opened to the possibilities created by anthropological research and the use of the comparative method'. Still as a young man, Frazer met William Robertson Smith, the controversial biblical scholar from Aberdeen and author of *Lectures on the Religion of the Semites* (1889), who became his adviser and close colleague. It was Smith's theories of clans, kinship groups and totems that most influenced Frazer's thinking and stimulated, at least in part, the writing of the first edition of *The Golden Bough*. In 1907, Frazer was appointed to the chair in the new field of anthropology at the University of Liverpool, which Alan Barnhard contends he regarded largely as an honorary post. Eric Sharpe (1986: 87–8) corroborates this point, adding that Frazer 'worked in the area of anthropology simply because he was intrigued by the problems presented by primitive religion and mythology, magic and religion'. Sharpe (1986: 90) explains that Frazer's main contributions in *The Golden Bough* were to have provided a working theory of magic, to have analysed the significance of the widely held belief in divine kingship and to have drawn links between deities of vegetation and myths of death and resurrection. Barnhard (2000: 37) underscores the immense significance *The Golden Bough* held for later scholarship, calling it 'one of the great books of anthropology' and noting that 'it was widely read by generations of intellectuals of all kind'.

My interest in Frazer in this context focuses on his conviction that humanity possesses a cognitive unity, a point which recently has been emphasized in an article written by the scholar of classical religions, Ulrich Berner (2004: 141–9). Berner refers to Frazer's inaugural lecture at Liverpool in 1908 in which Frazer reminded his audience that superstitions still prevail in many parts of Europe as 'survivals' of a past era. The study of myth, magic and folklore in primitive societies thus bears direct relevance for understanding contemporary practices and beliefs, since it confirms that many people living in so-called civilized societies 'though they are drilled by their betters into an appearance of civilization, remain barbarians or savages at heart' (cited by Berner, 142). Berner points out that this observation was based on Frazer's understanding of the comparative method, since he assumed 'that the human mind works similarly in all races of men' (Berner, 2004: 142). This idea resonates closely with Ridgeway's conclusion that 'the pristine barbarism of the aborigines of Europe was far greater' than the savagery of African tribes (1869: 53).

The Golden Bough carries the subtitle, 'A Study in Magic and Religion', but it does not begin with accounts of exotic practices performed by far-off African tribes. Rather, it opens by recounting stories circulated in pre-Christian Rome about the bizarre practices of the priest of Diana of the Wood, who in the grove of Aricia lived a life of fear. (This is now the modern Italian city of Ariccia, near Lake Nemi in the Albani hills, approximately 25 kilometres south of Rome.) Frazer describes how, according to the legend, one became a priest by murdering the incumbent, but then awaited his own successor who would in turn slay him. Frazer (1963: 1) writes: 'He was a priest and a murderer; and the man for whom he looked was sooner or later to murder him and hold the priesthood in his stead.' The priest was also a king, but it was a highly precarious rule: 'The least relaxation of his vigilance, the smallest abatement of his strength of limb or skill of fence, put him in jeopardy' (1963: 2). Frazer notes that this 'strange rule ... has no parallel in classical antiquity', but he sets it into a comprehensible context by relating other stories that shed light on it (1963: 2). After recounting a number of these, he concludes that 'it needs no elaborate demonstration to convince us that the stories told to account for Diana's worship at Nemi are unhistorical' and that 'they belong to that large class of myths which are made up to explain the origin of a religious ritual' (1963: 6). Historical legends, of course, can be connected to the Nemi myths, and archaeological evidence traces the sanctuary of Diana at Aricia to a period sometime around the fourth century BCE. Despite these ancient historical connections to the story of the priest of Aricia, Frazer argues, 'we cannot suppose that so barbarous a rule as that of the Arician priesthood was deliberately instituted by a league of civilized communities', which he contends the communities by the fourth century BCE certainly were. Rather, the story 'must have been handed down from a time beyond the memory of man, when Italy was still in a far ruder state than any known to us in the historical period' (1963: 6). It is only after reviewing the ancient barbarism in times preceding civilized Rome that Frazer moves in *The Golden Bough* to consider aspects of magic and religion as they are found in contemporary contexts amongst primitive societies. The point to be underscored here is that by beginning with the legend of the priest of Aricia, Frazer has connected the almost unspeakable savagery of ancient times to the legends and rituals of Roman civilization and through them directly to Christianity.

Frazer did not undertake this analysis to support a theory of cultural evolution, conceived as the inevitable advance of humans from a lower mental and moral state to a higher one. Rather, he maintained that all humans, whether of ancient times or in contemporary settings, who live by rude laws of superstition and barbaric behaviour, share the capacity to be uplifted to a higher level of understanding and to an elevated moral standard. In his view, Christianity was not an instrument in the modern era capable of promoting progress, but, like every religion, it perpetuates the survival of superstitious beliefs and magical ways of thinking. A clear example is found in the Christian Eucharist where believers think they are eating the body and drinking the blood of Jesus Christ, which in Frazer's mind clearly is derived from ancient rituals of eating the gods, such as occurred in the cult of the Greek god Dionysus. Frazer observes: 'It is now easy to understand why a savage should desire to partake of the flesh of an animal or man whom he regards as divine. By eating the body of the god he shares in the god's attributes and powers' (1963: 578). Although he does not mention Christianity by name in this section of *The Golden Bough*, his meaning is unmistakable: 'The drinking of wine in the rites of a vine-god like Dionysus is not an act of revelry, it is a solemn sacrament' (1963: 578). When such acts are perpetuated into the modern age, they maintain the ancient bondage to superstition and primitive mental error. He explains: 'Yet a time comes when reasonable men find it hard to understand how anyone in his senses can suppose that by eating bread or drinking wine he consumes the body or blood of a deity' (1963: 578). Ulrich Berner asserts that these comments were directed less against ancient ways of thinking as they were against Christianity, which falsely sees itself as detached from primitive beliefs and practices. Berner (2004: 147) observes of Frazer in the context of Africa: 'His way of speaking about African religions in terms of "savagery" and "superstition" is not to be seen as an expression of a contempt for Africans but as part of a critical discourse on religion in general that is finally targeted at survivals of superstition in the Christian culture of Europe.'

Frazer foresaw an era when religion would be replaced by science, banishing once and for all every 'survival' of primitive thinking in contemporary life. Towards the conclusion of *The Golden Bough*, he expressed just this sentiment: 'It is probably not too much to say that the hope of progress – moral and intellectual as well as material – in the future is bound up with the fortunes of science, and that every obstacle placed in the way of scientific discovery is wrong to humanity' (1963: 825). Although this stands in sharp contrast to the missionary message put forward by W.H. Ridgeway, it is not appreciably different in its underlying attitude towards indigenous societies. The superstitions of the primitive peoples who have not yet been brought into the light of civilization are superseded for Ridgeway by the forces of Christianity and its related social institutions. All humans, from ancient times onwards, share the same cognitive and moral capacities; they simply need to be freed from those false beliefs and practices that keep them in a state of backwardness. The difference between the missionaries and Frazer, of course, was that the liberating message for each was different: for missionaries, it was the message of Jesus Christ; for Frazer, it was the freedom from superstition and magic which comes from understanding and applying the true laws of causation disclosed by science.

Another important conclusion from Frazer's approach must be drawn. Although his analysis can be regarded as highly critical of religion, or at least as describing religion as just one further step from savagery towards enlightenment, his theory about the cognitive unity of humanity meant that Christianity, as a religion, must be treated in the same way as all religions. For this reason, the study of Indigenous Religions, in the case of Frazer, is a study of humanity and the history of human cognitive development, in which religion plays an important intermediary role between magic and science. No religion is privileged in such a study, apart from noting the cultural influences one religion may have exercised within a particular geographical location or time in history. Contemporary forms of Indigenous Religions, in so far as they are steeped in the superstitions of past times, may reflect the survival of magical thinking, but in this regard they are no different from any other religion and should not be treated as such in academic studies. In Frazer, therefore, we see repeated in a slightly varied form the same two assumptions that were articulated thirty years earlier by W.H. Ridgeway: (1) humans everywhere think alike and thus are capable of correcting wrong thinking (and acting); (2) primitive religions should be described and their practices classified in a scientific, comparative manner without privileging any religion over another, particularly when such a privileging is justified by a racist ideology.

These two overriding assumptions, shared by Ridgeway and Frazer, although expressed differently by each to reflect the contrasting aims of missionary scholars and early anthropologists, when taken together, served as foundational principles on which university courses in Indigenous Religions eventually were built. The first principle is derived from the conviction, shared both by Ridgeway and Frazer, in the essential unity of humanity and its universal capacity for moral improvement, which the study of primitive societies discloses. The second principle, which is related closely to the first, was exemplified in Ridgeway's discussion of the academic racism of his day and by Frazer's insistence that all religions, in a comparative sense, deserve equal scholarly treatment. The academic study of Indigenous Religions thus in one fundamental sense is rooted in the missionary movement, which helps to explain why academic programmes in Indigenous Religions often were initiated within departments with close connections to mission studies. Its claim to academic credibility, however, can be traced to the influence of early anthropologists, like Frazer, who maintained that humans everywhere are the same, and that the study of contemporary forms of primitive beliefs leads to an understanding of religion in general.

The Study of African Traditional Religion in Ibadan

The attempt to correct widespread bias against Indigenous Religions can be traced to the early writings of scholars of religion who maintained that a rudimentary belief in God can be found amongst indigenous peoples around the world. This view was voiced most explicitly by early missionary academics working in Africa, specifically Edwin W. Smith (1936, 1950) and E. Geoffrey Parrinder (see below), each of whom drew a line of continuity between the basic beliefs of African indigenous peoples and fully developed monotheism. Later, African scholars writing from within the Christian tradition, such as Parrinder's student E.B. Idowu (1962, 1973) and the Kenyan theologian John S. Mbiti (1969, 1970, 1975), used the idea of the universal belief in God to maintain that African Religions deserve to be treated with respect and to be studied as religions in their own right alongside the other religious traditions around the world. African Traditional Religion as a separate category was introduced first into an academic syllabus under the influence of Parrinder, who in 1949 was appointed as lecturer in an entirely new field called 'Religious Studies' at the University College Ibadan in Nigeria, almost twenty years before a similar department was established in the United Kingdom at Lancaster (Walls, 1980: 144).

In order to understand the history relevant to current trends in the study of Indigenous Religions, I begin with the pioneering work of Geoffrey Parrinder, who first went to Africa in 1933 as a missionary of the Methodist Missionary Society. Initially, he taught in Protestant theological seminaries in Dahomey (now Benin) and in the Ivory Coast, where he also worked as Superintendent of a Methodist Circuit. For three years, he served as Principal of the Protestant Theological Seminary in Porto Novo, Dahomey, after which he returned to England to complete a Bachelor of Divinity Honours degree, which was awarded in 1940 by the University of London. In 1943, he returned to West Africa as Principal of the Theological Seminary in Porto Novo, a post he held until 1946. During this time, he read R.S. Rattray's ethnographic study of the Ashanti (1923) and, according to Martin Forward (1998: 18), he explored 'in detail West African indigenous religion'. It was largely from material he obtained between 1943 and 1946 that he based his doctoral thesis submitted in 1947 to London University, and published in 1949 as *West African Religion*. In the same year of this publication, he accepted the post in Religious Studies at the University College Ibadan, which he held until 1958 when he was appointed Reader and later Professor in the Comparative Study of Religions in King's College, London.

Andrew Walls (2004: 209) explains that in West Africa, following the second world war, the Colonial Office in Britain established a commission to investigate the state of higher education in West Africa, resulting in the establishment of two new universities, one at Legon in the Gold Coast (Ghana) and the other at Ibadan in Nigeria. Both institutions were expected to attain standards equivalent to British universities and both were affiliated to the University of London, which granted their degrees. Walls (2004: 211) observes that the Principal of Ibadan, who was a scientist, initially had not considered introducing religion as a subject for study, 'but was surprised to find how vigorous was the student attachment to religion'. As a result, a course on 'Religious Studies' was approved in 1948, with Parrinder assuming the lecturer's post in this new subject area. He was joined in 1950 by James Welch, former Director of Religious Broadcasting for the BBC, who was appointed the new Professor of Religious Studies (Walls, 2004: 211; Forward, 1998: 21). As was agreed during his interview for the post, Parrinder began organizing the Religious Studies course immediately on his arrival (Parrinder, 1961: vii). Teaching began the following year when Welch arrived. Honours students were to sit nine papers on three topics: Old Testament, New Testament and 'the Indigenous Religious Beliefs of West Africa', with Parrinder teaching Old Testament and the course on West

African Indigenous Religions, and Welch taking responsibility for the course on the New Testament (Parrinder, 1961: vii). Martin Forward (1998: 22) observes that most students enrolled in a general degree, which meant that Religious Studies comprised one of three subjects, with students most commonly choosing English, History or Geography as their other subject areas.

In a traditional theology programme, the course structure would have included philosophy of religion or church history alongside the Old and New Testaments. By introducing West African Indigenous Religions as an integral part of the Religious Studies programme at Ibadan, Parrinder broke new ground by insisting that the study of the beliefs of African peoples, which had been transmitted from generation to generation through oral traditions, should be given the same academic status and credibility as the study of Christianity and its written scriptures. Andrew Walls (2004: 211) underscores the significance of this act: 'It was the first time that the subject had appeared at university level in the English speaking world.' Parrinder himself claimed that 'this was the first time that such a syllabus had been taught in any university' (Parrinder, 1961: vii). After 1950, the teaching of the religious traditions of Africa spread to other African universities making it, in Walls' (2004: 211) words, 'a viable university subject'. It also became a tool for African nationalism, as in Ghana, where Kwame Nkrumah, made the study of African Traditional Religion, again in Walls' words, 'an African necessity' (2004: 211).

The primary text for Parrinder's new course at Ibadan was his own book, *West African Religion*, since none other had been written on the topic (Parrinder, 1961: vii). This meant that in the first instance the students primarily were studying the traditions of the Ewe, Akan and Yoruba peoples of West Africa, on whom Parrinder had conducted his doctoral research. Nevertheless, by identifying specific groups of African peoples, Parrinder adopted a comparative approach, in which he could note differences of belief and practice and yet argue for a certain consistency among each. Walls (1980: 142) explains that Parrinder taught the course on West African Indigenous Religions under the conviction that 'African religion exists in a diversity of forms and yet with a certain common structure'. A brief examination of *West African Religion* will provide insight not only into the content of the course as he taught it initially at Ibadan, but it will also disclose the fundamental assumptions Parrinder employed in his approach to the subject.

West African Religion (1949: ix–xii) was written with two main objectives in mind: (1) to provide an overview for comparative purposes of the main religious beliefs of the Yoruba, Ewe, Akan and what Parrinder calls 'kindred peoples'; and (2) to correct prior descriptions of African religions that classify them as the religions of 'savages'. On the first point, Parrinder explains that most tribes of West Africa share 'common elements' which 'need drawing out and collating' so that students may have presented to them 'the nature of the chief beliefs and practices of these deeply religious peoples' (1949: 2). On the second point, Parrinder argues that the religions of the tribes comprising his study should not be confounded with the idea of a 'primitive religion' since each group has 'a religion which deserves consideration as a distinct entity and that it is well advanced beyond the first dawn of the religious sense' (1949: 12). In particular, the term 'fetish', along with its association in English with 'juju', is confusing and inaccurate, and thus should be 'relegated to the museum of the writings of early explorers' (1949: 14).

In the opening sections of *West African Religion*, Parrinder considers various theories about African religions, including those of Wilhelm Schmidt, who posited an original primal monotheism which had degenerated into polytheism, and E.B.

Tylor, who traced the development from a primitive animism to more developed forms of polytheism. Parrinder's aim, however, was not to engage in theoretical discussions concerning the origin of the religious impulse in humanity. 'It is not our purpose to enter into these speculations here' (1949: 15). Rather, he was concerned to classify West African religious beliefs according to a four-fold comparative scheme: a supreme God; the chief divinities, generally non-human and associated with natural forces; the cult of ancestors; and charms and amulets. He calls this a 'workable classification' based on distinctions already occurring within the 'African mind' (1949: 16–17).

In the chapter devoted to the 'supreme God', Parrinder poses two main questions: 'whether the conception of a "Supreme Being", a "high God", is native to West Africa' and 'whether such a God is worshipped, and to what extent' (1949: 18). Parrinder concludes that 'most tribes in our area believe in a high God', although variations exist regarding 'his worship' (1949: 29). In support of this conclusion, he cites the pioneering ethnologist, R.S. Rattray, as having shown conclusively that the supreme God is believed in by the Akan of Ghana, a fact further corroborated in Twi language designations for the high God. Rattray found evidence that God is worshipped amongst the Akan through the numerous altars dedicated to him. (On Rattray, see Platvoet, 1996b: 108.) Other groups in Parrinder's study of West Africa, however, seem not to worship the Supreme Being directly. Parrinder (1949: 29) observes: 'In other parts of our field, a supreme God is recognized by everyone, but his cult is not practised by all who take his name on their lips.'

Parrinder then asks if the designation 'Supreme Being' corresponds to the Christian usage of the same term. He notes, 'The word 'supreme' is easily comprehensible in European theology, but it may be fatally misleading to transfer our ideas into the African hierarchy. God the Father is supreme in Christian theology' (1949: 30). In West Africa this cannot be regarded as the case, since generally 'worship is scant enough'. Parrinder concludes: 'In short, while to us belief in God is the "highest" article of religion, and practised as such, it is not in the forefront of practised West African religion' (1949: 31). Whether or not this confirms Schmidt's theory of the degeneration of a primitive monotheism into polytheism, Parrinder says cannot be resolved on the basis of his evidence, but he claims to have found, just as the German missionary and linguist Diedrich Westermann had done before him, that 'the African's God is a *deus incertus* and a *deus remotus*', an unknown being who remains far away and uninvolved with day to day human details' (Parrinder, 1949: 32; Westermann, 1937: 74).

Parrinder applied this comparative approach to the whole of Africa, when in 1954 he published a much broader work under the title, *African Traditional Religion*, which clearly was written to supplant his more limited earlier work in his teaching at Ibadan. Subsequently, the book became a standard text for the teaching of African Traditional Religion throughout many parts of Africa, Europe and North America. Although his main approach remained the same in *African Traditional Religion* as in *West African Religion*, Parrinder simplified his basic categories for comparison whilst at the same time making them more detailed by introducing sub-categories beneath each. His book is divided into three main sections under the headings 'The Pantheons', 'The Social Group' and 'Spiritual Forces'. Under each of these, he separates his subject matter into eight chapters. Under the broad classification 'Pantheons', he devotes a chapter each to 'The Supreme Being' and to 'Nature Gods'; in the section on 'The Social Group', he has five chapters: 'The Ancestors', 'Divine Rulers', 'Communal Ritual'. 'Personal Ritual' and 'Sacred Specialists'; and under the section 'Spiritual Forces', he considers 'Magic and Sorcery', 'Witchcraft' and 'The Soul and Its Destiny'. In order to compare the whole of Africa under these classifications, Parrinder is forced to draw heavily on secondary sources, to supplement his own primary work on the Akan, Ewe and Yoruba. One central source for his work is Edwin W. Smith's edited volume, *African Ideas of God*, to which Parrinder contributed the chapter entitled, 'Theistic Beliefs of the Yoruba and Ewe Peoples of West Africa' (Smith, 1950: 224–59). Other sources are cited widely throughout the book, many drawn from early anthropological studies such as Evans-Pritchard's work on witchcraft amongst the Azande (1937) and Meyer Fortes' outline of the clan structure of the Tallensi (1945), or from philosophical perspectives, such as Placide Tempels' classic work on *Bantu Philosophy* (1959) (which Parrinder read in the French version published in 1945), and some which were strongly influenced by African nationalism, such as J.B. Danquah's *The Akan Doctrine of God* (1944). By drawing on these sources and putting them into comparative categories, Parrinder sought to build up for his students a composite picture of African traditional beliefs and practices, which could at the same time be substantiated by specialized studies of particular African peoples.

Parrinder was aware of the problem posed by trying to create generalizations about the numerous peoples of Africa under generic categories. In the Introduction to *African Traditional Religion*, he discusses the diversity of religion in Africa and admits that 'the desert nomad of Somaliland has little in common with the citizen of Dakar who knows no language but French, and the Cow Fulani of Nigeria must have a very different mentality from the miner of the Rand' (1954: 10). He responds to this problem first by arguing that the postulated homogeneity of other religions likewise is much more apparent than real. The beliefs and practices of Hinduism, Islam and even Christianity are highly varied, and yet they are taught and studied under a single classification as world religions. Similar variations amongst African beliefs and practices thus would not seem sufficient reason to reject teaching and studying them under a general classification. Even more significantly, a study of the traditional religions of Africa reveals much more in common than might at first sight be assumed. Due to the specific nature of anthropological studies, scholars have written about different African peoples as if each were unrelated and unique. 'But the resemblances are far more important than the differences' (1954: 11). Citing the work of Hilda Kuper (1947), an anthropologist who had worked with Bronislaw Malinowski at the London School of Economics and who had written an early ethnography of the Swazi peoples of southern Africa, Parrinder (1954: 11) notes that 'the piling up of ethnographic detail produces an impression of chaos where there is in fact only variation on a few themes'. This applies particularly in the sphere of religion where great similarities can be identified throughout Africa:

> A Supreme Being is worshipped both by Ashanti in the west and Kikuyu in the east, there are divine kings in Nigeria and Uganda, witches in Dahomey and Bechuanaland, a dowry system in the Ivory Coast and Basutoland, female circumcision in the Gold Coast and among the Half-Hamitic Masai, niche burial for Hottentots and Yoruba (1954: 11).

We thus find Parrinder supporting the study of African Traditional Religion in the singular in the first instance because other world religions, which are equally diverse, are also approached under a general heading (Hinduism, Buddhism, Islam, Christianity, Sikhism, Zoroastrianism and so on). Secondly, he insists that the sense of extreme diversity amongst African religions has been exaggerated by the methods of anthropological research, and that only a limited number of themes run throughout the whole of the continent, which can be organized usefully into categories for comparative purposes. In this way, his course on African Traditional Religion as he developed it over nine years at Ibadan was justified and its components constructed. He explains: 'We shall try, then, to treat African religion on a comparative basis, gathering material from various parts of the continent. The broad lines of religious belief will be sketched. For details the student must go to the studies of anthropologists' (1954: 11).

Parrinder's approach at Ibadan incorporated the same principles I noted in the earlier writings of W.H. Ridgeway and J.G. Frazer. African Traditional Religion should be treated on an equal basis with every other religion and not be subjected to an interpretation based on racial prejudice which designates African beliefs and practices as sub-human. Moreover, a clear continuity between African religions and other world religions (in line with the theory of the cognitive unity of humanity) is shown by comparative studies, particularly when it emerges that almost universally Africans believe in a Supreme Being, and with such variations of approach as occur elsewhere throughout the world. In the end, Parrinder simply brings into a modern context the central tenets of both Ridgeway and Frazer by contending that the study of African Traditional Religion constitutes a legitimate and necessary topic for academic research and teaching.

After arriving at Kings College, London in 1958, Parrinder's interests expanded beyond Africa. In particular, he began to direct his research towards Islam and Hinduism, and even studied Sanskrit at the School of Oriental and African Studies (Forward, 1998: 24). This broader interest is shown in some of his books comparing aspects of the world's religions, for example, *Jesus in the Qur'an* (1965) and *Sexual Morality in the World's Religions* (1980). Nevertheless, he made a fundamental contribution to the development of the study of Indigenous Religions when in 1964 he published a small book under the title, *The World's Living Religions*, which, as he explained in the Foreword, aimed at providing 'a short and impartial account of the major religions of the modern world' (1964: 7). Alongside chapters on 'Islam and the Arab World', 'Hinduism', 'Jains, Sikhs and Parsis', 'Buddhism in Southeast Asia', 'China's Three Ways', 'Japanese Shinto and Buddhism', 'Judaism' and 'Christianity', he inserted a chapter entitled 'Africans, Australians, and American Indians' in which he justifies considering 'non-scriptural faiths' (1964: 7) under one classification much in the same way he had done previously when discussing African Traditional Religion. Parrinder (1964: 125) notes: 'There is such great variety of tribes in many parts of the world, that one who wished to study a particular tribe must look for a specialist book on the subject.' But, he adds, 'there is enough similarity for comparative works to have been written, and these can now be referred to fairly easily'.

Parrinder (1964: 124) identifies the subjects of such studies as peoples as living in 'tiny groups' in North America, as those still inhabiting the Central and Southern American forests, as groups living in the Pacific Islands 'who still retain elements of their ancient faith', as the aborigines of Australia who number 'some 50,000', as the hill and jungle tribes of India, South-east Asia, China and Siberia 'that have for long resisted the encroachments of Hinduism and Buddhism' and, of course, the 'many tribes' of Africa 'which have their own religious practices, despite the inroads made in modern times by Islam and Christianity'. The categories Parrinder uses to compare such a wide grouping of peoples from around the world include 'God and Divine Power', 'Gods and Ancestors', 'Totem and Taboo', 'Magic, Witchcraft and

Sorcery' and 'Social Change'. To have included such a chapter in a book on the world's religions was highly unusual and inventive. By so doing, Parrinder created a category among the world's religions for the study of peoples, in his words, 'who do not follow one of the great historical religions, but have religious beliefs and practices that derive from ancient ideas and traditions' (1964: 124).

The Teaching of 'Primal Religions' at Aberdeen University

In the context of his teaching and research as a scholar of comparative religions at King's College, London, Parrinder anticipated the creation of entire courses devoted to the study of indigenous peoples. The first of these was established under the direction of Andrew Walls in the University of Aberdeen.[7] Walls, like Parrinder, had wide African experience. In 1957, he joined the Department of Theology in the University of Sierra Leone to teach Church History and in 1963 developed the same course in the Department of Religious Studies at the University of Nigeria, Nsukka (Turner, 1986: 1–4). In 1966, he was appointed to a post in Ecclesiastical History in the University of Aberdeen. Four years later, he founded the Department of Religious Studies in the University of Aberdeen's Faculty of Arts and Social Studies, the purpose of which he described as 'the study of religion, in its own terms and in its social, phenomenological and historical aspects' (Walls, 1990: 42). He soon surrounded himself with colleagues who had experience of working in Africa, first James Thrower, who had lectured at the University of Ghana, and soon afterwards, Harold Turner, who had been Walls' colleague in Sierra Leone and Nigeria (Shenk, 1998: 684). In 1976, they were joined by Adrian Hastings, who had worked extensively throughout east Africa and two years later by Lamin Sanneh, a scholar from the Gambia with a specialization in Islamic–Christian relations in West Africa. After the addition of Adrian Hastings, the department recruited Rosalind Shaw as a temporary lecturer, who had taught in West Africa, and it forged links with the University of Nigeria at Calabar through the contacts of one of its graduates, Rosalind Hackett. Hastings describes the period of the late 1970s 'as a wonderful time to be a member of the Aberdeen African Religions team brought together by Andrew Walls', whom, Hastings adds, had created a department with a 'remarkable balance, at least in African terms' (Hastings, 2004: 269). In 1967, just after taking up his post in Church History in Aberdeen, Walls founded the *Journal of Religion in Africa*, which he continued to edit until 1985, and in the process solicited numerous articles and book reviews from Aberdeen staff and postgraduate students (Hastings, 1986: 5–9; Hastings, 2004: 265–74).

In 1976, the Department initiated the study of what it called 'Primal Religions' by introducing a one year taught masters programme, 'The M.Litt. in Religion in Primal Societies'. The aim of the course was described in an appendix to John B. Taylor's edited volume, *Primal World Views* (1976: 128), as 'providing instruments for the study of the "primal" (or "ethnic" or "traditional") religions characteristic of many societies in Africa, the Americas, Asia and Oceania, the effects on belief systems, practices and religious institutions of the meeting of these religions with "universal" religions (notably Christianity and Islam), and the new religious movements arising after contact with Western influences'. It was claimed in Taylor's volume that 'there

---

[7]   For my earlier discussion of the academic programmes at Aberdeen and Edinburgh, see, Cox, 2004b: 255–64.

are considerable documentary resources on this field in Aberdeen, including what is probably the largest specialized collection in Britain of literature from and about the new religious movements; and the Department holds a large corpus of bibliographical and classificatory information on these movements, on primal religions generally, and on non-Western manifestations of Christianity' (1976: 128). This latter point was referring to an extensive research project which had been begun by Harold Turner aimed at describing, classifying and analysing new religious movements among primal societies.

The M.Litt. in Religion in Primal Societies was the first postgraduate course in any established university to offer a degree in the study of Indigenous Religions taken as a single world phenomenon. It was a taught course taken over twelve months full time, and was assessed by a combination of examinations and a short dissertation. It sought to recruit students who had completed first degrees in Anthropology, History, Religious Studies or what it called 'Area Studies', such as specialized courses in African or Asian studies. 'Exceptionally' it would consider students with 'significant experience of work in cross-cultural situations'. The course was comprised of instruction and examination in three areas: (1) Primal World Views; (2) The Penetration of Primal Societies by Universal Religions; (3) New Religious Movements in Primal Societies. The section on 'Primal World Views' considered 'the nature and structure of primal religion' and methods for studying it around the world. The element dealing with primal societies and universal religions analysed such themes as the conversion of primal peoples to Islam and Christianity and the adaptations of Primal Religions to 'new forms of belief, practice and institutions'. The final part of teaching on New Religious Movements examined 'Religious movements arising subsequent to the impact of Western and other external influences on primal societies' (Taylor, 1976: 128–9).

During the early 1970s the designation 'primal' was gaining widespread acceptance amongst academics and within church organizations closely connected to the history of the missionary movement. For example, it was incorporated into the World Council of Churches' sub-unit on Dialogue with People of Living Faiths and Ideologies at a consultation held in Ibadan in September 1973. John B. Taylor, who was the Director of the sub-unit during the consultation, explained that by using 'primal' rather than primitive, he meant beliefs and practices that were quite 'basic' and that 'lie below the surface' of religions everywhere (1976: v). Taylor added that primal world views have been the subject of great distortion over the years by being described in derogatory language through such biased terms as 'witchcraft', 'sorcery', 'mumbo-jumbo', 'superstition' or 'even "primitive religion"' (1976: v). Taylor's idea that the Primal Religions were basic to all religions became a fundamental tenet of the course at Aberdeen, and was used by Andrew Walls as a justification for treating them as a unit.

Two quite small, but highly influential, works closely connected with the Aberdeen programme supported this contention. The first, which was written in 1971 by Harold Turner while he was still in Leicester University, carried the title *Living Tribal Religions*, in which he identified common 'religious' characteristics shared amongst tribal societies. After arriving in Aberdeen, Turner, in close consultation with Walls, opted to promote 'primal' as the preferred term for what he was describing. A second important publication on this topic, *An Introduction to Primal Religions* was written by Philippa Baylis, who had been an undergraduate student in the Aberdeen programme under Walls. Although her booklet appeared much later than Turner's, the Aberdeen influence is apparent throughout. In the introduction, which formed part of a series of lectures delivered to the first year comparative religion course in the University of Edinburgh in 1987, Baylis largely re-stated the list of unifying features Harold Turner had identified previously. Baylis (1987: 2–3) argues that 'primal religion' can be treated as a single category because everywhere in the world it displays the following characteristics: (1) a primal religion 'cannot be separated from society as a whole; (2) it is local in character and hence 'culturally and historically ... unique'; (3) it is tolerant of other religions and sometimes 'borrows certain elements from them'; (4) it is 'ethnocentric' and 'and non-missionary by nature'; (5) it transmits its traditions orally rather than in written form; and (6) it is entirely non-creedal, since its beliefs are not articulated but remain 'implicit' in the society's myths and rituals.

In his 'Foreword' to Baylis' book, Andrew Walls (1988: v) argues that 'primal religions ... underlie all other religions'. He adds that 'though we think of ourselves as Christians, Buddhists, Muslims or unbelievers, we are all primalists underneath'. He then offers an insight into the development of his own course in Aberdeen by observing that 'no part of the formal study of religion is in general so unsatisfactorily treated' and complains that 'many a substantial book about the religions of the world ignores the primal religions altogether'(Walls, 1988: v). Walls outlined his own understanding of primal religions in an article appearing in a book published in 1987 on contemporary religions edited by Frank Whaling. In his contribution on 'Primal Religious Traditions in Today's World', Walls (1987: 250) admits that it is extremely difficult to compile 'a comprehensive statement on the primal religions', since they lack a 'central authority', possess 'no universally recognized texts'; are virtually impossible to number for statistical purposes and constitute a 'bewildering' diversity in culture and environment. Despite the problem of defining precisely what constitutes a primal religion, Walls re-states his conviction that primal religions lie at the base of all other faiths, and thus must be understood if we are to appreciate religion in the contemporary world 'long after adhesion takes place to Christianity or Islam, to Hinduism or Buddhism' (1987: 249–50).

Yet, in his discussion of the 'content and structure' of primal religions. Walls avoids oversimplification by stressing that primal religions, like every other religion in the world, undergo change in response to numerous internal and external factors. He discusses the 'structure' of religion according to Parrinder's fourfold pattern ('Supreme Being, divinities, ancestors and object of power'), but argues that the 'elements of religious life' are not the same as a religion's structure (1987: 253–4). He exemplifies this by referring to Aylward Shorter's 'six types of religion', each of which can be classified by the relative stress given within each model to the four elements in Parrinder's overall comparative structure (See Shorter, 1975: 8–13). Walls says that the study of religions shows that 'there appear to be God-dominated systems, divinity-dominated systems, ancestor-dominated systems, and systems in which the hypostatization of the transcendent is so slight that objects of power, or impersonalized power itself, dominate them' (Walls, 1987: 254–5). Following Shorter, he notes that some African religions are strictly theistic, whereas others approach a Supreme Being through intermediaries, whilst still others fail to acknowledge a Supreme Being overtly and yet ritually mitigate an overwhelming power that persistently threatens human experience. The structures of each of these differ, even though they can be compared according to the varying roles each ascribes to a transcendent reality or power (1987: 255).

Walls (1987: 258, 260) describes the structures of primal religions as being 'in flux' due to the impact of forces for change, often fostered by colonialism, missionary activity and the rise of nationalism within primal societies, the latter particularly since the second world war. If, for example, a religion directed towards ancestors comes into contact with God-dominated religions (like Christianity or Islam), a complex relationship between the old and the new emerges. The outward structure of the relationship with the transcendent may be reconfigured, but at its base the former way of relating to ancestors may persist. This becomes particularly apparent in the case of African Christianity, where dependence on ancestors seems to have been replaced by devotion to God, but this may be largely superficial since Christian rituals 'may impinge very little on the life of most members of the community' (1987: 254). It is equally important to remember that the religious elite may hold quite different attitudes from the majority of those living in the society towards either the new God-centred structure or the former ancestor-dominated one (1987: 258–9). This complex interrelationship of patterns of change warns against treating primal religions as if they were 'a static, timeless entity', unless we want to describe them in a quite dated anthropological manner by 'use of the "ethnographic present"' (1987: 253). For any analysis of such changing patterns to be credible, therefore, it becomes imperative that scholars acknowledge that primal religions 'underlie all other faiths' and that they continue to exercise 'an active life within and around cultures and communities influenced by those faiths' (1987: 250). The challenge for those who want to study, research or teach about primal religions, Walls concludes, is to acknowledge that such societies are no longer 'purely local or ethnic', but form part of 'a village all now know to be global' (1987: 278).

The interpretation of Primal Religions, as articulated by Turner, Baylis and Walls in the context of the courses at Aberdeen, clearly sought to overcome prior prejudices against the religious expressions of primal peoples by placing them in a pivotal position at the base of every religion. In this view, religion cannot be understood as a general category without a careful study of the primal sources within it. The characteristics of Primal Religions, outlined in a somewhat static way by Baylis, were interpreted in Walls' writings as dynamic forces interwoven into the world religions in complex ways, often expressed and practised differently by various groups within the same primal society. For Walls (1987: 253), this meant that if we want to understand Primal Religions, we ought not to restrict ourselves to studying peoples disclosed by the so-called 'ethnographic present', but we should pay close attention to the way the major religious traditions have been adapted into or have adopted aspects of Primal Religions. Although Primal Religions were depicted as continuous with the world religious traditions at Aberdeen, their importance was attributed not so much to their anterior position in relation to the world religions, but to the elemental place they occupied at the foundation of all religions. This latter point, when applied to the persistence of primal world views within the world's living religions, made the academic study of Primal Religions a credible research and teaching topic.

The concerns to avoid prejudice against indigenous peoples, voiced early on by Ridgeway in a missionary context, thus became fully articulated through the academic programme at Aberdeen, while at the same time it embraced the theory of the cognitive unity of humanity so central to Frazer's thesis. That the justification for the study of Primal Religions at Aberdeen was conceived by those coming from missionary backgrounds, like Walls and Turner and indirectly Parrinder, is no accident. The presentation of the concept primal as basic, foundational and elementary bears an unmistakable resemblance to the Christian theological position towards other religions known as '*preparatio evangelica*'. In this view, God had prepared people everywhere to understand and receive the Christian message when it was first presented to them by providing the rudimentary concepts in their own 'primal' religion that were anticipated and fulfilled in Christianity (See, Sharpe, 1986: 151–4; Hick, 1984: 145–64; Whaling, 1999: 226–74). If all of us are 'primalists underneath', clearly humans have always possessed the cognitive capacity to embrace Christianity as a world faith. In this way, Christianity was studied at Aberdeen as a religion without ethnic or geographical limits, but as containing within it the primal world view. At the same time, Christianity was depicted as transforming localized religious expressions, which were often dictated by kinship ties, into universal categories without losing sight of the adaptations into Christian life and practice that had been derived in primal societies from their own specific cultural and linguistic concepts.

In line with this fundamental approach to the study of Christianity and Primal Religions, in 1982, six years after he had begun the M.Litt in Religion in Primal Societies, Walls established within the Department of Religious Studies in Aberdeen a 'Centre for the Study of Christianity in the Non-Western World (CSCNWW)'. He described the new Centre as having been founded on the conviction 'that the churches of Africa, Asia, Latin America and the Pacific are now central to the Christian faith, and lie at the heart of most questions about the present and future of Christianity' (Walls, 1983: 10–11) Although on the surface the programme in Aberdeen looked strong at the beginning of the 1980s, financial cuts which had begun to affect departments of religion throughout the United Kingdom were beginning to be felt acutely by the non-theological programmes in Scotland. By 1985, it had become apparent that Religious Studies in Aberdeen, with its unique programme in Primal Religions and Non-Western Christianity, was no longer tenable. As a result, Walls entered into negotiations with the Faculty of Divinity in the University of Edinburgh to secure a home for the Centre for the Study of Christianity in the Non-Western World and to continue the study of Primal Religions (see Cox and Sutcliffe, 2006: 6–12). Agreements for the transfer were concluded in 1986 and the following year Walls moved to Edinburgh. The Religious Studies Department in Aberdeen was closed in 1986 and absorbed into the Faculty of Divinity, and with it the institutional interest in Primal Religions also transferred from Aberdeen to Edinburgh.

The Development of the Study of Indigenous Religions in Edinburgh

When Andrew Walls accepted an appointment in Edinburgh, as he had done originally in Aberdeen, he joined a Faculty of Divinity in an ancient Scottish University, but one that had a very different history of Religious Studies from that at Aberdeen. Religious Studies in the University of Edinburgh had been introduced in 1971, one year after Walls founded a separate department in the Faculty of Arts and Social Studies in Aberdeen (Cox and Sutcliffe, 2006: 14–19). In Edinburgh, a three year BA in Religious Studies degree was initiated as part of the overall programme of New College, the home of the Faculty of Divinity. New College had been created as a Free Church theological college at the time of the disruption of the Church of Scotland in 1846, but with successive mergers in the Scottish Church, had functioned since 1929 as the Divinity Faculty of the University of Edinburgh (Wright, 1993: 624). From its inception, therefore, Religious Studies at Edinburgh was managed from within a traditional Divinity Faculty with a long and prestigious history in training candidates for the ministry. Its strengths, aimed at students who enrolled in the Bachelor of Divinity degree, traditionally resided in Departments of Hebrew and

Old Testament, New Testament, Ecclesiastical History, Divinity and Dogmatics, and Christian Ethics and Practical Theology.

The scope for the study of religions at Edinburgh was broadened when Walls moved the Centre for the Study of Christianity in the Non-Western World to New College. Although the Centre primarily was a teaching and research institute for postgraduate students and postdoctoral researchers, it had an impact on the undergraduate programme by introducing for the first time into the curriculum a section on 'Primal Religions', and by making non-Western students a visible part of the overall New College community (Whaling, 1996: 158). Soon, additions to the staff in the Centre further strengthened the Primal Religions element within the Religious Studies programme. John Parratt, who had been Professor and Head of the Department of Theology and Religious Studies in the University of Botswana, was appointed to the Faculty of Divinity as Associate Director of the Centre in 1990. Parratt taught the section on Primal Religions in the first year survey of religions course, which Walls had initiated, and he pioneered for Honours students a specialization in Primal Religions (although initially very few students took this up). In addition, Parratt made the study of Primal Religions a central part of the new taught master's course in Non-Western Christianity. In 1993, I was appointed to the Faculty of Divinity from the University of Zimbabwe as Lecturer in African Christianity and as Co-ordinator of the African Christianity Project, which was located in CSCNWW. In 1994, T. Jack Thompson, who had for many years worked in Malawi, joined the University of Edinburgh as a lecturer in the history of Christianity in the non-Western World.

In 1996, I published an article in *Studies in World Christianity*, in which I attempted to de-construct the term 'primal' by associating it with unacceptable phrases used in prior literature to describe indigenous peoples, such as 'primitive', 'animistic', 'tribal', 'basic', 'pre-literate' and 'ethnic' (Cox, 1996a: 55). I asserted that although Walls and Turner had argued forcefully for primal as opposed to other designations, they did so largely for theological purposes, since the term was used to emphasize that primal religions are foundational for the world religions, antecedent to them and thus contain basic principles on top of which universal religions could establish themselves by employing primal world views for their own ends. As I have just noted, this was particularly useful for the Christian notion that God had prepared the way for the missionary message by providing 'primalists' with the essential categories of thought which would make them receptive to Christianity, particularly through the postulated universal belief in a Supreme Being (Cox, 1996a: 65–9). Although my article was intended to demonstrate that the term primal was non-empirical, just as were the other generalized descriptions previously employed in anthropological, theological and religious studies literature, I suggested at the very end of the article that the term 'primal religions' should be replaced with 'the religions of *indigenous* peoples' (emphasis in original article) (Cox, 1996a: 74). I warned against using this phrase in the same non-empirical way that primal had been employed, by stressing contextual studies, arguing that the scholar should note, where possible, 'geographical, ethnic and linguistic qualifiers' (1996: 74).

After I was appointed convener of the Religious Studies Subject Group in the University of Edinburgh's School of Divinity in 1999, I began to develop the dormant undergraduate 'primal religions' courses into a full-blown study of what the School of Divinity accepted as 'Indigenous Religions', which students could take singly as part of their overall Honours programme or study alongside other religious traditions: Hinduism, Buddhism, Islam, Christianity, Judaism, Ancient Near Eastern

Religions or Chinese Religions. This was done in some senses rather uncritically by simply re-naming the courses already in the Calendar on Primal Religions Africa and Asia as Indigenous Religions: Sub-Saharan Africa and Indigenous Religions: Asia. Other courses were added in the next few years under the broad category Indigenous Religions, including Shamanism, New Indigenous Religious Movements and Anthropological Approaches to the Study of Religions. Recently, courses have been introduced in Indigenous Religions under inter-disciplinary listings, such as 'Apocalypse Now: A Study of Millenarian Movements; 'Islam in Africa', 'The History of Christianity in Africa', 'The History of Christianity in Asia', and 'African Voices in the Study of Religions'. By building up credits in these subjects, and by completing the first year survey of religions course, which has five weeks devoted to Indigenous Religions, and the second year methods courses, students at Edinburgh University by 2003 could complete an Honours degree in Religious Studies with a specialization in Indigenous Religions.

The new Religious Studies track on Indigenous Religions at Edinburgh differed from the approach to teaching Primal Religions in Aberdeen precisely on the point of the theological assumption implicit in Walls' use of the term primal. The Indigenous Religions courses at Edinburgh were tailored to treat specific indigenous societies as, in one sense, unique to themselves, nonreplicable and worthy of study in their own right. In my own teaching and writing during the 1990s, I tried to raise suspicion about categories that had been used in earlier literature, particularly by Parrinder, that classified the religions of indigenous peoples by the way they understood and developed rituals in relation to a postulated transcendent, an approach that Walls did not escape despite his attempt to show the dynamic nature of primal traditions. In an article I published on the notion of the 'sacred' in Zimbabwean death rituals, which appeared in the journal *Religion* in 1995, I deflected the emphasis on God towards ancestors, whom people most commonly address during death rituals. I argued that my research had demonstrated that ancestors continue to dominate the lives of everyday people, despite the long history of Christianity in the country (Cox, 1995: 339–55). In my classroom teaching, I drew attention to the relation between means of subsistence in Zimbabwe and the way people construe powers beyond their control. Since Zimbabwe depends on agriculture and cattle for its main means of subsistence, regular rainfall is essential for maintaining the well-being of the people. I argued that the importance of rain rituals and conceptions of great ancestors as providing the rain could be traced to the type of subsistence economy operating in the country. In these ways, I sought to move the study of Indigenous Religions away from its association with 'primal', which I argued was a non-empirical term that had proved extremely useful for inserting Christian assumptions into the study of Indigenous Religions.

Despite this distancing away from Christian theology, the long tradition that seeks to remove prejudice from the study of indigenous peoples was firmly endorsed in the Edinburgh programme. By defining Indigenous Religions as a distinct tradition that students could take as the major part of their degree programme, Religious Studies at Edinburgh sought to avoid earlier academic biases that relegated such a study to departments of history, anthropology or missiology. Indigenous Religions were assigned a place for teaching and research on an equal footing with any other religious tradition. We have seen that similar motives were employed very early on by Frazer, but made explicit by Parrinder at Ibadan, and Walls at Aberdeen. By making Indigenous Religions in effect a 'world' religion, the Edinburgh programme also perpetuated the notion that 'Religion' constitutes a single category, reflecting the cognitive unity of humanity. Although the new track for the study of Indigenous Religions sought to avoid theologizing the subject, by maintaining a singular view of religion, it can be questioned whether such a separation actually was attained. It remains clear, nonetheless, that the twin assumptions running throughout the history of the study of primitive, traditional, non-scriptural, primal or now indigenous peoples persisted: (1) the attempt to overcome bias against the legitimate study of such religions; and (2) the assumption that they form a continuous part in the overall religious life, practice and beliefs of humanity.

Current Developments in the Study of Indigenous Religions

In the United Kingdom, no other academic institution apart from Edinburgh offers students an opportunity to specialize in Indigenous Religions as a separate category of study. At the Open University, which is dedicated to distance learning with around 150,000 undergraduate and 30,000 postgraduate students enrolled (nearly all studying part-time), a project called 'Belief Beyond Boundaries' was established in 2000 in the Department of Religious Studies as a research group focusing on non-institutional forms of religion. Its web site indicates that 'the group intends to facilitate the production of research in those religions and spiritual groups which fall outside the remit of mainstream or traditional religion (as temporally or geographically defined)', such as 'Paganism; New Age; New Religious Movements; spiritualism; traditionally Eastern beliefs in a Western setting (e.g. Western Buddhism); Hinduism and Islam in diaspora; vernacular religion; diaspora religion'.[8] Since its inception, the Belief Beyond Boundaries Research Group has sponsored conferences on such themes as 'Locating the Ancestors', 'The Development of Paganism' and 'From Vernacular Religion to Contemporary Spirituality: Locating Religion in European Ethnology'. Currently, it is planning a conference under the title, 'Indigenous Religions: Debates, Issues, Methods and Approaches'. The indigenous dimension within the Religious Studies programme at the Open University was strengthened by the appointment in 2003 of Graham Harvey to its staff. As I noted in the Introduction to this book, to date Harvey has done more than any other scholar to promote the concept 'indigenous' internationally as a legitimate category within Religious Studies. Previously, when Harvey was at King Alfred's College, Winchester, he developed courses containing elements relevant to Indigenous Religions, such as the MA in 'The Rhetoric and Rituals of Death', which has been retained in the Religious Studies programme at the recently renamed University of Winchester.

That the classification 'Indigenous Religions' is gaining acceptance generally within teaching contexts is supported by the third edition of *The New Lion Handbook: The World's Religions*, edited by Christopher Partridge, which contains a major section under the heading 'Indigenous Religions' (2005: 100–133). Specific articles have been written by those who have conducted research in various parts of the world, including 'Indigenous Religions in Asia' (by Barbara Boal), 'the tribal religion of the Foe of Papua New Guinea' (by Joan Rule), 'Australian Aboriginal Religions' (by Lynne Hume), 'Melanesia' (by Carl Loeliger), 'South American Indigenous Religions' (by Andrew Dawson), 'Native North Americans' (by J.W.E. Newberry), 'Norse Shamanism' (by Veikko Anttonen), 'The Bangwa' (by Fiona Bowie), 'the Zulu' (by Axel-Ivar Berglund) and two articles I have written, one on 'The Inuit' and

---

[8]   www.open.ac.uk/Arts/relstud/index/html.

the other on 'African Indigenous Religions'. Graham Harvey's general introduction to the section on Indigenous Religions follows articles on theory and method in the study of religion and 'The Religions of Antiquity', but precedes sections dealing with the major religious traditions around the world, classified in largely customary ways, such as 'Hinduism', 'Buddhism', 'Jainism', 'Christianity' and 'Islam'. In his introductory article to the section on Indigenous Religions, Harvey argues that 'Indigenous Religions are the majority of the world's religions' (2005b: 100), and thus they continue to be 'of considerable importance in the Study of Religions and Anthropology' (2005b: 104).

Further corroboration of the now widespread use of 'Indigenous Religions' as a category amongst scholars of religion is found in a book by Mary Pat Fisher called *Living Religions*, which includes a separate chapter entitled 'Indigenous Sacred Ways' (1997: 38–68). This is particularly striking since the other chapters in the book employ traditional categories for the world's religions. In her more recent book, *Religion in the Twenty-first Century*, Fisher begins the chapter on 'Religious Traditions in the Modern World' with a section on 'Indigenous Spiritual Traditions' (1999: 29–37), which she follows again with discussions of the conventionally titled world religions. Fisher indicates that she is concerned with the 'spiritual ways practiced by indigenous people who still live close to their land', usually in 'small-scale societies in remote areas of the planet' (1999: 28). She adds that these 'are not literate cultures with written scriptures' and that their religious frame of reference is their own environment' (1999: 29).

Both the *New Lion Handbook* and Fisher's books are intended to introduce students generally to the study of the world's religions. By including substantial sections devoted to the category 'Indigenous Religions', each publication has reinforced the classification as fully worthy of detailed and lengthy discussions comparable to those dealing with the 'world' religions. Neither the contributors to the *New Lion Handbook* nor Fisher adopts the earlier line promoted at Aberdeen that Indigenous (Primal) Religions occupy an elemental status in human religious experience, although Fisher (1999: 30) admits that 'these ancient ways once existed everywhere'. She adds that for the most part 'they have been suppressed by, or fused with, the religions of cultures which are more politically powerful, such as Christianity or Hinduism' (1999: 30). This observation derives from Fisher's analysis of power relations between local societies and globalizing forces, rather than implying a theological connection between Indigenous Religions and the universal religions. The development of new academic programmes and publications related to Indigenous Religions, such as those at the Open University and that of the *New Lion Handbook* and Fisher's introductory texts, supports my contention that 'Indigenous' now has overtaken 'Primal' as the preferred designation amongst religious studies scholars, although, as we will see, much clarification and further analyses are needed if this trend is to be sustained and legitimated.

Conclusion

In this chapter, I have not sought to present a global overview of academic programmes and the growing number of textbooks associated with them that incorporate aspects in the study of Indigenous Religions. These can be found in some form now in many universities, often in courses relating to the particular cultures in which the academic institutions are set. Rather, I have tried to show that, where such studies follow generalized and comparative approaches, they can be traced to the much older ideas, derived from nineteenth-century missionary attitudes and early anthropological literature, that humanity shares a common cognitive capacity and that the religions of humanity, even in their most primitive forms, should be treated for comparative reasons as containing the same basic elements. I have shown how these principles were applied to the study of Primal Religions in the 1970s at the University of Aberdeen and how currently they have been adapted into both undergraduate and postgraduate programmes on Indigenous Religions in the University of Edinburgh. In recent years, the idea of Indigenous Religions as a category alongside the other religions of the world has gained further credibility in publications used to introduce students to the study of religions. In such books, Indigenous Religions, despite their geographical diversity and localized expressions, are described as sharing enough features in common to be treated under a single classification.

This gradual acceptance of Indigenous Religions as a viable category within the field of religious studies is accompanied by numerous theoretical problems. In this chapter, I have drawn attention to my own earlier critique of the term primal as useful for theology, but I have admitted that problems with this designation have not been overcome simply by inserting 'indigenous' as an alternative classification. In the next chapter, I outline some of the most critical and persistent problems associated with studying 'Indigenous Religions' as a comparative category within a world religions paradigm. I do not address directly the problem of 'religion' in the next chapter, but postpone this discussion to Chapter 4, precisely because in the next two chapters, I want to disentangle the theoretical difficulties attached to the terms 'indigenous' and 'world religions' from the quite distinct, but highly contentious methodological problems associated with the category 'religion'.

Chapter 2

Essentialism and the World Religions Paradigm

In the last chapter, I traced the development of the academic study of Indigenous Religions, beginning with nineteenth-century ideas, advancing to the innovations introduced into this field by Geoffrey Parrinder in African contexts and concluding with a review of teaching programmes devoted exclusively to this field in the universities of Aberdeen and Edinburgh. Before I can consider the category 'indigenous' as a viable field within the study of religions, I must in this chapter examine the prior concept 'world religions' as a pervasive, but problematic term that continues to be used rather uncritically within the academic study of religions despite efforts to undermine it or to qualify it. This becomes an increasingly important question for the central discussion of this book, since, as we have seen, in academic programmes and recent publications, 'Indigenous Religions' as a separate category is increasingly being fitted neatly into a 'world religions' paradigm. Although it is only after a critical review of the assumptions associated with this expression that questions about the legitimate use of Indigenous Religions as another 'world' religion can be addressed, at the conclusion of this chapter, I will argue that an even more fundamental problem has surfaced, that of religion itself.

The Emergence of the World Religions Paradigm

By the world religions paradigm, I am referring to the study of religions under classifications commonly defined by Western scholars as the major traditions of the world. In a recent book outlining how the term 'world religions' developed out of nineteenth-century academic contexts, Tomoko Masuzawa (2005: 2–3) argues that by creating systems for classifying the so-called great world faiths, scholars intended primarily 'to distinguish the West from the rest'. This, she argues, has been done by creating either binary or tripartite divisions. The binary classifications place religions into the categories of 'East' and 'West'. An excellent example of such an approach is found in Frederick Spiegelberg's *Living Religions of the World*, in which the author separates the world's religions rather conveniently into 'the Semitic-Judaic-Christian tradition in the West' and 'the religions of the Orient' (Spiegelberg, 1956: vii). Masuzawa argues that the tripartite system of classification organizes the world's religions according to geography, dividing them into religions that originated in the Ancient Near East (primarily Judaism, Christianity and Islam); the religions of South Asia (almost always including Hinduism, Buddhism and Jainism, but sometimes adding Zoroastrianism); and religions that developed in the Far East (Confucianism, Taoism and Shinto). Masuzawa contends that the geographical division, although appearing scientific and neutral, actually is tainted by 'a racialized notion of ethnic difference'. She cites John Clark Archer's *Faiths Men Live By* as an example of this. In the introduction to his book, Archer (1938: 1) claims that the world's religions are represented by what he calls 'three major "racial" strains': '(1) the Turanian, for example, Taoism, Confucianism, and Shinto; (2) the Indo-European, for example, Hinduism, Parsiism, Jainism, Buddhism and Sikhism; and (3) the Semitic, Judaism, Christianity, and Islam.' Masuzawa notes that many books on the world's religions also include a section often referred to as the 'pre-historic' or 'primitive' religions, which she says are widely regarded by scholars as 'an ever-receding region of the premodern lurking at the edge of the world historical stage' (2005: 3–4).

Masuzawa observes that courses on the world's religions following these broad general patterns began to appear in North American university curricula during the 1930s, which she says 'marks something of a watershed' since such courses were accompanied by the 'visible increase in the publication of books on this general topic' (2005: 37). She cites two early works published in the United States, Richard Ernest Hume's *The World's Living Religions* (1924) and Archer's *Faiths Men Live By*, as prefiguring the relatively uncritical acceptance of the term 'world religions' that now characterizes its widespread use both in academic and popular contexts. Masuzawa fails to mention the highly influential book by John B. Noss, whose volume of over 800 pages entitled *Man's Religions*, played such an influential role in classroom teaching, particularly in the United States, after 1950. Noss developed this monumental survey out of lectures he delivered in courses on world religions during the 1930s at Franklin and Marshall College, a small liberal arts institution located in Lancaster, Pennsylvania. With the help of his younger brother, David, the book first appeared in 1949 (Noss, 1949). The eighth edition, which was re-named *A History of the World's Religions* (1990) by David Noss, was altered to include contemporary themes, such as women in the religious traditions of the world. This version of the book, which now lists David Noss as the main author, currently is in its eleventh edition and remains popular as an undergraduate text, primarily in North American universities. John Noss's original design described the religions of the world much along the lines Masuzawa refers to as the geographical distribution of the religions, but in Noss's case, also according to a detailed analysis of historical developments. Noss divides the historical geography of the world's religions into four classifications: 'Some Primitive and Bygone Religions', 'The Religions of India', 'The Religions of the Far East' and the 'Religions of the Near East'. Under the first category, he includes two sections, one on 'religion in prehistoric and primitive cultures' and 'representative national religions of the past'. The remainder of the book outlines for his students how the world's religions came to occupy their present place in world history, with studies of early and later Hinduism, Jainism, Buddhism in its earlier and later phases, Sikhism, Taoism, Confucianism, Shinto, Zoroastrianism, Judaism in its early biblical period and in its later history, Christianity in the time of the early Church followed by descriptions of its subsequent doctrinal and ecclesiastical splits, and Islam, with its main divisions and regional variations.

In the preface to the first edition, Noss notes that he wrote the book to meet two specific needs: to introduce the world's religions in a way that contains 'adequate amounts of descriptive or interpretative details from the original source materials' (1963: xiii) and to present 'man's most noteworthy faiths in a time-setting that will do justice to their development as well as to their origins' (1963: xiii). The third edition of the book, which appeared in 1963, was called by Noss a 'thorough revision' since it attempts 'to treat several of the religions in greater depth', particularly Buddhism. He also acknowledges having reconsidered the features of 'primitive religions … in the light of recent anthropological research' (1963: ix). The preface to the third edition also makes it clear how Noss intended his book to be used in university courses on religion. He draws to the attention of 'teachers' the large number of entries in the Index, which he notes could be useful as topics for assigning term papers.

> Entries such as 'Ancestor worship,' 'Angels,' 'Asceticism,' 'Atheism,' 'Christianity,' 'Christology,' 'Church,' 'Creation,' 'Ethics,' 'Future life,' 'God,' 'Gods,' 'Heaven,' 'Hell,' 'Incarnation,' 'Magic,' 'Man (doctrine of),' 'Monism,' 'Mysticism,' 'Prayer,' 'Priesthood,' and 'Sacrifice,' contain references to many faiths of the world. A comprehensive essay based on any of these entries,… could prove of great value to the student (1963: x).

He admits that the book is probably too large 'for a one-semester course', but urges teachers who are limited by time constraints to 'select for study particular chapters or groups of chapters'. He adds that 'first-rate supplementary reading is now possible', much of which is now beginning to appear in less expensive paperback editions (1963: x).

One widely-read study of the world religions, which as a paperback proved extremely popular in classroom settings, was Huston Smith's *The Religions of Man*, first published in 1958 and included in Noss's list of recommended readings. Smith, who was Professor of Philosophy at the Massachusetts Institute of Technology, developed his book out of lectures he presented in 1955 on an educational television station in St. Louis, Missouri, which he claims reached over 100,000 viewers (1965: ix). His aim in the published form of his lectures was to 'move more rapidly than the usual survey into the *meaning* these religions carry for the lives of their adherents' (emphasis his) (1965: xi). Smith claims that no single book had yet been written which could 'carry the intelligent layman into the heart of the world's living faiths to the point where he might see and even feel why and how they guide and motivate the lives of those who live by them' (1965: xi). Smith explains that his book was written to achieve this goal by adhering to three central principles: (1) to treat religion as a world-wide phenomenon; (2) to take religion seriously as a potent force in the contemporary world; and (3) to communicate the meaning of religion in a way that will prove relevant to the everyday lives of his readers (1965: 6–12). The religions considered by Smith include separate chapters in the following order on Hinduism, Buddhism, Confucianism, Taoism, Islam, Judaism and Christianity. Since Smith adopted a popular approach to the study of the world religions, leaving out much historical and textual material, it is evident why Noss listed it as a supplementary text for students that could prove useful in courses unable to consider in such depth what his own text was written to achieve. Smith's book, nonetheless, attained remarkable popularity in its own right, with numerous re-prints occurring over the years, eventually resulting in a renewal of the copyright in 1986 as part of Harper's Perennial Library series. As such, it did much to re-enforce the world religions paradigm, not only in undergraduate courses, but more widely amongst the general population, again particularly in the United States.

In the United Kingdom, an early contributor to the study of world religions was E. E. Kellett, whose academic credentials stretched widely from that of a translator of German literature into English to literary criticism. His book, *A Short History of Religions*, which was first published in 1933 by Victor Gollancz Ltd in London, was re-issued in 1948 by the same publisher and then reprinted in 1963 as a Penguin paperback, provides an early example in Britain of a survey of the world religions that was intended to reach a wide public audience. In his 'prefatory note', Kellett explains that he has written the book 'not to satisfy, but to stimulate, the interest of serious-minded people in its theme'. He adds that 'there are many signs that the world is awaking to a renewed sense of the paramount importance of religion', which cannot be understood unless each religion is placed into its context as part of world history. Although he admits that it would be impossible for him to approach his subject with 'absolute impartiality', his aim is to treat each religion sympathetically (1948: prefatory note, no page number). Nevertheless, the Christian bias in the book is evident by the treatment given to Christian history and its subsequent divisions, which constitute well over half the 565 pages in the volume. Separate chapters are devoted to 'The Reformed Church of England', 'The Church of Scotland', 'The Sects' (including Baptists, Quakers, Methodists and The Salvation Army), and 'Some other Sects' (including among others Mormons, Spiritualists, Christian Science, and even a segment on scientific positivism as a religion). Just one chapter is dedicated to 'The Religions of the Far East', constituting 63 pages, and dealing with what the author classifies as Hinduism, Brahmanism, Jainism, Buddhism, Confucianism, Taoism and Theosophy.

Kellett begins with a discussion of the nature and origin of religion, relying heavily on theories of magic and superstition derived from J.G. Frazer (1948: 12–15). He then discusses Judaism before reviewing Roman, Greek and Germanic Religions, which he follows by five chapters on the early development of Christianity. One chapter each is devoted to Zoroastrianism and Islam. In the conclusion, Kellett makes his partiality to the Christian religion evident by arguing that in the modern world Christianity can accommodate itself 'better than any other' since the meaning of Christ will never be exhausted' (1948: 572–3). Nonetheless, he praises all religious teachers, including the Buddha, for lightening 'the load of humanity' and for 'strengthening those hopes without which it would have fainted and fallen' (1948: 576). He concludes: 'If our study has led us to honour these teachers as they deserve, and to rid ourselves of the narrow parochialism which thinks itself in sole possession of all truth, it will not have been in vain' (1948: 576). The significance of Kellett's work lies precisely in its popular appeal. It possesses a thorough academic grounding, but aims at making a scholarly approach to the history of religions accessible to serious readers who do not necessarily possess specialized knowledge of the religions. In this way, just as Huston Smith's book did later in the United States, Kellett helped advance the world religions paradigm into broader circles in the United Kingdom than ever before had been attempted.

Another important contributor to the development of the world religions paradigm in Britain was A.C. Bouquet, whose book *Comparative Religion*, first published in 1942 in paperback by Penguin, was intended to provide what he called 'a plain tale, inspired by scientific method' (1950: v, prefatory note to the first edition). Bouquet, who was an Anglican priest and Army chaplain during the first world war, wrote *Comparative Religion* after having been appointed a lecturer in the History and Comparative Study of Religions in the University of Cambridge. The front cover of the third edition, published in 1950, calls the book 'a survey and comparison of the great religions of the world, and an examination of their significance today'. In the preface to the second edition, published in 1945, Bouquet expresses gratification at the way his 'little book' has been received (1950: vi), and in the note to the third edition indicates that the only substantial change within any of its three printings has been the addition of 'some valuable suggestions made by a scholar in Islamics, Dr Heinz Zilcher', whom Bouquet explains had written to him as a prisoner of war 'from a camp in the Eastern Mediterranean' (1950: vii–viii).

In *Comparative Religion*, Bouquet follows an approach similar to the one adopted by Noss, but in a much more popular and less extensive way, by beginning with the question 'How did religion start? (1950: 38). After a largely psychological explanation, which considers 'the self or ego' and 'the world or environment of the self' (1950: 38), Bouquet considers the explanations of these phenomena from the perspective of 'earlier races' (1950: 42). His method is not historical, but largely a projection from his own experience into what he would expect to be the understanding of pre-historic humans, as exemplified in the statement: 'Early man would seem to have drawn but little distinction between himself and his animal, bird and reptile cousins' (1950: 44). His next chapter considers the religions of antiquity, dealing briefly in a few pages each with Mesopotamia, Egypt, Central America, Greeks and Romans, Northern and Central Europe. Bouquet includes in the midst of this discussion a chart, which he claims shows comparatively the varieties of polytheism operating throughout each of these ancient religious traditions, from versions of the sun-god to the High God (1950: 94–5). He then discusses in turn in subsequent chapters 'the phenomenon of India', 'China and Japan', 'Hebrew and Christian Religion', 'Islam' and 'Mysticism'. Although the chapters on Asian religions are divided geographically, they retain the traditional designations throughout, with references to Hinduism, Buddhism, Sikhism, Confucianism, Taoism and Shinto.

Bouquet's concluding 'epilogue' (1950: 293–302) considers theories of religion, in which he lists briefly ideas associated with a wide variety of scholars, including Frazer and Freud (whom he describes as having maintained views against religion), those who promoted a 'radical exclusiveness' based on a religious confession, advocates of a 'radical relativity' who see all religions as pathways to higher truth, and finally the 'detached and descriptive' approaches, exemplified through a wide range of methods from the philosophy of history in Hegel to the classifications of religion outlined by the Swedish Archbishop Nathan Söderblom in his 1931 Gifford Lectures delivered in the University of Edinburgh (Söderblom, 1933). Bouquet concludes by asserting full agreement with a theological interpretation of religion, support for which he cites the writings of the Dutch phenomenologist, Gerardus van der Leeuw, who, in his classic book *Religion in Essence and Manifestation* (1938: 679) described the 'essence' of religion, for believers, as coming 'only from above, beginning with God'. Bouquet expressed his own version of this sentiment when he wrote: 'The sweep of man's quest for the Eternal and the Real seems a fine and venturesome and not wholly fruitless endeavour, and those who proclaim a Response and an Initiative upon the part of the Eternal have an even nobler tale to tell, whether we assent to it or not' (1950: 302).

Around the same time that Hume and Archer in the United States and Kellett in Britain were writing on the world's religions, similar books were beginning to appear on the European continent. For example, in the late 1920s Carl Clemen of the University of Bonn, in collaboration with eleven colleagues, ten of whom were working in German universities or related institutions (the other in The Netherlands),[1] published a book under the title, *Religions of the World: Their Nature and their History*, which was translated into English in 1931. Clemen explains in

---

[1]   In addition to Clemen, the contributors include Albert Schott of Bonn, writing on Babylonian Religion; Günther Roeder, curator of the Hildesheim Museum, on Egyptian Religion; F.E.A. Krause of Göttingen, writing on Chinese Religion and Japanese Religion in separate chapters; Otto Strauss of Kiel, on Indian Religion; Friedrich Pfister of Würzburg, on Greek and Roman Religion; Franz Rolf Shroeder from Würzburg, on Teutonic Religion; Karl H. Meyer from Münster, on Slavic Religion; Rabbi Leo Baeck from Berlin, on the 'Religion of the Hebrews'; Heinrich Hackmann from Amsterdam, on Buddhism; Erich Seeberg from Berlin, on Christianity; and Frans Babinger from Berlin, writing on Islam. Beyond editing

his preface that 'the main purpose of this work is to provide the general reader with an account of the history of the various religions of the world' by avoiding 'all unnecessary technicalities of expression' (1931: vii). He adds that the authors have 'confined themselves to the main features of the various religions' and in the process have 'emphasized chiefly those aspects of them which are really important for their adherents' (1931: vii). The outline of the book follows a pattern similar to those appearing in comparable North American and British publications of the time by beginning with two sections, both written by Clemen, one on 'Prehistoric Religion' and the second on 'Primitive Religion', although these taken together constitute less than 40 pages in a book of nearly 500 pages. The third section on 'Ancient National Religions' is broken into ten chapters and includes separate articles written by different experts in the fields of Babylonian, Egyptian, Chinese, Indian, Persian, Greek and Roman, Celtic, Teutonic, Slavic and Japanese religions. Some contributions to the third section are extremely short, such as the article by F.E.A. Krause of the University of Göttingen on Japanese Religion, which comprises a mere seven pages. This can be contrasted to the detailed discussion of Greek and Roman Religion written by Friedrich Pfister of the University of Würzburg consisting of 61 pages. The fourth section of the book is entitled 'World Religions', and, although large portions in most chapters are devoted to the history of the religions discussed, each author tries to address the situation at the time of writing, largely in terms of doctrines currently advanced. The four 'world religions' considered include separate chapters on 'Religions of the Hebrews', 'Buddhism', 'Christianity' and 'Islam'. The uneven distribution of space given to the religions is just as evident in this section as it is in the first part on the ancient national religions with, for example, 32 pages devoted to Islam while the chapter on Christianity contains 100 pages. A notable exception in approach to the other contributions is found in the article written on the 'Religion of the Hebrews' by Rabbi Leo Baeck of Berlin, who describes Judaism not in historical terms but theologically under three main themes: 'The One God', 'Man' and 'The Individual and the Community'. The Clemen's volume demonstrates that the German contribution during the 1920s to the study of world religions was overwhelmingly historical and on balance was concerned with discussing those 'ancient national religions' that bore a direct relationship to the development of European civilization and that treated world religions in a way that was heavily weighted towards Christianity. The translator, A.K. Dallas from Edinburgh, explains (1931: v) that he had worked with Carl Clemen to produce the book in English 'for general readers' because 'the last decades have witnessed a distinct revival of interest in the study of comparative religion'. He admits that many books have appeared in recent years on this subject and have been incorporated into 'most modern commentaries on the books of the Bible'. He argues that Clemen's volume nonetheless will prove of considerable interest to readers in English because the editor has made a firm endeavour 'to bring out clearly the broad outlines of the various faiths'.

Although by 1960 attempts were being made to vary the way the world religions paradigm was interpreted in textbooks following the model established by Noss and Smith in the United States, Kellett and Bouquet in the United Kingdom, and before them by Clemen in Germany, many simply further reinforced the general view that religions need to be studied according to the main religious traditions of the world.

---

the book and writing the sections on 'Prehistoric Religion' and 'Primitive Religion', Clemen contributed separate chapters on 'Persian Religion' and 'Celtic Religion'.

For example, in 1960 John A. Hutchinson and James Alfred Martin, Jr, published *Ways of Faith: An Introduction to Religion*. The title was intended to demonstrate that religions contain far more than beliefs, and that they are best understood as pathways of life. Despite this attempt to break from the traditional historical and doctrinal approaches to describing the religions, Hutchinson and Martin persist in dividing the 'ways' into traditional categories: 'the classical ways of China', 'the ways of Hinduism', 'the ways of Buddhism' 'the way of Judaism' and 'the way of Islam'. Christianity is given special attention in the volume, with separate chapters devoted to the ways of faith in the Roman Catholic and Protestant traditions. They thus did little more than dress the world religions paradigm in a slightly different guise, without making any substantial changes to what had gone before.

In light of this brief sampling of influential texts aimed at undergraduate students and the serious layperson, it would be fair to conclude that, by 1960, religions were conceived widely in undergraduate teaching in the United States and Britain (and other European contexts), and more broadly amongst the informed public, in terms of the divisions classified as the major faiths of the world. During the 1960s, two influential scholars, Wilfred Cantwell Smith and Ninian Smart, writing from quite similar perspectives, challenged many of the foundational assumptions which had motivated and informed most prior books on the world's religions. Had their primary aim been to undermine the world religions paradigm and had they offered viable alternatives in its place, the study of religions as an academic field might have undergone far-reaching methodological revisions in the years that ensued. That Smith and Smart ultimately proved unsuccessful in uprooting conventional approaches to the study of world religions, as we will see, resulted largely from their own 'religious' interpretations of religion.

Challenges to the World Religions Paradigm: W.C. Smith and Ninian Smart

Wilfred Cantwell Smith, who originally was an Islamicist working in India, by the early 1960s had become interested primarily in exposing the problematic way religion had been conceived and studied in Western academic contexts. He described his book, *The Meaning and End of Religion*, first published in 1962, as urging a radical methodological revision in the study of religions. by exposing the gradual objectification of 'personal faith' into the category 'religion' (1964: 18). He believed this process had originated at the time of the Western Enlightenment and had come to define the basis on which the world's religions were currently classified. In another book, *The Faith of Other Men*, also first published in 1962, Smith illustrated his method for attaining understanding of religions of which one is not a part, offering his easily grasped analysis as a popular alternative to prior objectivist approaches. The other important contributor to this debate was Ninian Smart, who in 1967 founded the first Department of Religious Studies in the United Kingdom at the University of Lancaster. By stressing the multi-dimensional nature of religion, Smart attempted to re-direct the study of religions away from the inherent doctrinal and historical biases he had discovered in most prior studies.

In *The Meaning and End of Religion*, Smith argues that the term 'faith' denotes in a far better way than 'religion' what human beings intend when they perform rituals, recite scriptures, tell sacred stories and adhere to communal traditions. He contends further that the term 'religion', under the increasingly hegemonic influence of Western scientific and dualistic thinking, has become 'reified' and thus nowadays is treated commonly as if it were entirely objective and static (1964: 72; 123–4). Smith asserts that religion is not a 'thing', but a living reality better described in terms that refer to actions, such as 'piety', 'devotion' or 'faith'. He acknowledges that students of religion cannot observe the inner life of adherents; indeed he admits that faith is nearly impossible to define. Nonetheless, he insists that personal faith constitutes the 'locus' of religion, and that without such an understanding, scholars have no clue about the true nature of religion (1964: 167–8). In order to safeguard the study of religion against reification, Smith posits that researchers should investigate and describe the 'expressions' of faith. These include such phenomena of religion as rituals, myths, community structure, scripture and religious specialists (1964: 155). The scholar observes these outward forms of religion, but must always keep in mind that they reflect an inner reality for adherents. The dynamic nature of religion for Smith is enshrined in the term 'cumulative tradition', which refers to the various ways faith has been expressed not simply in ancient practices, but how it responded to changing circumstances by incorporating new stories, ideas and rituals into the overall tradition (1964: 139–41). Although academics are tempted to describe the world's religions as if they were static and unchanging, such a critical error can be avoided by acknowledging that religious traditions over time accumulate new and impressive additions that make the tradition fuller and richer than before.

If the concepts associated with 'faith', 'expressions of faith' and 'cumulative tradition' provided a methodological revolution in the study of religions for Smith, he needed to demonstrate how this might work in a quite practical way to aid genuine understanding. He attempted to do just this in *The Faith of Other Men*, which he wrote to provide a clear methodological alternative to the reifying tendencies within the world religions paradigm. At the outset, Smith notes, 'a certain pattern has developed, in which the panorama of human religious life across the world is described under a series of headings: Hinduism, Buddhism, Confucianism, and the like – a number of separate systems, each called a religion' (1998: 28). He admits that a great deal of progress has been made in researching and reporting on 'the outward facts' (1998: 26) of the great traditions, but asserts that 'it is possible to know a good deal about what are called the various religious systems, and still not to understand the people whose lives they help to form' (1998: 28). This problem can be overcome, not by describing religious systems, but by encouraging the reader to gain an understanding of the faith of religious people. To achieve this, Smith isolates a central symbol for each faith, which discloses its inner nature. This symbol varies in each instance, from 'an image, a phrase, a ceremony', but it provides for the reader 'some inkling of how what seems to us at first unfamiliar, and even odd, may on inquiry suggest to us how other people look at the world' (1998: 29).

Smith then explains that he will confine his attention to four groupings: 'Hindus, Buddhists, Muslims and Chinese', which, when coupled with Jews and Christians 'cover at the present time perhaps eighty percent or so of the world's population religiously' (1998. 30). The key symbols offering the deepest insight into each of these four faiths include: the phrase '*tat tvam asi*' ('that thou art'), referring to the Brahman-Atman unity in classical Hinduism; the *Shin Byu* ceremony (or going out ritual) for Buddhists, whereby young men retreat to a monastery as a re-enactment of the Buddha's great renunciation; the intensely felt testimony of faith for Muslims, the *shahada*, 'there is no God but Allah and Muhammad is His apostle'; and the *yin-yang* symbol that explains the coincidence of opposites in Chinese religious philosophy. By exploring each of these symbols, Smith sought to open a window of understanding, primarily to his Christian (and in some sense Jewish) readers, by enabling them to grasp the central meaning at the core of each faith. Smith admitted that this method sacrifices 'extension of coverage' in favour of gaining an appreciation of the profundity within each religious tradition (1998: 30).

Smith's approach can be illustrated aptly in the case of the Islamic 'creed', the Shahada. He employs the word 'creed' deliberately in order that his Western audience can understand the profound difference between reciting a formal list of beliefs and the witness to what fundamentally constitutes Islamic faith. For a Muslim, according to Smith, the verbal expression indicates that God's word has been revealed and incarnated into the holy Qur'an, just as Jesus Christ is the incarnate word in human form for Christians. For Muslims, this explains why the Qur'an is regarded with such deep respect, and why its central testimony to the unity of God and the role of his apostle helps the outsider gain an understanding of inner Islamic devotion. We see the reverence accorded to the word in the art form calligraphy in which the text of the Qur'an is written in a beautiful Arabic script (1998: 64). In addition, Smith notes, when the Shahada is recited, it is always done in Arabic, with its own lilting resonance, also indicative of a kind of art form (1998: 65). Moreover, the Shahada overcomes what Westerners would call the sacred-secular divide, uniting all of life in full devotion to God (1998: 66). Most significantly, the Muslim creed bears witness to a profound and elemental reality. Smith underscores this point when he asserts that for the Muslim, the two parts of the Shahada are 'not merely true, but profoundly and cosmically true, ... the two most important and final truths in the world, and the most crucial for human beings and their destiny' (1998: 70). When his reader grasps the utter significance of the simple proclamation of Islamic faith, Smith contends that at least some measure of understanding will have been attained, not of the history and doctrine of a religion, but of the 'locus' of what it means to be a Muslim, that is, the personal faith of the adherent. What Smith does in the case of Islam, he repeats for Hindu, Buddhist and Chinese faith, so that by the end of *The Faith of Other Men*, the reader's understanding will have been transformed into something akin to a deep empathy.

Smith's attempt to break out of the world religions paradigm was based on his own conviction that religion consists of inner experience and that it should not be presented, as it had been done so widely in texts on the world's religions, as if understanding could be attained by mastering facts. Smith's aim was to liberate the study of world religions from its slavery to historical surveys and the presentation of static doctrinal systems by showing that it is far more important to understand the people who practise within these traditions than it is to attain knowledge of the outward structures of their religious systems. As innovative and critical as Smith's approach was, we look very hard to find him challenging the categories whereby the religions of the world have been placed into distinct units. He still speaks of the faith of 'Hindus', 'Buddhists', 'Muslims', 'Christians', 'Jews' and 'the Chinese' as if these comprise single categories which the reader can distinguish from the others by grasping the key symbol within each. In the end, Smith failed to confront the world religions paradigm itself and in some ways, legitimated it. Rather than dismantling the categories for classifying world religions, he stressed instead the 'religiousness' of religion by placing the inner faith of adherents at the core of his method.

One of the most prolific writers on the world's religions during the latter third of the twentieth century was Ninian Smart, whose volumes have been read widely and have influenced methodological approaches within the academic study of religions. Smart challenged customary approaches to the study of world religions in his text, *The Religious Experience of Mankind*, first published in 1969, by viewing religions through the lens of 'experience'. In this important book, Smart argues in the first instance that religion as such cannot be observed. Of course, he admits that people's religious acts can be seen through the 'externals' of religion, such as the way various rituals are performed or by the manner in which moral laws are interpreted and enforced within religious communities. Nonetheless, at its core, religion is experiential, the significance of which can be understood only as an expression of 'the inner life of those who use these externals' (Smart, 1977: 11). The student of religion thus must do much more than put to memory a chronological sequence within the history of any tradition; the student must 'enter into the meaning of those events' by penetrating 'into the hearts and minds of those who have been involved in that history' (1977: 11). For Smart, the externals are best described as the 'dimensions of religion', which include the ritual, mythological, doctrinal, ethical and social dimensions, and conclude with the 'experiential' dimension. (1977: 21). By employing these categories, students are unlikely to reduce religion to any one aspect, such as doctrines or societal structures, but instead are inclined to view them holistically as expressions of the inner faith of religious devotees.

Smart (1977: 25–9) admitted that his stress on experience, due to its subjective nature, could be criticized by those within scriptural traditions who regard the most important aspect of religion as an objectively articulated divine revelation. In particular, he had in mind theological controversies within Christianity which pit the instability of beliefs based on personal apprehensions of the truth confirmed by experience against what God has revealed and enshrined in scripture. Smart explained that as a scholar of religion he is not concerned with the 'truth' of religion. If a religion, like Christianity, asserts a particular theory of revelation, this will be studied under the doctrinal dimension. Moreover, many religions, including Hinduism, maintain a belief in a verbally inerrant revelation, but all forms of revelation are mediated through humans, such as prophets, and thus in the end can be fitted under the experiential dimension.

Although in *The Religious Experience of Mankind* Smart sought to reconfigure prior methods in the study of the world's religions, he continued to employ traditional classifications to describe religious experience. In a way resembling the earlier outline in Noss's volume, Smart begins his analysis with the category Primitive Religions, including 'prehistoric' religions, and then describes the 'Religions of India', 'Religions of the Far East and 'Religions of the Near East'. Under each category, he reinforces the conventional ways the world religions have been classified, outlining historical developments in each region, in India, for example, from the Vedic tradition through Jainism and Buddhism to Classical Hinduism. He does the same in other geographical regions, so that by the conclusion, the reader has been provided with descriptions of the 'world religions', which in the introduction to the book, Smart catalogues as 'Christianity, Judaism, Islam, Buddhism, Hinduism and Confucianism', to which he adds, 'Taoism in China, Shintoism in Japan, the Jain and Sikh religions in India, together with certain modern offshoots from Christianity in the West such as the Latter Day Saints' (1977: 14). Smart's experiential approach, which he used to create the dimensions of religion, thus reinforced in the minds of students and scholars alike the notion that religions should be classified along broad lines corresponding to the world's religious traditions. Although he intended the dimensions of religion to broaden the scope of religious studies by including in its remit secular world views, such as Marxism, ultimately he failed in this early book to challenge the categories that constitute the basic elements within the world religions paradigm.

In a much later book, entitled simply *The World's Religions* (1989, paperback re-print 1992), Smart clearly gave priority to the dimensions of religion as a methodological scheme for classifying religions without insisting that they be understood primarily in terms of experience. To each dimension he applied a dual designation to emphasize its flexibility, and he moved the experiential dimension to second place on the list, coupling it with the term 'emotional'.[2] In addition, he inserted a new category, which he called the material dimension, the only one he discussed without providing it with a dual label. He drew attention to the complexity and diversity of religions, and challenged the presentation of each religion as if it were a distinct unit by underscoring the many divisions found within each religion. In the Introduction to the book, he illustrates this by contrasting a Baptist chapel in Georgia with an Eastern Orthodox church in Romania, noting that these very different expressions of religion are lumped in most books under a single rubric called Christianity (1992: 11). Affinities of adherents within the religions also may vary. In his own case, Smart admits to feeling closer to Buddhists in Sri Lanka 'than I do to some groups in my own family of Christianity'(1992: 11–12). By stressing the dimensions of religion and by dropping any reference to experience in the title to this later book, Smart seems to have rejected his earlier emphasis on experience as the key to understanding religion, while at the same time moving away from describing religions as if they were entirely self-contained.

The World's Religions carries the sub-title, 'Old Traditions and Modern Transformations', a phrase denoting the two main sections of the book. In Part One, Smart discusses 'Earliest Religion' and then painstakingly outlines religions in various parts of the world from South Asia through China, Japan, Southeast Asia, The Pacific, The Americas, The Ancient Near East, Persia and Central Asia, The Greek and Roman World, Classical and Medieval Christianity and Judaism, Classical and Medieval Islam and concludes finally with what he calls 'Classical African Religions'. In Part Two, he examines how in each of these geographical areas religion has been transformed in the modern world, particularly by colonialism and its demise and the concurrent rise of secular world views, including the intense change fomented by globalising forces. The first part of Smart's book, just as in *The Religious Experience of Mankind*, follows almost identically the pattern set forth in many earlier works on the world's religions by adopting a geographical approach to religious history, such as we have seen in the works of John B. Noss, E.E. Kellett and Carl Clemen. In the second part, Smart demonstrates in a remarkably comprehensive way the manner religions have responded to enormous changes over the past 400 years or so, since the age of exploration and travel first began on a global scale. He argues that the contemporary world now has become a market place for competing worldviews, including scientific humanism, Marxism, existentialism and nationalism (1992: 21). The central issue emerging from the discussion in the second part of his book becomes evident when Smart considers if secular worldviews constitute religions in their own right or if religions are better conceived as worldviews. Smart responds by noting that his newly named seven dimensions can be applied equally

---

[2] His revised list of the 'dimensions' include: the practical and ritual dimension; the experiential and emotional dimension; the narrative or mythic dimension; the doctrinal and philosophical dimension; the ethical and legal dimension; the social and institutional dimension; the material dimension. Amongst the dual names assigned to these dimensions, he speaks only of the relationship between narrative and mythic by using the term 'or', as if these two dimensions referred to the same phenomenon.

to secular worldviews as they can be to religions. In the case of nationalism, for example, since 'the nation today is like a religion ... it is then reasonable to treat modern nationalism in the same terms as religion' (1992: 24).

It would seem then that in *The World's Religions*, written twenty years after the first edition of *The Religious Experience of Mankind*, Smart not only abandoned the priority he had given earlier to experience for interpreting religion, but actually broadened what he meant by religion to include worldviews. On closer examination, however, it becomes apparent that this is not precisely what he intended. We must remember that for Smart the dimensions referred to religion; they were dimensions *of religion*. Moreover, Smart used the dimensions, as he explained, 'to make sense of the variety and to discern some patterns in the luxurious vegetation of the world's religions and subtraditions' (1992: 12). That he intended his categories to apply strictly to religions becomes unambiguous, when, after discussing the relevance of the dimensions to Marxism, he tellingly observes: 'Though to a greater or lesser extent our seven-dimensional model may apply to secular worldviews, it is not really appropriate to call them religions, or even "quasi-religions"' (1992: 25). He explains that Marxists do not regard themselves as religious at all, but as anti-religious and thus for scholars of religion to refer to Marxism as a religion would disparage the very ideology Marxists espouse. It is much more honest to refer to this as a worldview, which can be subjected to the same form of analysis as can any of the world's religions. This demonstrates, in Smart's words, that in the contemporary world 'the various systems of ideas and practices, *whether religious or not*, are competitors and mutual blenders, and can thus be said to play in the same league' (1992: 25) (emphasis added). Quite obviously then a worldview is not identical to a religion. Since Smart does not define religion in this context, we are only left to guess why not, other than by calling secularists 'religious' against their own preferred self-designation, Smart would contradict his lifelong commitment to privileging the insider's point of view. At the end of this monumental treatment of the world's religions, therefore, despite the breadth Smart suggests within his worldview analysis, the world religions paradigm emerges unscathed.

Both Cantwell Smith and Ninian Smart sought to break new ground in the study of religions, but in the end neither succeeded in uprooting the basic model associated with 'world' religions, partly because both held prior commitments to their own 'religious' interpretations of how religions should be studied, taught, communicated and eventually understood in academic circles and more widely in popular perceptions. Both agreed that religion should not be studied simply by referring to observable facts, either through historical studies or by describing contemporary religious activities. Religion must be seen from the perspective of believers, which never equates to external actions, but always reflects an inner experience that points to something greater than its outward expression. Although both Smith and Smart affected the direction the study of world religions took after 1970 by raising consciousness about the need to understand religion from the inside and by informing students that religions need to be conceived in multi-dimensional, dynamic and interdisciplinary ways, their methodological advancements were not matched by changes in the way the world religions paradigm was conceived. It is no surprise then that the idea has persisted to the present day that the religions of the world can be written about and taught according to the geographical regions where they are dominant, conceived, as Masuzawa asserts, largely along racial or ethnic lines, or under the conventional categories originally designated as the major traditions of the world, broken into a binary opposition between West and East.

Critical Problems with the World Religions Paradigm

It will already be clear that Tomoko Masuzawa intended that her book should expose the culturally biased construction of the world's religions as it developed historically within Western academic circles. I will return to her important critique shortly, but, significantly, some twenty-five years earlier, Jonathan Z. Smith of the University of Chicago attacked the concepts beneath the world's religions on grounds very similar to the ones Masuzawa later articulated. In his book, *Map is Not Territory* (1978), Smith delineates his own theory of religion, which he casts in the language of power and location. He explains: 'What we study when we study religion is the variety of attempts to map, construct and inhabit … positions of power through the use of myths, rituals and experiences of transformation' (1978: 291). Paradoxically, the world religions paradigm constitutes one such expression of power, although ostensibly it simply classifies religions according to objectively neutral criteria. Smith argues that the history of Western academic disciplines is rooted in the ancient Greek distinction between 'us' and 'them', or as it was put in 'Greek anthropology' between Greek and barbarian. 'To be, in a cultural sense, non-human was to be a barbarian' (1978: 294). This same approach to the 'other' was transposed into intellectual attitudes in the nineteenth and twentieth centuries 'out of Western imperialist and colonialist experience and ideology' (1978: 294). History has been written by Western academics from such a perspective, since the world is divided between those who 'make history whom we call human' and 'those who undergo history whom we call non-human' (p. 294). What Smith dubs 'the moral of this oft repeated tale' thus becomes self-evident: 'The West is active, it makes history, it is visible, it is human. The non-Western world is static, it undergoes history, it is invisible, it is non-human' (1978: 295).

This analysis of the power relations between the West and the remainder of the world serves as a preamble to Smith's biting criticism of the world religions paradigm. He argues that in conventional studies in the West a religion qualifies as a 'world' religion if 'it is a religion like ours'. This means that it must have 'achieved sufficient power and numbers to enter our history, either to form it, interact with it, or thwart it'. The world religions thus 'correspond to important geo-political entities with which we must deal' (1978: 295). Of course, this means that the 'primitive' religions are classified as 'minor', and attain importance only in so far as they adapt to the characteristics of the major religions or are adopted within them, as is the case with many of the so-called Independent Churches of Africa or some new religious movements in the West. To qualify as a world religion, primitive societies must demonstrate that they can be characterized by the same criteria we assign to world religions and thereby enter the world's geopolitical stage. Smith then alludes to the type of critique of the world's religions suggested by Wilfred Cantwell Smith and Ninian Smart, who sought to overcome the Western bias in the study of religions 'by exploring and, above all, by valuing the religious life of other men' (1978: 296). Despite this attempt to re-conceive the nature of religion, Smith argues, such attempts have failed: 'We have set forth a new cartography, but it remains uncomfortably close to being a mirror image of the "mainstream map"' (1978: 296).

Smith's conclusion that world religions have been constructed by the West to exert power over the rest of the world defines one of the central theses beneath Masuzawa's argument. She expands this idea by asserting that the uncritical manner by which we now refer to world religions came to prominence between the first and second world wars, which, for the West at least, was a time characterized by a series of global crises. Many authors during this period deemed it more important to speak of living religions rather than the historical religions, because to understand and deal with international threats to peace and stability required a general knowledge of the religious dimensions within an increasingly volatile geo-political context (Masuzawa, 2005: 39–41).[3] Masuzawa contends that it was thus from a sense of vulnerability that Western scholars of religion began to describe and interpret religions in terms of their global importance. This view corroborates J.Z. Smith's contention that it is only when the 'other' achieves sufficient power to engage the West on its own terms that it is accorded a visible place in Western intellectual discourse. For this very reason, according to Masuzawa, the rise of interest in the world's religions was accompanied by a relative reduction in the attention given to 'primitive' religions, a fact that is amply confirmed both by Noss's volume, in which out of 777 pages of text, just 49 deal with 'primitives', and by the limited attention given to 'primitive religion' in the collection of German contributions on the world's religions edited by Carl Clemen.

Masuzawa's second major critique of the world religions paradigm charges its advocates with the error of describing 'religion' as an essential unity, a universal core out of which its various expressions around the world are thought to have proceeded. The Christian theological assumptions beneath this idea are obvious, when, for example, it is compared to the doctrine of the incarnation, where God enters into the world in a human being as the fullest manifestation of his eternal essence. The theological notion of general revelation follows a similar model, whereby God is thought to have revealed himself in various worldly phenomena so that his nature can be recognized and acknowledged, in some measure at least, by all humanity. To speak of world religions in a similar manner asserts that a common essence belongs to them all, which can be traced to a universal core called 'religion'. With this Christian model before them, Western scholars of religion studied and classified expressions of the essence (not the essence itself), such as myths, rituals and ritual specialists, which could be compared according to their similarities and differences. Masuzawa (2005: 9) contends that survey courses on the world's religions commonly followed up to this day in North American and British universities begins 'with the scholastically untenable assumption that all religions are everywhere the same in essence, divergent and particular only in their ethnic, national or racial expressions'. She attributes the widespread acceptance of this non-critical approach to the spate of textbooks used in such courses, many of which were developed before 1960, or at least took their inspiration from them. So widespread has the essentialist assumption about religion become in popular perception, in Masuzawa's view, that it defines one of the strongest factors motivating the large numbers of students who populate 'our classrooms year after year' (2005: 9).

The essentialist dogma deftly combines the assertion of Western power in relation to non-Western cultures with the theologically-loaded idea of a universal religious essence. Masuzawa argues that these twin assumptions had produced numerous exponents by the end of the nineteenth century, such as Robert Flint, Professor of Divinity in the University of Edinburgh, who argued in his St Giles lectures of 1882 that a scientific study of the world religions demonstrates the superiority of

---

[3]   Masuzawa (2005: 40-41) draws attention to Sydney Cave's *Christianity and Some Living Religions of the East* (1929), whom she cites in the following quotation as an example of one writing out of a sense of international crisis: 'Without peace there can be no security, and peace depends not on one nation but on all.'

Christianity over all others (Flint, 1882). Masuzawa observes that from our current perspective it seems 'remarkable that so many nineteenth-century authors ... assumed ... that their enterprise of comparing religions without bias was not only compatible with but in fact perfectly complementary to their own proudly unshakable conviction in the supremacy of Christianity' (2005: 103). According to Masuzawa, the fact that religions still are taught as a means of uncovering divergent expressions of the same universal essence can be explained by this nineteenth-century Christian theological assumption which has never been exposed adequately through careful historical analysis.

The Resilience of the World Religions Paradigm

Thus far in this chapter, we have seen how during the early part of the twentieth century the world religions paradigm became embedded in textbooks which their authors intended for use both in undergraduate teaching and for popular consumption. We have observed also that the paradigm emerged from contexts of power between Western and non-Western religions and that it surreptitiously derives from a Christian theological assumption, which postulates a universal essence as the source for every world religion. We have also seen how these two assumptions are interrelated, since to qualify as a world religion, a faith must in some sense be comparable to Christianity, either by possessing components that can be translated into Christian terms, like scriptures, doctrines or festivals, or by mounting a strenuous challenge to Christianity, such as occurred in the proselytizing activities of Islam or that became evident as Westerners encountered the intellectual sophistication of philosophical Hinduism. In each case, the 'success' of the 'non-Christian' religions elevated their status within Western renditions of history. If Masuzawa is correct that this approach still prevails, both students of religion and the general public continue to maintain largely unreflective views towards the world's religions which are politically charged and intellectually indefensible.

Three notable examples of textbooks, which have appeared within the past ten years in the United Kingdom, demonstrate that the world religions paradigm has survived earlier critiques and is alive and well in the twenty-first century. The first, clearly written within the field of Religious Education and associated with the Shap working party in Britain,[4] is entitled *World Religions: An Introduction for Students* (1997), edited by Jeaneane Fowler, Merv Fowler, David Norcliffe, Nora Hill and Diane Watkins. The editors specialize in particular religious traditions, have worked together in the Department of Philosophy and Religious Studies in the University of Wales, Newport and have been involved in writing texts for teaching Religious Education in schools. In the Preface to the book, the editors explain that it has been published in an attempt to supplant earlier confessional approaches associated with Religious Education and replace them with methods developed in Religious Studies, which they call 'the study of religion' (1997: ix). They indicate that the book should prove particularly useful for students who need a broad introduction to the religions

---

[4]   The Shap Working Party on World Religions in Education was founded in 1969 in Shap, Cumbria, England to promote the study and teaching of world religions in schools, colleges and universities. The founding members included such notable figures as Ninian Smart, Eric Sharpe and Trevor Ling. In 2004, scholars serving on the committee, who are noted specifically for their work in Religious Studies, included John Hinnells, Ursula King, Peggy Morgan, Clive Erricker, Owen Cole and Wendy Dossett.

of the world before specializing in one or two traditions, as often occurs at university level. They indicate that their approach entails an understanding 'of the *essence* of the religions', particularly since religion 'is a universal phenomenon' (1997: 2) (emphasis theirs). In order to do this, they 'provide basic information on six major world faiths … for the purpose of assisting teachers who need the background material to inform their Religious Education curriculum, as well as students who are approaching Religious Studies' courses' (1997: 3). The six traditions studied include in order of their treatment, Judaism, Christianity, Islam, Hinduism, Buddhism, and Sikhism, none of which is presented in a comparative way but, as the editors explain, each is treated 'discretely' (1997: 3).

In fairness to the editors, their aim is to reach an audience involved either in teaching or studying at a pre-university level. Nonetheless, their approach does little to alter the fact that, in their words, 'Religious Education has … not enjoyed an honoured position in the post-modern educational curriculum' (1997: ix). The book incorporates in the most glaringly obvious way the essentialist assumptions about religion that Masuzawa cites, and it does so by identifying 'major' faiths of the world and treating them largely as homogeneous and in isolation from the others. The student and teacher who use this book come away with the same impression that marked the texts written more than 50 years before, that religion is a singular entity expressed in various ways amongst adherents within self-contained traditions. The approach of the editors minimizes history in favour of describing living religions, but this is not done in a way that encourages readers to reflect on the categories the authors employ. Rather, it confirms Masuzawa's assertion that university classrooms are now populated by students who have chosen to study religions with an entirely uncritical attitude towards popular assumptions about the ways religion is expressed and organized. Just as the Kellett and Bouquet books had done in the 1930s and 1940s in Britain, *World Religions: An Introduction for Students* reinforces the widespread notion that there exist major religions of the world, that they can be studied as discrete units and that the essence of religion can be grasped through its varied expressions.

A much more sophisticated text has appeared in the past few years under the title *Religions in the Modern World* (2002), edited by Linda Woodhead, with the assistance of Paul Fletcher, Hiroko Kawanami and David Smith, all of the Department of Religious Studies in the University of Lancaster. Unlike the volume edited by Fowler and her associates, this book was written for use in university teaching. In some ways, it is modelled on Ninian Smart's earlier book, *World Religions*, and it is not without significance that the book was conceived by staff at Lancaster University and is dedicated to Smart. Its sub-title, 'Traditions and Transformations' bears an uncanny similarity to Smart's own sub-title, 'Old Traditions and Modern Transformations'. And like the Smart volume, the Woodhead book is divided into two parts, one which may be regarded as a largely traditional approach to the world's religious traditions and the second which seeks to engage religion with contemporary issues, such as secularization, globalization, politics, gender and spirituality.

In her introductory chapter, Woodhead (2002: 1) explains that the first part of the book 'centres round the concept of religious "traditions" such as Hinduism, Buddhism, Christianity'. She admits that these 'are treated as relatively self-contained and discrete entities which should be explored in terms of their characteristic phenomena'. It is in the second part of the book that the editors have sought to relate the study of religions to contexts dictated by the modern world. Woodhead (2002: 1) explains that in the second section less attention is given to 'the concept of traditions and world religions', since the focus has shifted to 'religion in relation to wider society'. Here religion is conceived not in its own terms, but from the perspective of sociology, as in the theories of secularization that are explored, or from the viewpoint of anthropological and ethnographic studies of 'particular small-scale communities, cultures or other aspects of religious life' (2002: 1). Part one of the book, with its traditional approach to distinct religious traditions, constitutes over two-thirds of the text, comprising 12 chapters, whereas the broader treatment of religion in relation to contemporary themes consists of five chapters totalling less than 100 pages.

On the back cover of the book, Irving Hexham of the University of Calgary, an expert on new religious movements, is quoted as commending the Woodhead volume for providing 'at last an introduction to Religious Studies that is not a clone of 1960s textbooks'. This comment is particularly apt, since there can be little doubt that the editors intended to present contemporary religions as dynamic and as engaged with social conditions in global contexts. Yet, since the book persists in conveying the impression that religions consist of self-contained, homogeneous units, no challenge is presented to the basic categories that were developed in much earlier texts. Part one of the book deals quite explicitly with the major traditions of the world under conventional titles, each chapter having been written by an expert in the specific religion discussed. The 12 chapters of the first section are broken into categories in the following order: Hinduism, Buddhism, Sikhism, Chinese Religions, Japanese Religions, Judaism, Christianity, Islam, Religion in Africa, Native American Religions, New Age Religion, New Religious Movements. As we have seen, to have included sections on Africa and Native American traditions was not new, since Geoffrey Parrinder had done the same thing in his small book on the world's religions as early as 1964. Nonetheless, by including sections on the religions of these two indigenous societies, and by adding chapters on New Age Religion and New Religious Movements, the editors have underscored the notion that these constitute separate religious traditions that can be studied as topics in their own right as self-contained units. This is an issue to which I will return in detail in Chapter 3, since it defines one of my primary concerns in this book. The point I wish to emphasize here is that even in a volume where the editors have made a self-conscious effort to supplement the conventional approach to the study of world religions by introducing issues that in many ways embed religion in social contexts, they have insisted on giving priority to the world religions paradigm.

Not only does the Woodhead volume follow a precedent established more than a decade earlier by Ninian Smart, but in some ways it reflects a pattern followed in a third important book, *A New Handbook of Living Religions*, published in 1997 and written by a team of international scholars under the editorial direction of John Hinnells, an expert on Zoroastrianism and the founding Head of the Department for the Study of Religion in the School of Oriental and African Studies in London. Just as Woodhead and her colleagues sought to do, the Hinnells volume insists that any study of the world's religions must treat seriously contemporary developments in an increasingly globalized society. The *New Handbook*, now in its second printing, reflects substantial changes from the original *Handbook of Living Religions*, also edited by Hinnells, first published in 1984. In his 'Introduction to the *New Handbook*', Hinnells (1997: 1) explains that as editor he has sought to update the original 1984 volume with the most recent scholarship. For example, the section on China has been doubled in size and the chapter on Native American peoples has been entirely rewritten. The most significant series of changes in the new version can be found in the introduction of new chapters on what Hinnells (1997: 1) calls 'cross-cultural issues', such as gender and spirituality, themes that were also addressed in the Woodhead volume, and by the addition of seven new chapters dealing with religious communities in diaspora, including groups from Africa, Australia and South Asia. In the case of South Asian migration, the authors consider in separate chapters the spread of South Asian communities to Britain, Canada and the United States. Hinnells explains that these chapters have been added because 'teachers of religion have often emphasized that the subject [diaspora] has immediate relevance in the West because of the local presence of Asian religions' and because few academic works on the migration of South Asian peoples to Britain and North America 'have studied the religions of these communities' (1997: 1).

In his original Introduction to the First Edition of the volume, Hinnells identified problems that had plagued previous books on the world's religions, some of which had been noted both by Wilfred Cantwell Smith and J.Z. Smith, and later by Tomoko Masuzawa. He asserts in the first instance that 'a real danger for a book on religions is that it can too easily assume, wrongly, that there are always definable, separate phenomena corresponding to the labels popularly used, such as Christianity and Hinduism' (1997: 5). He counters this naïve assumption by drawing the reader's attention to the fact that divisions between religions are often exaggerated by notions that each religion considers its faith to be 'right' and all others to be wrong. In fact, he observes, many people belong to more than one religion at the same time, such as is commonly practised in Japan. New religious movements, many of them developing out of 'primal religions' in Africa, provide another example of the fluidity between religious ideas and allegiances (1997: 5). As such, Hinnells argues, his book attempts to challenge many prior assumptions in the study of religions: 'that India is changeless; that Christianity is a single, easily recognized phenomenon; that religions are monolithic wholes; that Jainism and Zoroastrianism are dead religions; that Islam is a "Near Eastern" religion; or that Buddhism is an abstract philosophy' (1997: 5). Finally, Hinnells asserts, since the *Handbook* is intended for the general reader as well as the specialist, it has been necessary for each contributor to have provided 'a brief account of the different scholarly methods and assumptions which have influenced the study of their subject' (1997: 5).

Despite Hinnells's attempts to qualify the notion of world religions and to present each as responding dynamically to emerging global situations, the *New Handbook*, just as the original had done, perpetuates the world religions paradigm. Part One, entitled 'The Religions', uses conventional titles almost always associated with the major faiths of the world, including separate chapters on Judaism, Christianity, Islam, Zoroastrianism, Hinduism, Sikhism, Jainism, Buddhism, Chinese Religions, Japanese Religions, and Baha'ism. In addition, separate chapters consider what might otherwise have been called the 'primal' or 'indigenous' traditions including Native North American Religions, Religions of the Pacific, African Religions, New Religious Movements in Primal Societies and Modern Alternative Religions in the West. That studies in the religions of indigenous peoples and new religious movements are included, just as they were in the later Woodhead volume, under the category 'The Religions', suggests, following the argument of J.Z. Smith, that these have become important because they now are engaging with the West in such politically significant ways that they have become 'visible' to Western scholarship. In addition, despite Hinnells's protestations to the contrary, the majority of the book is devoted to classifying the world religions as 'isms', which conveys to the general reader the notion that these exist, at least for purposes of classification, as separate or discrete units. Moreover, very little is done to dispel the popular notion that the many geographical, ethnic and localized religions described throughout the book are derived from a single source or universal essence.

Numerous other books have appeared on the study of the world's religions in the past ten years, so many that it would be impossible to do anything other than list a few of them.[5] I have selected the three in this section as notable examples to demonstrate that the longstanding approach to classifying religions, what I am calling the world religions paradigm, continues unabated well into the twenty-first century. Both Woodhead and Hinnells clearly acknowledge the problems inherent in this paradigm, just as W.C. Smith and Ninian Smart had done many years before. They have sought to overcome the deficiencies in the paradigm by showing how the world religions are engaging with contemporary social themes and by describing how they have become increasingly diverse during the latter half of the twentieth century as they have spread beyond narrowly defined geographical limits, largely through the migration of peoples, but also through modern methods of travel and communication. Nonetheless, neither volume escapes the categories which for nearly a century have prescribed the boundaries within which the religions of the world are studied. In fact, they have re-enforced them by adding to the list the 'religions' of 'primal' or 'indigenous' peoples and by including new religious movements within the same classification. Certainly, Woodhead and Hinnells have edited essays that discuss the world's religions in much more sophisticated ways than in prior volumes (although this is clearly not the case with the book edited by Fowler and her associates), but the basic paradigm dividing the religions into discrete categories persists, leaving virtually unchallenged the underlying political and theological assumptions associated with such classifications.

Conclusion

In the closing stages of her detailed analysis exposing how the category 'world religions' was invented by a handful of nineteenth-century 'philologists, Orientalists, and amateur comparativists', Tomoko Masuzawa asks if she ought to suggest some alternative terminology to replace a notion she believes has now been discredited so thoroughly (2005: 307–8). She defers to others on this point, since the aim of her volume, she explains, has been to provide largely an intellectual history. For her, the twentieth century requires a quite different analysis since 'the discourse of world religions is now truly in the public domain' (2005: 308). Now, the debate about the best way to describe and interpret religions extends far beyond 'the sphere of intellectual history proper', but involves a diverse range of scholars working in the social sciences and those more concerned with 'institutional history' (2005: 308). She admits that her work has done much to unmask the nineteenth-century roots beneath the essentialist notions within a 'pluralist episteme, couched in the language of world religions', but she is 'under no illusion that this study fully accounts for the installation of that discourse in its historical entirety' (2005: 309). Instead of providing an alternative, or even a conclusion, Masuzawa opts instead to explore the

---

[5]   For example, see: Richards (1997); Morgan and Lawton (1996); McCloughlin (2003); Burke (1996); Coward (1997); Eliade, Couliano and Wiesner (2000); and Partridge (2004). These can be supplemented by the Shap Calendar of Religious Festivals, appearing annually, listing major religious observances in the Christian, Muslim, Buddhist, Baha'i, Sikh, Hindu, Chinese, Zoroastrian, Rastafarian and Japanese traditions and available from the Shap Working Party's Religious Education Centre in London.

thought of the early twentieth-century liberal theologian, Ernst Troeltsch, as a way of tapping into the larger question for thinkers at the conclusion of the nineteenth century and which arguably persists even today: 'Whether and how Europe, or the West, might continue to assume the subject position in the unfolding of world history' (2005: 309). Masuzawa thus leaves the world religions paradigm in place by default, and, if her reasons are accepted, she does so because the task of reconstructing the study of world religions belongs not to intellectual historians but to those working directly in religious studies.

After the considerations of this chapter, we are left with one central conclusion: the world religions paradigm persists today in scholarly and popular circles, despite recent efforts to mollify its position of power *vis-à-vis* the non-Western world and notwithstanding concurrent attempts to distance it from its incipient theological roots. I have not yet demonstrated that the re-configuration of 'primitive' religions first into 'primal' and then into 'indigenous', which I described in Chapter 1, suffers from the very same political and essentialist errors inherent in the world religions paradigm. This defines my task in the next chapter, but, at this point it is important to note that the problems residing at the core of both concepts, 'world' and 'indigenous', cannot be resolved finally until the assumptions within the category religion itself are exposed and addressed. If a case for re-conceiving religion can be made, by stripping it of its position of power over the non-Western world and by liberating it from its traditional obeisance to theology, the study of religions in global contexts may attain levels of academic credibility that contemporary scholars like Masuzawa argue it has never before deserved. If my proposal for re-conceiving religion, which I outline in Chapter 4, is successful, the world religions paradigm will be shattered once and for all, not by exposing its irrecoverable flaws, but by substituting a different model altogether in its place. Only after this is accomplished will it be possible in the remainder of the book to discuss intelligently the appropriate place for the study of Indigenous Religions within the larger domain of religious studies.

Chapter 3

Defining 'Indigenous' Scientifically

In Chapter 1, I traced how the study of Indigenous Religions came to achieve, largely after 1970, its present status in academic circles where it is commonly treated as a tradition in its own right amongst the other world religions. I noted that increasingly sections on books describing the major world faiths now include discussions of Indigenous Religions and that in some institutions, like the University of Edinburgh, following in the tradition of Aberdeen's taught master's programme on religion in primal societies, it is possible for students to specialize in courses devoted exclusively to the study of Indigenous Religions. In Chapter 2, I outlined how the world religions paradigm developed in the early twentieth century and argued that the assumptions beneath it veil an imbalance of power between the Christian West and the religious traditions of the non-Western world and that it is based on the theological notion that religion derives from a universal essence. I drew attention to the fact that many books on the world's religions prior to 1950 included a section on pre-historic and primitive religions, but these usually were depicted as providing clues to the later development of the major religious traditions and as indicating how religion began in early human societies. In this chapter, I consider further how Indigenous Religions currently are defined, understood and constituted as a unified tradition comparable to other world faiths, like Hinduism, Buddhism, Islam and Christianity. I then offer my own definition of the term 'indigenous' as a prelude in Chapter 4 to re-interpreting the term 'religion' in socio-cultural contexts. By the end of this analysis, I will argue that the worthy intentions of those who have sought to uplift popular and academic perceptions of Indigenous Religions to levels equivalent with the 'major' religions suffer from the same fatal flaws that infect the world religions paradigm.

Indigenous Religions in Current Literature

In Chapter 1, I drew attention to my own article criticizing the widespread use of the term 'Primal Religions'. As we have seen, at the conclusion of the article, I recommended substituting 'indigenous' in place of 'primal', but at the same time, urged that when this nomenclature is used, it should be accompanied by 'geographical, ethnic and linguistic qualifiers (1996: 74). In many current texts on the world's religions, this is precisely the approach that is adopted when discussing localized indigenous societies, but this is done frequently without considering the theoretical implications of doing so. A generic term for indigenous peoples is avoided in such books, presumably because the problems entailed by trying to find common elements amongst so diverse a range of religious expressions are regarded as insurmountable. Nonetheless, by outlining local studies without reflecting on why they are included in a text on world religions, and by assuming that each shares characteristics in common with the other, the authors commit the twin errors of perpetuating the world religions paradigm and of approaching the study of indigenous peoples under hidden essentialist assumptions.

An extremely good example of the issues I am raising is found in a somewhat unusual recent publication on the world religions, edited by Sean McLoughlin of the Department of Theology and Religious Studies in the University of Leeds, under the title *World Religions: A Source Book* (2003). The book, which is intended for a popular audience, adopts a geographical approach, dividing its chapters under sections on Asia, Africa, Americas, Near East, Europe and Oceania/Pacific. What have been called previously world religions are considered under the sections on Asia and the Near East, seemingly for historical reasons, although they are recognized as not being restricted any longer to the regions of their origin. Indigenous Religions are interspersed throughout the sections of the book, and comprise the majority of the chapters, although the disparity in topics is not matched by the number of pages devoted to each. For example, Buddhism comprises sixteen pages, Christianity nineteen pages, and Islam twenty-one pages, but the longest section on any 'indigenous' society is that devoted to African Traditional Religion and Australian Aborigines, each comprising nine pages. The arrangement of the topics by geography means that Ancient Egypt is considered under the same heading as African Traditional Religion and that sections on the Americas and Oceania/Pacific deal exclusively with indigenous peoples. The chapter on Europe devotes sixteen pages to Ancient Greece and Rome, and is followed by short discussions of Celtic, Germanic, Slavic and Baltic Religion.

The rationale for this rather atypical ordering of the world's religions is explained in the introduction by McLoughlin as an attempt to avoid confining such a study to 'the usual suspects', by which he means the list of religions commonly included in such books: 'Christianity, Islam, Hinduism, Buddhism, Sikhism and Judaism' (2003: 7). This book, by contrast, is intended to be 'more inclusive' by organizing the material according to 'geographical area' (2003: 7). Of course, McLoughlin acknowledges that substantial chapters are devoted to 'the major world faiths mentioned above, all of which trace their origins to Asia or the Near East' (2003: 7). Religions that are often overlooked, like Confucianism, Taoism and Shintoism, are also included within the geographical divisions. McLoughlin then draws the reader's attention to the large sections of the book devoted to the study of 'the beliefs and practices to be found in more small-scale African, Native North American, Aboriginal and Maori "tribal" religions' (2003: 7). Finally, he notes that no book on the world's religions should be limited exclusively to 'the living traditions that continue to prosper into the twenty-first century'. There must be room also for 'an account of the religions of ancient civilizations, from Greece and Rome to the Egyptians in Africa and the Incas of the Americas' (2003: 7).

McLoughlin argues that the geographical approach presents the study of religions according to their place of origin and thus establishes for the reader a knowledge of the historical roots of each. This avoids the common error of describing religions as 'isms' or as discrete entities, since 'an emphasis on region provides an opportunity to reflect on the relationships between traditions, both in terms of the cross-fertilization of ideas and the formation of identity through polemics' (2003: 7). This is exemplified in the cases of Jainism and Buddhism, both of which trace their histories to 'the complex weave of "Hindu" traditions in India' (2003: 8). Or, in the case of Judaism, it would be impossible to understand the firm monotheism enshrined in Jewish tradition without relating this to the polytheism of the older Canaanite religion (2003: 8). Moreover, McLoughlin explains, the book underscores the fact that religions change not only across time, but also spatially, sometimes by overt conversion of peoples from different areas of the world, as in the cases of

Islam and Christianity, and in more recent times, through migration of peoples from one part of the world to another (2003: 8). The book closes in a somewhat odd way by providing first a timeline of the world's religions that is restricted to the major faiths (or their derivatives): Buddhism, Confucianism, Hinduism, Jainism, Judaism, Taoism, Zorastrianism, The Baha'i Faith, Islam and Sikhism (2003: 296–7). This is followed on the next page with a summary of the numerical adherents within world faiths, including atheists, adherents to new religions, the non religious, and followers of 'tribal religion' (2003: 298). The text concludes with a list of festivals practised among the major traditions of the world (much in line with the Shap publications) (2003: 299–301) and by providing a list of the sacred texts of the world religions, which, by definition, excludes the many oral societies which comprise the majority of sub-headings in the book (2003: 302–3).

McLoughlin's source book of the world religions is much more likely to confuse the reader than to dispel the errors of previous texts which he accuses of presenting religions as 'isms' and as discrete units. The world religions are still defined in quite separate categories from 'tribal' or 'small-scale' societies, which are organized according to geography, but largely without explanation or connection to any other tradition. No reason is provided for including some traditions or for excluding others, despite McLoughlin's historical-geographical justification for his methodology. For example, in the chapter on the Americas, a few pages is devoted to the Huichol people of Mexico (2003: 146–9), but amongst other Native American traditions, no section considers just one people, since all are treated generically, as are Traditional Religions of Africa. The section on Asia is introduced with a short discussion of 'shamanism', which the book presents as 'the world's oldest religious tradition' (2003: 12), and is placed immediately ahead of the section on Hinduism, not as a predecessor to Hinduism, but because, the author claims, it is 'known to have originated in Siberia', and thus falls under the chapter on Asia (2003: 12). It is clear that McLoughlin did not prepare this book for use in educational contexts, certainly not in universities, but 'as an informative and accessible reference work intended for a general readership' (2003: 6). As such, it should not be judged for its lack of academic sophistication (even the authors of the sections remain unnamed), but it can be held up as another in a long line of books dating back to the early part of the twentieth century that re-enforces the widespread popular belief that religions can be studied according to the divisions comprising major faiths, including 'small-scale' localized groupings as historically antecedent to the major world faiths. Admittedly, most Indigenous Religions are presented as still practising their ancient traditions, but this is done in a way that largely ignores the global interpenetration of religious movements. Presumably, such inter-relations are neglected in favour of considering the religions of indigenous peoples in their own right, but, if this is the case, it is never stated explicitly.

A second example of a book published in the past ten years that incorporates a section on religions in indigenous societies into a larger discussion of world religions is *The Illustrated Encyclopedia of World Religions* (1997), edited by Chris Richards, who at the time the book was published was a senior adviser on Religious Education located in Northamptonshire, England. Unlike McLoughlin's book, the *Illustrated Encyclopedia* lists the authors of the articles, some of whom are leading experts in their fields, such as Brian Bocking, an authority on contemporary Japanese religions and Head of the Department of Religion in the School of Oriental and African Studies in London; Peter Clarke, a sociologist of religion with specialisms in new religious movements and African religions; and Denise Cush, a scholar of Buddhism and Head of the Religion Department at Bath Spa University. The popular appeal of the book is underscored by the first words of the introduction, in which Richards, as editor, declares that its purpose is to bring 'the world's major faiths vividly to life' and to help the reader 'answer basic questions about religion' (1997: 6). The *Encyclopedia* begins with a chapter on 'Primal Religions', written by Peter Clarke, and follows with separate chapters on Hinduism, Judaism, Confucianism, Buddhism, Jainism, Christianity, Islam, Shinto, Sikhism, Taoism, The Baha'i Faith and Rastafarianism. It concludes with a chapter devoted to 'other sects and denominations' (author or authors unnamed), which considers, without explanation, an assortment of groups, including, among others, 'Voodoo', 'Transcendental Meditation', 'Zoroastrianism', 'Hasidic Judaism', 'Soka Gakkai' and 'Methodism' (2003: 244–7).

In his opening statement outlining the aims of the book, Richards asserts that 'this encyclopedia has been written to give the reader insights into some of the beliefs and practices of major and influential religions in the world today' (2003: 10). He admits that the volume could not include every religion in the world, but, in an even more telling comment, he remarks that not 'all the religions qualify to be called world religions' (10). In fact, he asserts, only Christianity and Islam 'have the significant and widespread distribution of followers which entitles them to be called world religions' (10). The other religions are included in the book because 'they are of particular interest, or because of the influence they have had, and in some cases still have, on the world and its beliefs' (10). The article on Primal Religions, as I noted above, is written by the distinguished sociologist of religion, Peter Clarke, who recently retired from a professorship at King's College, London but who retains an active involvement in the academic community as a Research Fellow in Wolfson College, University of Oxford.

Clarke's article considers Primal Religions under two categories: Australian Aboriginal Religions and African Religions. He introduces the chapter by asserting that the most commonly used terms to designate the religions of such peoples, 'traditional' and 'primal', are 'controversial', since they often are 'wrongly taken to refer to static, unchanging and primitive, or unsophisticated religions found in underdeveloped societies' (Clarke, 1997: 14). Clarke counters that he is not using the terms in this way, but as referring to 'those religions that have always been an integral part of the culture of a society', which, because they have been confined to that society, can be contrasted to religions 'with global ambitions such as Christianity and Islam' (1997: 14). Due to limitations of space, Clarke explains that he has restricted his accounts to the Australian Aborigines and to African Religions, but the reader should understand that 'traditional religions abound' and include also 'Maori and Melanesian religions, Native American religions such as Navajo and Hopi … and a considerable range of Central and Latin American religions, including Inca and Aztec religions' (1997: 14).

Clarke treats the cases of Australia and Africa in separate sections and notes that, although 'in Africa we find some parallels with Aboriginal religions', there exist many differences (1997: 18). The similarities and differences can be observed by the headings Clarke employs to describe each. He addresses the category 'myth' in each religion and also examines ideas of a supreme being, although he distinguishes sharply between Aboriginal and African views of the transcendent. He deals specifically with Aboriginal rights, but in the African section focuses on sacrifices, healing rituals, ancestors and witchcraft. He admits that there are many and diverse expressions of traditional religions in Australia and Africa. In the case of Africa, specifically, there are 'many hundreds' of traditional religions 'closely bound up with particular linguistic and ethnic groups' (1997: 18). Despite the heterogeneity of religious practice in Africa, Clarke argues that 'African religions have much in common', a fact which justifies his treatment of African religious diversity under broad themes, so that in a few pages he is able to exemplify common characteristics by referring to groups as varied as the Dinka of southern Sudan, the Yoruba of western Nigeria, the Dogon of Mali, the Zulu of South Africa, indigenous peoples in Madagascar and the Igbo of Nigeria (1997: 19–22). At the conclusion, Clarke tells his reader that the old way of viewing traditional religions as 'irrational' and 'superstitious' is wrong and that the purpose of these 'highly complex systems of belief and ritual' is the same as religion everywhere: 'to explain and attempt to deal with the problems – emotional, existential, environmental, medical and social – of everyday life' (1997: 23).

Very little explanation is provided by Richards or Clarke as to why the topic 'Primal Religions' is included in an encyclopaedia of world religions. Clarke implies that this topic is of interest because Primal Religions persist today as 'integral' to their local societies, and because they stand in sharp contrast to the universal aims of missionary religions, chiefly Christianity and Islam (1997: 14). Clarke refuses to describe Primal Religions as antecedent to the world religions in any evolutionary scheme, but the editorial decision to place them first in the book suggests to the reader that in some ways they are basic or foundational for the religions that are described in the articles that follow. Clarke qualifies his definition of Primal Religions by restricting his discussion to two geographical regions, but he contends at the outset that the term applies to all small-scale, local communities which existed prior to the global expansion of the world religions, which he calls 'newer arrivals' (1997: 14). Finally, although he refers to the diversity of Primal Religions, and even to the variety of religious expressions amongst the two groups he is considering, his thematic approach conveys the view that in broad terms all Primal Religions share certain concepts in common. If his treatment in the article has been restricted in scope primarily due to limitation of space imposed by the editor, the reader is correct to conclude that Primal Religions everywhere, although varied and local, can be understood under a few central topics. In the end, 'Primal Religions' emerge as a discrete tradition, fully worthy of study in their own right, and well suited for inclusion in a popular text on the world's religions.

A third book, which specifically includes sections on Indigenous Religions, is Christopher Partridge's edited volume, *The New Lion Handbook: The World's Religions*, to which I referred in Chapter 1 as providing evidence that Indigenous Religions now have been accepted widely in academic and popular literature as a category comparable to other world religions. A closer look at the way Indigenous Religions are organized and presented in this recent volume will indicate how their diversity of expression has been consolidated into a unitary scheme of classification that fits comfortably within a world religions paradigm. In his Preface to the volume, Partridge (2005a: 9) describes the book 'as a collection of insightful, stimulating and accessible introductions to the histories, beliefs and practices of religions from pre-historic times to twenty-first century developments'. He explains that the volume 'is particularly suitable for teachers, students, interested laypeople, and professionals who need clear, accurate, comprehensive overviews of the world's principal religious beliefs and practices' (2005a: 9).

Partridge has compiled a remarkable collection, with articles from leading scholars in Religious Studies, the social sciences and history. Part One of the book is devoted to methodological issues, with clearly written articles on such themes as

'What is Religion? (by Russell McCutcheon) (2005: 10–13), 'The Anthropology of Religion' (by Fiona Bowie) (2005: 19, 22), 'The Sociology of Religion' (by Malcolm Hamilton) (2005: 23–5), 'The Psychology of Religion' (by Fraser Watts) (2005: 26–8), 'Critical Theory and Religion' (by Jeremy Carrette) (2005: 28–31) and Partridge's own article on 'Phenomenology of the Study of Religion' (2005b: 14–18). Many of these represent quite sophisticated attempts to overcome the essentialist assumptions within religion, such as is found in Russell McCutcheon's attempt to relativize the term by calling religion 'a historical artefact that different social actors use for different purposes (2005: 13), or Jeremy Carrette's insightful comment that 'the ways we think about religion are caught inside questions of power' (2005: 31). Such nuanced discussions of theory and method in the study of religion place the *New Lion Handbook* head and shoulders above many previous popular editions, such as McLoughlin's *Source Book* and Richard's *Illustrated Encyclopedia*. Nonetheless, some telling cracks appear as the book moves into actual discussions of the religions of the world, and, Indigenous Religions, in particular.

Just as in the Richards' volume, the *New Lion Handbook* presents a timeline of the development of the world religions (2005: 36–7) and shows a map indicating what it calls 'the approximate present-day distribution of the world's religions' (2005: 34). The timeline extends from an undesignated period before 2500 BCE to the present day. Religions that existed before 2500 BCE are listed as the Old Kingdom of Egypt, Indigenous Religions and Vedantism. Only Indigenous Religions are presented as an uninterrupted line extending up to the present; the Old Kingdom of Egypt is shown to develop through the Middle to the New Kingdom before arriving at the period of ancient Egyptian religion that ends around 100 BCE; Vedantism slides into Hinduism around 500 CE. On the surface, by glancing at this chart, the casual reader would think that Indigenous Religions persist unchanged from pre-historic times. The map showing concentrations of adherents similarly is confusing. No numbers are attached to the religions, but the map is divided according to the following designations: Indigenous Religions (majority of population claiming to be adherents), Hinduism, Buddhism (with Shinto in Japan), Sikhism, Zorastrianism (Parsis), Judaism, Christianity, The Religions of East Asia and areas of low population ('undifferentiated or tribal religions') (2005: 34). A close look at the map discloses that the areas assigned to Indigenous Religions are confined largely to small regions in western and southern Africa. Mixed allegiances are shown on the map as well, so that the reader is led to understand that in some parts of Africa adherents are split between Indigenous Religions and Christianity or Islam. In the case of Korea, the split is between Indigenous Religions and Buddhism. Vast areas of the globe are regarded as having such low population that they are designated as 'undifferentiated or tribal'. These include the whole of Siberia, parts of central Asia, regions of South and North America, as well as the desert regions of northern Africa. This most misleading visual picture of the distribution of the world's religious population can be noted in the case of Alaska, which since the early twentieth century has been almost entirely Christian, with churches having been established throughout the state, and having achieved virtual unanimity of assent since the 1930s (see Cox, 1991, Chapters 1–3). Yet, the map shows only the region around the largest city, Anchorage, as Christian, entirely ignoring the domination of Orthodox Christianity around the capital Juneau and along the Aleutian Islands, and the overwhelming Christian allegiance (either Protestant, Catholic or new evangelical) everywhere else. The editor can argue, of course, that the map and time chart are simply approximations providing general information, which the articles in the book both qualify and clarify. This objection is shown to be vacuous by the ordering of the articles, which conform to a now all too familiar pattern: Part Two is devoted to 'Religions of Antiquity' followed by 'Indigenous Religions' in Part Three. The reader would be forgiven for thinking that Indigenous Religions have emerged unchanged out of antiquity, that they have preceded the world's living religions, and that they exist now in pure form only in isolated pockets of the globe, or in areas of such low population that traditional 'tribes' have not yet been displaced by the forces of modernity.

As we saw in Chapter One, the section on 'Indigenous Religions' in *The New Lion Handbook* is introduced by Graham Harvey, whose article I will consider here as an example of the essentialism I identified in the last chapter as a hallmark of the world religions paradigm. I will refer later in this chapter to some of Harvey's other works in which he discusses the meaning of Indigenous Religions in a deeper way than he intended in this general summary. At the outset of his introduction, Harvey considers practitioners of Indigenous Religions 'altogether', but acknowledges, in a similar way as Peter Clarke had done in Richards's volume, that 'just as there are hundreds of indigenous languages in North America or in Papua New Guinea, so there are many different ways of being religious' (2005b: 100). So, then, how is the reader to understand what the 'case studies' which follow his introduction hold in common? As a precondition to considering this question, Harvey tells us, we must not think that Indigenous Religions 'are fossilized remains of the earliest or first religions' (2005b: 101). If the reader had been given that impression from the way the articles in the book are organized or by the map and chart at the beginning, this assumption must be dismissed. Harvey even contradicts the terminology of the map, by noting that 'it is unhelpful to speak of groups that might include millions of people as "tribes" and of their religions as "*tribal religions*"' (2005b: 101) (emphasis his). What seems to make it possible for Harvey to speak about Indigenous Religions generally in the first instance results from their sharing similar histories. Indigenous Religions preceded in time 'the spread of transcultural or global religions (e.g. Buddhism, Christianity and Islam)' (2005b: 100). As such, they have been severely affected by colonialism with varying results, including their disappearance in some places, and in others, by their adapting to or adopting parts of the invading religions. Despite this, he suggests, Indigenous Religions 'continue to provide resources for people surviving and thriving in the new globalized world' (2005b: 101).

By noting that Indigenous Religions are antecedent in time to the spread of missionary faiths, Harvey implies that they are neither missionary nor global, but, as yet, we are not told precisely what traits delineate such religions from others. This is soon rectified when Harvey produces a list of characteristics found among indigenous societies virtually everywhere. The first Harvey calls 'respect', particularly for elders and ancestors, but also in ordinary social occasions, as occurs when one meets a person for the first time. A second characteristic of Indigenous Religions entails their very broad understanding of personhood. In many indigenous societies, the concept of a person extends beyond human beings to include God, ancestors, other spirits and 'animals, plants, rocks, clouds and more'(2005b: 102–3). Harvey notes that the term 'other-than-human persons', coined by the anthropologist Irving Hallowell from his work amongst the Ojibwa people of south-central Canada, applies within many indigenous views of the world (See, Hallowell, 1960: also Harvey, 2002a: 17–49). 'There are human-persons, tree-persons, rock-persons, cloud-persons and so on' (Harvey, 2005b: 103). A third characteristic of Indigenous Religions is found in the act of exchanging gifts, which are 'given as signs of respect and love to those more powerful or esteemed than us' and 'received as signs of support, help and compassion from those more powerful or esteemed than us' (2005b: 103). Closely associated with gift-giving in indigenous societies is what Harvey calls 'the dynamics of power' (2005b: 203). This should not be understood as people trying to induce a mystical force to influence natural events for selfish ends, but as confirming social events by 'empowering' people with the ability to perform certain roles such as 'making pots or speeches', acts which are necessary for the welfare of the community as a whole (2005b: 103).

Thus far, Harvey has presented a picture of Indigenous Religions as founded on community respect, symbolized by an enlarged view of personhood that is often cemented by the giving of gifts and the empowering of those with specific social roles to perform. The last category Harvey considers refers to religious specialists in indigenous societies, such as shamans, diviners, witches and sorcerers. The use of such specialists, he admits, often involves a search for explanations for misfortune or community disruption. Specialists often possess esoteric knowledge, which enable them to perform rituals in a particular way, to reveal the causes of particular problems and to prescribe proper remedies. Harvey says that outsiders often ask if such activities are superstitious, but for the indigenous person such a question is irrelevant. What is important is to find out why an unwanted event occurred to a particular person at a specific time and to rectify the cause of the event. Usually, the cause has to do with a lack of respect for persons and/or other-than-human persons, and thus the resolution involves gift-giving, often in the form of sacrifices, to renew the bond of respect that has been violated. Harvey concludes in a way that echoes the earlier view of Peter Clarke: 'Indigenous Religions, like all other religions, may be considered to be ways in which particular groups of people seek the means of improving health, happiness and even wealth for themselves, their families and communities' (2005b: 104).

As I noted in Chapter 1, Harvey's introductory article is followed by eleven 'case studies' that describe the religions of selected indigenous peoples around the world. If the essence of Indigenous Religions centres around the term 'respect', as Harvey suggests, the case studies are intended to demonstrate for the reader how the essence is manifested in the particular instances described. In reality, the case studies do not incorporate Harvey's definition of the 'essence' of Indigenous Religions, since each was written independently and without collusion with Harvey, but it is clear that Partridge, as General Editor, arranged the material in such a way as to introduce the reader to the generic term before providing cases intended to exemplify its diverse expressions. Although Russell McCutcheon sought to distance the study of religion from such forms of essentialism, it remains the underlying assumption beneath the entire presentation of Indigenous Religions in the book. What appears as a focus on specific, localized cases thus emerges as a re-invention of a model that portrays an indigenous core with manifold expressions. That this idea extends to religion as a whole is confirmed by Harvey's concluding comment in which he defines religion in general as 'largely about the etiquette by which people relate to one another' (2005b: 104). The essence of Indigenous Religions thereby is extended to the essence of religion generally, and Indigenous Religions, understood as a discrete unit, becomes just one among many expressions of a universal religious core. In this way, we find Indigenous Religions elevated to the same status as other world religions, since each 'world religion' embodies 'etiquette or respect' as its central, defining characteristic. We thus see a model repeated by Harvey that is employed also by Clarke and to some extent McLoughlin, that begins by identifying common elements in Indigenous Religions, which then are illustrated and confirmed by a series of localized case studies derived in some instances from detailed field research, and presented in support of an inclusive approach to the comparative study of religions.

A Scientific Scheme for Classifying Indigenous Religions: J.G. Platvoet

Two critical questions emerge from these recent attempts to elevate Indigenous Religions to the status of a world religion: (1) Are the defining characteristics of Indigenous Religions derived from prior theoretical notions maintained by scholars before any empirical investigation has begun? (2) Is it possible to compile a sufficient number of studies of specific indigenous societies to identify enough common elements amongst them to justify placing them within a comprehensive category? The first question asks if the notion beneath Indigenous Religions as a world religion is obtained deductively; the second asks if it can be substantiated using inductive or empirical methods. If a researcher is committed to creating the classification 'Indigenous Religions' for altruistic motives, that is, in order to redress academic imbalances that for nearly one hundred years have favoured so-called world religions, this must be regarded as a deductive approach. The classification has been fashioned in order to justify the scholar's prior ethical convictions. Likewise, if a scholar includes Indigenous Religions as a world religion based on the supposition that a universal essence resides at the core of 'religion', and that its manifestations are found everywhere, the resulting classification can be traced to the scholar's prior theological commitment. If, on the other hand, the characteristics of indigenous societies around the world can be shown to have resulted from empirical investigations and that the defining elements themselves have been derived from comparative field studies, the category may be said to stand on verifiable (or indeed falsifiable) scientific methods. It is only in this second way that Indigenous Religions can be accepted within the scientific community as a legitimate category; the former approach belongs to the fields of ethics and theology, which rely on quite different methods of investigation and persuasion than those generally employed in empirical studies.

In the writings of various scholars on this topic, the application of an inductive, scientific method for classifying the characteristics of an 'indigenous' religion seems consistently to produce a list, which at a minimum, comprises the following three features: (1) indigenous societies are local, or at least self-contained, and thus have no interest in extending their religious beliefs and practices beyond their own limited environment; (2) they are based primarily on kinship relations, and hence usually have a strong emphasis on ancestors; (3) they transmit their traditions orally, resulting in a fundamentally different attitude towards beliefs and practices than is found amongst traditions derived from and based on authoritative written sources. J.G. Platvoet, recently retired from the University of Leiden, has written extensively about what he calls African Traditional Religions using these categories. Although he normally restricts his discussion to the religions of sub-Saharan Africa, it seems fair to review his approach as exemplifying the work of a scholar who defines the religions of diverse peoples, extending over vast areas, as localized, kinship-based oral societies. I have chosen Platvoet to illustrate these conclusions because, as a scholar of religion, he self-consciously employs an empirical method based on historical studies in which he contends that 'all religions developed traits after the type of society in which they were practised' (1992: 11).

Platvoet maintains that religions can be divided between those that are primarily 'community' religions and those that are 'transnational'. A community religion is 'particular to a single society' and thus is 'practised by all the members of the society and no one outside it' (1992: 12). This means that such religions are 'co-extensive with single societies', and refer also to what otherwise might be called 'ethnic or national religions' (1992: 12). He argues that before 250 BCE this type of religion was the only kind of religion in existence and 'most religions since then belong to this category' (1992: 12). One is born into this sort of religion, and, since such religions are void of any concept of conversion, they are entirely non-missionary in nature. Such religions can be contrasted to the 'transnational religions', which have appeared relatively recently in history 'when Buddhist monks first spread the teachings of the Buddha beyond India' (1992: 12). They include Buddhism, Christianity and Islam, and more recently movements as diverse as 'Mormonism, Baha'i, TM (Transcendental Meditation), Bhagwan, Scientology, New Age' (1992: 13). Transnational religions, as the term suggests, are 'world religions' as opposed to the more restricted concerns characteristic of 'community' religions.

Platvoet divides the 'community' religions into 'literate community religions' and 'community religions of oral societies'. The former category began somewhere around 3500 BCE in Egypt, Mesopotamia, Northern India and later in China, Mexico and Peru. Such societies developed agricultural methods of production and established states with an elite upper class developing alongside a population of labourers. Writing was devised initially for record keeping of goods used in trade, but later it evolved into many other functions, including the codification of laws, the recording of myths and for regularizing ritual practices (1992: 14–16). Community religions of oral societies, by contrast, are the 'oldest group of religions' and 'are lost in the mists of the roughly four million years of the genesis of humankind from prehuman primates' (1992: 16). The earliest mode of economy of such societies entailed nomadic food gathering, which in turn was reflected in the religious life of the people. Later, a more sedentary way of life developed as animal husbandry was adopted, but this still entailed moving the livestock to locations where feeding grounds were plentiful. Later, full-blown agricultural societies developed. In each case, the means of production were mirrored in religious beliefs and practices, as life came to depend less on abundance of game and more on the ability of the people to nurture crops and animals. As such, mystical trances to encourage animals to surrender to the hunter, as evidenced in early forms of shamanism, yielded to the performance of sacrificial rituals aimed at persuading ancestors and deities to provide plentiful rain to ensure a fruitful harvest (1992: 16–17).

It is clear that Indigenous Religions, taken as a whole, are included in the category 'community religions of oral societies'. Platvoet explains: 'The category of the "African traditional religions" comprises all the "community religions" of the indigenous societies of Africa since palaeolithic times' (1996a: 51). He adds: 'They were the normal and normally the only, religions in Africa south of the Sahara before the heyday of European colonialism (1920–1950)' (1996a: 51). He refers to the cosmologies in such societies as comprising 'small ... mental worlds' that can be contrasted to 'the macro mental worlds ... of modern society', since the rituals and beliefs of the African community religions developed in local settings and resulted from 'long ages of restricted outward communication' (1996a: 51). This does not mean that all African indigenous societies are the same. On the contrary, they are 'heterogeneous' having developed religious ideas and practices in accordance with their means of subsistence and modes of economy, the oldest, as we have seen, being the 'religions of the nomadic food-gathering societies', such as the San people of the Kalahari desert in southern Africa (1992: 17).

The localized nature of African Indigenous Religions means that adherents direct their attention towards community deities or spirits, which generally are kinship based. Platvoet (1992: 18) contends that the traditional societies of Africa 'are organised in primary, especially in kinship, relationships' and that 'they live in complex micro worlds'. Most people are 'familiar only with the territory in which they themselves live and part of that of neighbouring communities' (1992: 21). Even when territorial boundaries are extended in traditional societies, they are interpreted in kinship terms since all institutions are 'structured on the model of kinship' (1992: 21). Platvoet then makes what I regard as his central point about the Indigenous Religions of Africa: 'Kinship … rules religion' (1992: 21). He reaches this conclusion because 'the deceased, for as long as they are ritually approached as ancestors, are treated as the foremost members of the social worlds of these societies' (1992: 21–2). Even non-ancestral spirits, called by Platvoet 'other meta-empirical beings', are given 'quasi-kinship status'. (1992: 22) As community-based, kinship-orientated oral societies, therefore, the religions of sub-Saharan Africa clearly fit into a larger scheme of classification that includes similar communities in other parts of the world.

Because religions everywhere determine their beliefs in response to their modes of production and their related political organizations, Platvoet argues that we can begin to build classifications of religions that are typical of the society of which each forms a part. It is thus possible to extend our understanding of Indigenous Religions beyond the elemental properties of locality, lineage and orality to include their more substantial features, which in turn can be contrasted with the fundamental content of transnational or world religions. The main additional features of Indigenous Religions, for Platvoet, include the following (1992: 22–7):

1. Rituals are central to their religious practice;
2. Their beliefs are not articulated, and thus are vague and oftentimes contradictory;
3. They are recipients of a 'constant revelation' through direct communication with spiritual beings obtained in various ways such as dreams, visions, trances and spirit possession;
4. Their concept of salvation is tangible and material, aimed at securing benefits in this world rather than in a life after death.

Transnational or world religions can be contrasted with community or Indigenous Religions. Such religions also share certain characteristics in common (1992: 13):

1. They believe their teachings provide the only way to salvation;
2. They regard themselves as recipients of a final and complete revelation;
3. Correct ways of believing define their central concern, and they often have disputes over the defining nature of orthodoxy;
4. Salvation is located in another world or another realm of experience quite distinguishable from this life.

Platvoet assigns these characteristics to religions that preach an exclusive message, primarily Buddhism, Christianity and Islam, and hence refers to them as '*transnational exclusive religions*' (1992: 13) (emphasis his). He regards the newer religious movements associated, for example, with the New Age, as '*transnational inclusive religions*' since believers understand their revelation as supplementary to earlier revealed truths and they encourage their adherents to respect other religions (1992: 13) (emphasis his). They even invite people to participate in more than one form of religion at the same time as a means of meeting a myriad of personal and social needs. Such religions are transnational, nonetheless, since they spread their message around the globe, oftentimes by establishing bookshops or by using forms of evangelism that are less aggressive than those traditionally employed within the exclusive world religions.

The connection between economies, politics and religion can be seen particularly clearly in the case of African Indigenous Religions, which have developed in societies that are small-scale with relatively low-level technologies. Of course, all societies everywhere at one time were at a similar stage of development. Platvoet acknowledges that to speak of the traditional societies of Africa in this way provides his reader with a sense of what they were before the relatively recent large scale encounters with Western colonialism and missionary religions. Nonetheless, it is still possible to speak of such societies in the present tense, since they persist in traditionally recognizable forms throughout many parts of Africa. In such small-scale societies, based on kinship relations, almost every activity possesses a religious dimension, and each has a personal and social connection. The welfare of the community depends on proper relations within society, which, Platvoet explains, 'is not only a concern among the living but also between the living and unseen beings, foremost the ancestors' (1992: 22). Moreover, because in such societies control over the natural environment is low, beliefs must be capable of many interpretations and applications. Misfortune, which is a commonplace occurrence, must be explained, but not necessarily consistently or uniformly. Religious beliefs thus are characterized by a strong pragmatic element aimed at securing health and well-being for the community, usually through ritual activity (1992: 23). This requires specialists who can receive communication from the spirits, interpret the cause of any misfortune, provide a diagnosis and prescribe a prognosis. The way to rectify the causes of misfortune normally involves gift-giving in rituals, sometimes through libations or sacrifices, with, once again, certain social obligations entailed. Reciprocity between the spirit world and the human community is central to restoring well-being and avoiding various further or persistent calamities (1992: 24). Reciprocity extends also to the relationships within the society, including proper respect for chiefs and elders, and adherence to strictly defined roles for members of the community. Because the religions of such societies are pragmatic and their beliefs implicit, rather than articulated, they have been able to adapt to the spread of the transnational religions, often by adopting elements from them without surrendering their own reciprocal relationship to their localized and kinship-based spirit world (1992: 25).

The claim that Platvoet has employed empirical methods beneath his way of classifying Indigenous Religions derives from his hypothesis that the means of subsistence and political structure of any society determine the broad outlines of the religion or religions operating within it. This theory can be tested against available evidence, both in contemporary ethnographic studies and in historical accounts. As such, if evidence is found that contradicts the hypothesis, it is subject to re-formulation and re-testing. In Platvoet's case, his argument consists in the claim that small-scale, low technology, kinship based oral societies produce religions which aim at securing and protecting communal well-being, are pragmatic and thus possess only vague and inarticulate beliefs whilst at the same time emphasizing the importance of rituals in maintaining reciprocal relationships among the living members of the community, including and perhaps primarily, the ancestor spirits. In this way, on the basis of a scientific method, the category Indigenous Religions is portrayed as signifying those characteristics shared amongst all societies around the world that fit into a similar economic and political mould.

'Indigenous Religions' in the Work of Graham Harvey

Thus far in this chapter, I have been dealing with the broad methodological problems created by claims that world-wide phenomena can be lumped together within a common classification I have designated 'Indigenous Religions', and that such a classification can be fitted into a larger scheme I have called the world religions paradigm. In the process, I have raised issues focusing on theological essentialism and non-empirical methodologies. If we follow Platvoet's line of thinking, we are brought back directly to the problem of nomenclature. We have seen that Platvoet uses the term 'community religions of oral societies' to designate a type of religion found in small-scale, kinship-based communities. I have inserted the term 'indigenous' as a synonym for Platvoet's word 'community', just as I have done with expressions that have been used in prior literature to designate broadly the same thing, such as 'tribal', 'primitive', 'traditional', 'primal' and 'ethnic'. I have indicated a preference for 'indigenous', but, as yet, I have not justified why I have selected this term over others. Clearly, inferences have been made in the literature I have discussed that some usages, such as 'primitive', 'tribal' and 'ethnic' carry negative connotations that are best avoided when seeking to employ a descriptive category. I have also argued that the word 'primal' conveys theological ideas closely linked either to essentialism or to a Christian missionary theory called 'preparatio evangelica'. Even if I can establish that 'indigenous' is to be preferred amongst the many labels that have been employed previously, a critical problem emerges from my analysis of Platvoet's argument, since the characteristics Platvoet assigns to what he calls community religions seem not to correspond in all cases to what generally is meant by 'Indigenous Religions'. I want to consider this anomaly in more detail near the conclusion of the chapter, but in order to clarify the term 'indigenous', I want to review the writings of Graham Harvey on this topic, since he, more than any other scholar of religion, has championed the use of 'Indigenous Religions' as descriptive classification suitable for academic studies.

Harvey has edited or co-edited four books with 'indigenous' in its title: *Indigenous Religions: A Companion* (2000); *Indigenous Religious Musics* (2000), with Karen Ralls-MacLeod, *Readings in Indigenous Religions* (2002a) and *Indigenous Diasporas and Dislocations* (2005), with Charles D. Thompson Jr. In each of these books, Harvey has written or co-written an introductory article outlining what he means by 'indigenous' and why he has chosen it over other terms. In the case of *Indigenous Religious Musics*, he applies the term with reference to the ways indigenous peoples express their religions through various forms of music, and, in the book he co-edited with Thompson, Harvey is concerned to examine the significance of the spread of indigenous peoples to regions far removed from their homeland. Each book provides different perspectives on how Harvey understands and interprets Indigenous Religions as a viable category within the academic study of religions and thus helps us build up a composite picture of his own definition of the category. I shall consider three of the books in this context, ignoring *Indigenous Religions: A Reader*, since, largely as a selection of readings drawn widely from the history of the field, it is intended to be used alongside the *Companion*, which contains descriptions of indigenous societies written by contemporary scholars.

Harvey introduces *Indigenous Religions: A Companion* by discussing religion in general, which he defines as a universal concern with 'health, wealth and the pursuit of happiness' (2000: 1). He observes that what people value as producing health, wealth and happiness differs from religion to religion, but, fundamentally, 'religions are structured, orderly, socially sanctioned ways of reaching out to those things, or that thing, which people most want' (2000: 1). If this defines religion in general, we are left asking what 'indigenous' societies hold in common when they pursue well-being. This proves a particularly difficult question for Harvey, since he acknowledges that although 'indigenous religions are the majority of the world's religions', they represent an amazing diversity in language, culture and in their means of subsistence (2000: 3). Many of them hold specific beliefs and practices that apply exclusively within local contexts (2000: 3). Despite their local character, Harvey notes that indigenous peoples have interacted with other indigenous peoples throughout history and in recent times with the wider world to produce an even greater diversity of belief, practice and expression, leading him to conclude: 'This book does not homogenize … all indigenous religions … into one single indigenous religion' (2000: 6). Yet, unsurprisingly, given the title of the book, Harvey suggests that 'it is possible to find considerable common ground that justifies the use of the label' (2000: 7). This is particularly true when Indigenous Religions are considered alongside traditional approaches to the study of 'world religions', which equally are imprecise and broad (2000: 7).

Harvey rejects numerous terms that have been used in prior literature to describe indigenous peoples including: 'primitive', which implies that Indigenous Religions are 'simple' and 'mere fossils from the earliest evolution of humanity' (2000: 7); 'pre-literate' or 'non-literate', terms that unnecessarily dismiss 'the power and adequacy of oral/aural, artistic, dramatic or other means of communication' (2000: 8); 'primal', since it implies 'archaic' and 'foundational' and thus is 'evocative of those museums in which indigenous artefacts are displayed alongside "Natural History"' (2000: 9); and 'traditional', which masks 'a polemic in which indigenous religions are berated for being backward-looking and static' (2000: 9). Harvey then considers the term 'indigenous' and admits that too frequently it has been described negatively, as an 'absence' of universality, but this, he argues, is misleading since indigenous peoples have never been restricted to just one small village or community. They 'have always spoken with their neighbours, visitors and others', and in contemporary times they have become truly universal, for example, by engaging in land disputes in international courts of law and by their active participation in presenting their cultural traditions to outsiders on the Internet (2000: 10). Finally, we reach Harvey's own understanding of the term. He claims that Indigenous Religions celebrate 'the experience of continuity of people and places' by respecting 'the almost ubiquitous centrality of elders and ancestors as holders and sharers of tradition' (2000: 12). This respect extends also to the lands on which the people live, which in many senses are venerated, as we have seen from his contribution to the *New Lion Handbook*, as 'other-than-human persons' (2000: 12; Harvey, 2005b: 103). Although these factors help to characterize Indigenous Religions, the term itself is largely meaningless if it is disconnected from the history of Western colonialism, which has fostered the 'genocide' of indigenous peoples and expelled them from their traditional lands. In an indigenous understanding, genocide includes attacks on the land and thus extends to the killing of 'other-than-human persons' (2000: 12).

In the introduction to their co-edited book on *Indigenous Religious Musics*, Karen Ralls-MacLeod and Harvey adopt a somewhat different strategy when defining the term than Harvey, when writing alone, did in his introductory article in *The Companion*. Ralls-MacLeod and Harvey justify employing the word 'indigenous' on the grounds that now it is used as a term of self-designation, that is, it is widely applied by people who call themselves 'indigenous' (Ralls-MacLeod and Harvey, 2000: 4). Generally, 'indigeneity' as a self-designating term means 'belonging *to* a place' (2000: 4) (emphasis theirs). It is not always possible to live in the place to which one belongs, but 'indigenous peoples are "native", born to (if not always in) lands among relatives' (2000: 4). The term 'relatives', again in Harvey's terminology, includes not only kinship relations amongst the living and ancestral spirits, but extends to those persons who are not human. Distinctions found in the West between 'humans', 'non-humans' and 'super-humans', as well as dichotomies between 'culture' and 'nature' are absent in indigenous thought (2000: 4–5). The West dominates nature, whereas indigenous peoples 'live within environments, not over against them' (2000: 5). Again, we see the necessity in Harvey's work of defining indigenous over against Western colonialism and Western ontologies, a tactic he regards as a requirement of history.

In his most recent book dealing specifically with this topic, Harvey and his co-editor Charles Thompson, Jr, contrast the term 'indigenous' with the word 'diaspora', which they admit at first glance may appear as antithetical concepts (Harvey and Thompson Jr, 2005: 1). This is because diaspora refers to a condition of being uprooted, disconnected or spread out, whereas indigenous is largely understood as local, being from here, related or rooted. By focusing on indigenous diasporas, Harvey and Thompson are dealing with a contemporary phenomenon where indigenous people travel far from their homes, settle in alien environments and are forced to integrate their old traditions into their new living situations. Although they are discussing a movement of peoples largely in contemporary circumstances, because they separate the term 'indigenous' from 'diaspora', Harvey and Thompson are required to define 'indigenous' by identifying specific groups they regard as fitting into the category 'indigenous communities in diaspora'. At the outset, they acknowledge that 'indigenous peoples and religions are, as if by definition regularly associated with tradition, stability, boundedness, authenticity, rootedness, organicism, topophilia, particularity, integration and communalism' (2005: 2). These characteristics are closely linked to the way academics have described 'pre-modern' societies and thus they are contrasted regularly in scholarly writings with the traits assigned to modernity, such as: 'syncretcism, creolization, hybridity, migration, transmigration, globalization, trans-nationalism, multiculturalism, utopianism, artificiality, universality, alienation and rootlessness' (2005: 2). Harvey and Thompson object to such stark dualistic descriptions, where indigenous translates into the opposite of modern. They argue that by designating pre-modern indigenous cultures as 'closer to nature, native and natural' in contrast to the 'cultured, civilized, progressive and technological' character of modern Western society, various scholars working in the social sciences and the philosophy of religion have oversimplified the real situation in order to exercise power over an invented 'other' (2005: 2–3). These polarized constructions need to be confronted by re-presenting 'indigeneity' as always having been 'about movement', and by counteracting stereotypical renditions of 'tradition' by describing it as always having entailed 'a dialogical process of making ancestral heritage relevant to the next generation' (2005: 3). By challenging members of the academic community to re-think their prior assumptions, Harvey and Thompson hope to correct the longstanding misrepresentation in scholarly literature of indigenous peoples as isolated and purely local.

Although Harvey and Thompson have provided a biting criticism of dominant Western attitudes towards Indigenous Religions, they also consider in a positive way how the phrase should be employed legitimately in academic writings. Their definition is couched in language Harvey has used elsewhere and falls under two points, one methodological and the other content specific: (1) indigenous is a term of self-designation; and (2) it applies to those who have originated from and thus belong to a particular place. By taking self-descriptions seriously, scholars will learn to approach academic research as 'relational, participatory, dialogical engagements' with 'real people in real situations' (2005: 4). The dialogical approach takes away the power of the researcher over the objects of research and ensures that academics remain accountable to those 'generous hosts' who have invited them into their midst (2005: 4). This in turn requires that academics reflect accurately and fairly the self-perceptions of the people about whom they ultimately publish books or discuss in lectures. When people, either in particular local situations or in contexts of diaspora, refer to themselves as 'indigenous', it is thus incumbent on researchers to accept this claim largely at face value. Following the definition Harvey and Ralls-MacLeod suggested earlier in *Indigenous Religious Musics*, Harvey and Thompson argue that indigeneity is best defined as '"belonging *to* a place"', though the person who claims to be indigenous to that place 'may or may not live in it' (2005: 10). Not living in the place to which one belongs carries important ramifications for the practice of the religion associated with that place. It is not possible, for example, in situations of diaspora to perform rituals that are connected intrinsically to particular geographical features such as sacred mountains, streams, rivers, pools or trees. Nonetheless, indigenous people, who belong to a location without living in it, can carry the stories surrounding such locations anywhere and repeat them over and over again in their newly founded communities.

We thus reach Graham Harvey's final definition of 'indigenous': it refers to people who identify themselves as belonging to a place. If we consider this alongside Harvey's discussion in *Indigenous Religions: A Companion*, we understand also that indigenous describes people who maintain a fundamental respect for a long-standing tradition as embodied in elders, ancestors, the land and 'other-than-human persons'. When combined with his definition of religion, we are led to conclude that amongst self-defined indigenous peoples respect for the tradition of the place to which they belong (although not necessarily live in) is celebrated ritually and remembered orally in order that the community may experience optimal health and well-being.

Towards an Adequate Definition of Indigenous

It will be clear that Harvey's definition of 'indigenous' omits some of the main characteristics in Platvoet's description of 'community religions', primarily the instrumental value for religious belief of the means of production and the importance of revelation as a constant source for communicating what needs to be done within such societies to preserve or restore well being. We find Harvey agreeing with Platvoet that such societies focus on health and well being and that they traditionally place a high importance on ancestors, and hence on kinship relations.

For Harvey, however, all religions direct attention towards obtaining health, wealth and happiness, whereas Platvoet characterizes these, in material terms at any rate, as belonging primarily to community religions. Both acknowledge that Indigenous Religions need to be described in historical terms, including their interaction with colonialism, and their dynamic relationship with contemporary globalizing forces, but for Harvey, Platvoet characterizes indigenous societies too readily by their technological level, by their forms of political organization and by their non-literate methods of communication.

Despite these differences, Platvoet and Harvey are referring to the same phenomenon when they use the terms 'community' and 'indigenous'. Of course, Harvey stresses that location is not to be interpreted as being bound physically to a place and he blurs the boundaries between scientific descriptions and declarations of faith by insisting on giving priority to self-designations and by employing phrases like 'other-than-human persons'. By contrast, Platvoet could be accused of a type of scientific reductionism by explaining religion largely as a product of human economic and political processes. Nonetheless, for both, to be indigenous is in some sense to identify with a particular locality, to be from it, to be native to it and hence to belong to it. In Platvoet's language, this is couched in terms of locality and kinship; for Harvey, it refers to a self-declared place of identity, both in personal and communal terms. Since to belong to such a community entails kinship relations, religion focuses primarily on ancestor spirits, which by definition are restricted to a place and bound by lineage. 'My' ancestor spirits guard and protect me and members of my kinship group; they do not guard and protect those outside it, since others have their own ancestors to perform the same function. By definition, kinship-based religions are not and cannot be universal.

Following Harvey and Platvoet, I am now ready to propose a minimum definition that outlines what I regard as the major characteristic of Indigenous Religions and, which isolates the one central belief found among indigenous societies everywhere. On my definition, the primary characteristic of Indigenous Religions refers to its being bound to a location; participants in the religion are native to a place, or in Harvey's words, they belong to it. The single and overriding belief shared amongst Indigenous Religions derives from a kinship-based world-view in which attention is directed towards ancestor spirits as the central figures in religious life and practice. As such, Indigenous Religions are restricted cosmologically because their spirit world is organized around a system of lineage. Ancestors are known by name; they belong to a place just as their descendants do, and they relate to living communities as spirit conveyers of ancestral traditions. In this sense, Platvoet is right: amongst indigenous peoples, kinship rules religion; it defines its fundamental characteristic and dictates the one belief all Indigenous Religions share in common.

This central characteristic and defining belief, when considered together, explain why I prefer the term 'indigenous' to any other designation. Kinship and ancestor relations are tied to a place of origin, a location that those who belong to it regard as their own. They are native to it; their ancestors also belong to the place and continue to interact with their descendants, even in diaspora communities, through shared myths and rituals. The term does not necessarily imply that indigenous people are 'original' in the sense of being the first ever to inhabit the land, but it does suggest that those who are native to a place resort to a long tradition, sometimes including stories of migration to the land, that associates them with the particular locality and distinguishes them from those who do not belong to it. In this sense, the meaning of the term 'indigenous' carries a clear positive content that extends beyond objections to an inherent bias in terms like 'fetishism', 'tribal', 'primitive', 'primal', 'traditional', 'non-literate' and 'ethnic' that have been expressed by scholars I have discussed, from Geoffrey Parrinder to Graham Harvey, The category 'indigenous' on my definition is no longer characterized by its reaction against previous distorting images, but refers accurately to kinship-based, localized religious traditions.

My limited description of 'indigenous' also clears away much confusion that has surrounded prior attempts to define it. As we have seen, many scholars writing in this field, Platvoet chief amongst them, have insisted that Indigenous Religions are united by numerous features, including the fact that they convey their traditions orally, that their thinking is pragmatic and this worldly, that they explain misfortune oftentimes in complex, unanalytical and hence contradictory ways, that they are tolerant and non-missionary by nature, and that religion cannot be separated from the rest of social life. If we consider these point by point, it becomes clear that none of these attributes singles out characteristics exclusively applicable to Indigenous Religions nor points to any substantial belief held uniquely within indigenous societies.

As we have seen, in his outline of the historical development of religions, Platvoet insists on stressing the oral or non-literate nature of Indigenous Religions. This can be quite misleading, since most 'world' religions also at one point in their development relied on oral transmissions before they began writing down their traditions, and, in many situations amongst such religions, a preference for oral communication still prevails. The telling of a central story of faith occurs in most religions in ritual contexts, and very frequently also in informal settings. The Christian Eucharist is a case in point. The central story relating Christ's death and resurrection is re-told each time the sacrament is celebrated, and the events surrounding the death and resurrection are re-enacted in the breaking of the bread and drinking of the wine. Of course, by writing down traditions, religions change the mode of their expression, sometimes transfixing them into unchanging dogmas, but this is not true in every case, nor do written scriptures ever totally replace forms of oral communication. This point has been made in the case of Islam by the anthropologist of religion, Fiona Bowie: 'Islam places great emphasis on the sanctity and authority of the holy Qur'an, but the scriptures were originally *recited* to Muhammad, and the recitation of the Qur'an from memory in Arabic remains central to Islamic worship' (2000: 26–7) (emphasis hers). It is also important to note, as Harvey has pointed out, that indigenous peoples today have begun writing down their traditions, partly in order to assert authoritative land rights in courts of law, in other cases to preserve an ancient tradition and in still other instances to communicate to a wider audience what traditional culture entails. I would argue that whether they express their traditions in written forms or not does not affect the claims of such people to an indigenous status.

Other qualities often assigned to Indigenous Religions similarly fail to delineate them from other religions. Platvoet has argued that Indigenous Religions focus on this-worldly concerns, particularly by using spirit forces to protect against misfortune or to provide a remedy for persistent afflictions. Whereas this generally is true, it is not unique to indigenous peoples. On some theological interpretations of Christianity, for example, Christ's teaching on the Kingdom of God could imply a fully this-worldly focus, with material health and well-being defining its ultimate goal (Penulhum, 1997: 31–47). Even the Hindu idea of the transmigration of souls could be interpreted in material terms, where an embodied soul that submits to the law of karma enjoys progressively better re-births through improved degrees of physical comfort and social status (Rambachan, 1997: 66–86). Platvoet contends that indigenous peoples employ complex ways of thinking that frequently are multi-stranded, and unanalytical. This suggests that contradictory explanations for inexplicable occurrences are restricted to Indigenous Religions, whereas this certainly could be applied to most religions, particularly when the causes of suffering and misfortune are attributed to the mysterious workings of God. Platvoet adds that Indigenous Religions are tolerant of other religions, since they have no interest in converting them to their own faith. Instead, they often adapt to encounters with missionary religions by incorporating elements of the new religion into the original one. This phenomenon certainly also occurs in cases where the world religions interact with one another, often resulting in a mutual exchange of ideas. Moreover, it is wrong in every case to characterize Indigenous Religions as being entirely tolerant of outside forces. What is true in Platvoet's rendition of Indigenous Religions is that they are non-missionary by nature, but this is attributable directly to their kinship status rather than to their inherent tolerance. Many so-called world religions, like Hinduism and Judaism, likewise embody non-missionary traditions. Finally, Platvoet's claim that Indigenous Religions are 'co-extensive' with their societies can hardly be regarded as an exclusive trait. As Fiona Bowie observes, 'Most fervent practitioners of "religions of the book" claim that religion penetrates all aspects of their lives – there is no experience or part of the day that does not come under its jurisdiction' (2000: 27). It is quite misleading therefore to suggest that indigenous peoples do not distinguish 'religious' practices from non-religious aspects of their lives; otherwise, there would be no point in singling out as sacred certain ritually important times and places as opposed to normal or ordinary time and space.

I noted earlier that Platvoet has attempted to construct a scientific method for determining religious beliefs by arguing that religions represent responses to the levels of technological sophistication within societies in support of the means of production. When societies operate at low levels of technology, as occurs in hunting and gathering economies, beliefs about spirits will correspond to the threats people experience to their means of subsistence. As modes of production change, so too do the functions of the spirit world. It would be difficult on such an analysis to restrict Indigenous Religions to certain types of economic systems and political structures, since drawing a simple line from one type of economy to ancestral beliefs is difficult to substantiate. What seems more evident is that when societies are limited by their locations, and when their well-being depends on proper relations with ancestors, religious codes, beliefs and rituals share similar foci. There is little doubt that agricultural societies foster conditions that encourage people to appeal to a spirit world to create optimal conditions for productivity, but this is attested equally by the beliefs of universal religions, where the God of the harvest is praised just as ancestors are thanked within indigenous agricultural societies. It would seem, therefore, that an indigenous religion is not characterized by its means of production, but by its location and kinship system.

The Apparent Exceptions of 'Regional' and 'Non-Kinship' Indigenous Religions

My definition of Indigenous Religions may appear overly restrictive, particularly in cases where locality and kinship seem to have been overtaken by regional concerns, although not by global issues. For example, such great West African kingdoms as the Yoruba in Nigeria (Abimbola, 1991: 53), the Asante in Ghana (Parrinder, 1949: 5) or the Kingdom of Benin in present-day Nigeria (Kaplan, 2000: 114-51). clearly encompass numerous kinship groupings. Normally, the religions of these societies would be would be classified as indigenous, but they appear not to fit within the limitations I have imposed on the definition of the term. The contemporary Mwari (Mwali) or High God shrines in southwest Zimbabwe provide another instance that seems to contravene definitions of indigenous as local and kinship-based. In this case, a complex network operates in which messengers representing various chieftaincies throughout south and south central Zimbabwe regularly carry gifts and petitions to the shrine centres, where they hear the voice of Mwari from deep within caves located in the hills. In his recent book on this topic, Leslie Nthoi (2006: 1) describes these activities as 'a non-textual traditional religious cult' the domain of which 'extends across international boundaries from Zimbabwe into Botswana, the Republic of South Africa, Mozambique and possibly into Tanzania'. People of numerous ethnic identities relate directly to the shrines including 'the Karanga, Kalanga, Shona, Venda, Khurutshe, Nyai, Nyubi and Ndeble' (2006: 2). Following Richard Werbner's pioneering work on the Mwari shrines (1977: 179–218), Nthoi refers to them as regional cults 'of the middle range', since they are not global, but still extend 'far wider than a federative or territorial cult, whose sphere of influence is almost co-terminus with territorial administration or national boundaries' (2006: 2). If we follow the thinking of the American anthropologist, Sally Falk Moore, the Mwari shrines do not constitute a rare exception to the otherwise dominant place of kinship-based religious expressions in traditional societies. Moore (1993: 13) warns social scientists not to reduce African societies entirely to kinship and lineage systems, in support of which she cites research conducted in the 1940s and 1950s by Daryll Forde in southern Nigeria which, she says, 'provided unsettling evidence of the great importance of secret societies and other non-kinship-based associations' (see Forde, 1950: 285–332).

On my definition of Indigenous Religions, seemingly we would exclude contemporary expressions of the Mwari cult and other such regional trans-kinship and non-kinship-based religious practices from the category. The situation, however, is much more complex than appears on the surface. For example, the present configuration of the Mwari cult cannot be divorced from its development over 150 years alongside Christianity and colonialism. Although the origins of the cult are disputed, if they can be traced to the ancient empires associated as early as the eleventh century CE at Great Zimbabwe (near the current city of Masvingo), a case can be made for Platvoet's contention that even macro-deities in what he calls national community religions (which include the Asante and Benin kingdoms) bear the marks of great ancestors (1992: 22). The kings or paramount chiefs derive their authority from national ancestors whose spirits continue to affect the welfare of the whole kingdom. I will consider the hierarchical structure of other regional cults in Zimbabwe in considerable depth in my case study in Chapter 6, but I would stress at this point that Mwari is best understood in relation to a much wider oral tradition that relates how the Shona people migrated into present-day Zimbabwe under the guidance of the 'voice' of a foundational ancestor (see Beach, 1980, 1–51). It would be incorrect, of course, as Sally Falk Moore argues, to insist that Indigenous Religions have no other elements within them apart from locality and kinship. This is not my argument, since I am concerned to provide a definition that at a minimum delineates what I mean by the category. In this light, it is highly significant that amongst the religions of West Africa, including devotion to the many non-kinship deities or *orishas* in Yoruba religion, or amongst secret societies throughout West Africa, kinship exists alongside other forms of religious expression (Mbiti, 1969:

75–91). In this sense, ancestral relations in the broadest sense define indigeneity; other factors complement this one central characteristic, and are found in varying degrees or not at all in differing indigenous societies.

The Next Task: Separating 'Religion' from the World Religions Paradigm

I have intended in this chapter that my restricted definition of 'indigenous' should undermine an essentialist model that portrays the religious life and practice of indigenous societies as if they formed part of one core element, called 'religion'. Kinship implies a way of organizing society; belonging to a place locates where particular kinship relations originate and towards which they continue to direct their attention. Although certain patterns may be shared in common by kinship societies, particularly their relationship to ancestors, strong differences of belief about the roles and functions of ancestors occur amongst such diverse but similarly organized groups. An empirical approach to this topic insists that the broad parameters constituting an indigenous religion need to be filled in with specific content, including due attention being paid to the historical, cultural, economic, geographic, political and social variables that determine how kinship and place affect religious language and practice. In other words, I am not beginning with a pre-determined core definition of indigenous based on theological or ethical assumptions. I have adopted instead a modified inductive approach, one that is based on prior research, but entirely capable of being falsified and hence modified or discarded altogether. I call it a modified or qualified inductive approach because, as I have argued elsewhere (1999: 267–84), empirical studies do not and cannot begin as if the mind of the researcher were a blank tablet. We must follow certain intuitive, but informed, preliminary principles that guide the direction of our research. For this reason, I have sought to provide a minimal definition of indigenous, so that at the very least researchers can know what field is being investigated. Without such a preliminary, guiding definition, scholarly work cannot proceed intelligently.

My approach clearly differs from that adopted by Harvey in the *New Lion Handbook*, and endorsed by Partridge as editor, which assumes that indigenous societies everywhere express an identical core or essence called 'indigeneity'. This essence is entirely unverifiable, since it is derived from an ethical assumption that indigenous peoples have been maligned in colonial history and victimized by scholarly constructions of 'the other'. As a result, Harvey's core idea that indigenous implies 'respect' for all life (including other-than-human persons) bears the mark of quasi-theological essentialism based on unstated ethical presuppositions. I have argued that this same model applies to the world religions paradigm, where religion is conceived as a universal source for particular expressions everywhere. The study of the expressions makes it possible to identify and label the core of religion. Hinduism, for example, conveys certain essential characteristics that are diffused into its many expressions, so that it is possible to speak of its universal essence, as we saw in Wilfred Cantwell Smith's rendering of '*tat tvam asi*' (1998: 35–48). The same applies to Islam, Christianity, Buddhism and all other world religions, each of which can be described in terms of its core or essence. Taken together, these 'essences' point towards an 'ultimate' essence, the transcendental source of religion itself. This model, as I have contended, reflects a thoroughly Christian theological interpretation, and cannot be called a science of religion. Insofar as Indigenous Religions are treated in the same way, their study merely perpetuates a fundamental error that has plagued religious studies for over one hundred years by surreptitiously smuggling a theological agenda into the social sciences by disguising essentialist concepts in empirical terminology.

In order to break new ground in the study of Indigenous Religions, therefore, I must do more than provide a scientifically accountable definition of the word 'indigenous'. The world religions paradigm itself must be replaced, and this requires a re-direction of the category religion away from essentialist assumptions towards a socio-cultural contextualized interpretation. Obviously, I am not arguing that the study of Indigenous Religions should be abandoned. The contrary is the case. If the study of religions in general is to move beyond its intimate alliance with theology, a new approach is required, one which will break the stranglehold the world religions paradigm has maintained for nearly one hundred years over religious studies, and will pave the way for a genuine *science* of religion, which *includes* the academic study of Indigenous Religions. The dismantling of a theological interpretation of religion in favour of an empirically testable scientific definition prescribes the crucial task I confront in the next chapter.

Chapter 4

Towards a Socio-cultural, Non-essentialist Interpretation of Religion

Thus far I have argued that by fitting Indigenous Religions into a world religions paradigm, scholars have employed a form of theological essentialism, conceived as a universal core reality, which, although the same everywhere, manifests itself in diverse ways in locally specific social and cultural contexts. In order to discredit such a theological interpretation of Indigenous Religions, I have defined 'indigenous' in a quite limited manner by restricting it to location, or the place to which a people 'belong', and to kinship, including the central role attributed in indigenous societies to ancestor spirits. I have argued further that this restricted definition derives from an entirely empirical methodology that undermines once and for all the essentialist assumptions beneath the world religions paradigm. In order to substantiate this position, while still allowing for a classification called 'Indigenous Religions', in this chapter I propose a socio-cultural definition of religion, which radically decouples the category 'religion' from its longstanding link, amongst scholars of religion at least, with surreptitious theological assumptions.

A Pragmatic Approach to Defining Religion

In his introduction to the volume *The Pragmatics of Defining Religion*, which he co-edited with J.G. Platvoet, the Dutch scholar of religion Arie Molendijk argues that 'we cannot do without stipulative definitions, in order to demarcate the subject in a particular context' (1999: 3). A stipulative definition for Molendijk is a pragmatic one, developed 'for the sake of a specific undertaking' (1999: 9). In the context of defining religion, therefore, we are not looking for a 'true' definition, but for an appropriate and useful definition that at the same time corresponds to actual usage. This does not mean that our definition must conform to language used by religious practitioners, but it must be capable of furthering academic clarity whilst remaining recognizable to wider, non-academic audiences, including those who fit into the definition proposed. Molendijk notes that a pragmatic approach develops definitions for particular purposes, in service, for example, of legal, political or cognitive ends (1999: 9). Hence, the value of pragmatic definitions depends entirely on their utility in promoting the practical applications for which they are intended.

If we follow this largely utilitarian interpretation, in the context of this book, my aim is not to achieve any number of worthy or noble ends, such as fostering world peace, encouraging inter-religious dialogue, elevating dispossessed peoples to positions of power or of substantiating philosophical or theological arguments. My aim is to provide a framework for identifying those human activities, which can be called 'religion', and for making assertions about these activities that can be tested empirically. The value of such a definition of religion depends entirely on its usefulness in promoting scientific knowledge. This means that religion cannot be defined, for example, as an experience which God induces in people who are portrayed as responding to an overwhelming power, as proposed by the theologian Rudolf Otto (1926: 5–8) or the phenomenologist Gerardus van der Leeuw (1938: 23–8), or as a community fostered by divine interventions in history, as advanced by theologians like C.P. Tiele (1973 [1897]: 98). Religion, in other words, cannot be defined by a transcendental referent, but only in terms of concrete, observable socio-cultural activities, which are rooted in historical and political processes. Any theories about such socio-cultural activities must remain fully testable using well-defined and accepted empirical methods.

Following the thinking of Karl Popper (1959 [1935]), for a theory to be fully scientific, it must be falsifiable. If whatever idea being considered cannot be falsified, it operates outside the bounds of scientific investigation, and belongs to another, non-empirical realm – such as the metaphysical, theological or spiritual. If something cannot be verified, this does not make it unscientific. Many theories cannot be verified, at least according to known evidence, but in principle, they could be falsified. Popper famously used the example of an inductive method to test the proposition: 'All swans are white'. Obviously, this proposition cannot be verified finally, unless every swan everywhere could be accounted for and confirmed as white (1959: 27, 101).[1] Such a proposition, however, can be falsified, and indeed has been, by a species of black swans native to Australia. The proposition, 'All swans are white', in this sense is not verifiable, but fits fully into the category of a scientifically testable statement, since it can be falsified. This, of course, reflects what has been called a 'naïve' use of the inductive method, using the principle of falsifiability, but Popper preferred to apply the concept to theoretical considerations by contending that theories which cannot be falsified must be placed outside the process of scientific consideration (Smart, 1999: 265; Kippenberg, 2003: 159). The 'Big Bang' theory about the origin of the universe as we know it, for instance, as yet cannot be verified, and in the end may be incapable of verification, but it is open to testing, including the use of mathematics, and thus falls under the purview of scientific investigation. In other words, the 'Big Bang' theory could be falsified, or modified, according to further evidence, and thus is judged according to its proximity to known facts. This same principle cannot be applied to the theory of 'intelligent design', which posits that by studying the world, we are led to the conclusion that it was created by an ultimate mind. Although this theory often is couched in scientific language, those who pursue such a 'creationist' agenda have a prior commitment to the reality of a non-falsifiable deity, who stands outside all forms of empirical testing. I am not arguing that no such entity could exist, but by its very nature, it cannot be falsified, and hence does not belong to the realm of scientific enquiry. I do not intend here to go into detailed discussions in the philosophy of science, in which Popper plays an important historical role, but, following the pragmatic approach of Molendijk, I am suggesting that for purposes of a scientific definition of religion, the principle of non-falsifiability performs a utilitarian function in circumscribing a scientific approach to the study of religions.

---

[1]   Popper observes: 'No matter how many instances of white swans we may have observed, this does not justify the conclusion that *all* swans are white' (emphasis his) (1959: 27).

My own definition of religion, which I have now revised from my earlier contribution to the Platvoet and Molendijk volume (1999: 272), concentrates in the first instance on the key phrase: an identifiable community's beliefs about and experiences of postulated non-falsifiable alternate realities. The principal elements in this formulation include an identifiable community or socially recognizable group, what that community believes and claims to have experienced about and in response to what it collectively postulates to be realities that are clearly distinguishable from ordinary beliefs about the world and everyday experiences in it. I regard this way of referring to religion as one side of a two-pronged definition. The other, based on the work of the French sociologist, Danièle Hervieu-Léger, situates religious communities in historical, social and cultural contexts by insisting that religion transmits an authoritative tradition, or what Hervieu-Léger calls 'a chain of memory' (1999: 89). This two-sided approach, at once focusing on what adherents themselves postulate, while at the same time emphasizing patterns of community authority, provides a definition of religion freed from theological associations. In the remainder of this chapter, I will analyse these constitutive parts and in the process assert that the reformulation of religion I finally propose is fully empirical and pragmatic, since its assumptions are testable and its usefulness for identifying a specific field of study can be demonstrated.

Part One of the Definition: Focus on the Community's Beliefs and Experiences

The first part of my definition of religion restricts the study of religion to 'identifiable communities', which means that religion is always, in the words of Jeppe Jensen (2003: 117) a 'social fact'. Theories about religion, of course, as Jensen (2003: 118–21) argues further, are also social facts, which means that scholars of religion must always conduct their research in a self-critical, reflexive and transparent manner. Nonetheless, when we speak about religion, we are describing and interpreting that which is observable and testable as part of identifiable social systems. The scholar of religion cannot study individual experiences as religion, unless the experiences are somehow embedded in shared social constructs that are codified, symbolized and institutionalized in communities. In the case of individuals who testify to intense experiences of an extramundane reality, these can be treated as religion only if the individual incorporates the experiences into the life of an already existing identifiable community, or, as in the case of many charismatic leaders or prophets, forges the experience into a new religious movement comprising a definite group. Individual experiences are interesting to psychologists or to those who wish to classify types of experiences, but on my definition, without the community element, they cannot be included within the category 'religion'. The term identifiable refers to the requirement that a scholar place limits around communities under study, using sometimes historical methods, at other times defining them geographically, or in other contexts restricting them according to social or cultural criteria. In the end, we must be able to locate, delimit and contextualize the groups about which we are speaking.

The identifiable community often entails far more within it than 'religion', but in its religious dimension, it possesses certain characteristics. Its primary focus points towards what members of the community postulate collectively as an alternate reality or realities. The term 'postulate' favours the view of the outside researcher, since it attributes to the alleged source of a community's beliefs and experiences the status of a theory, or even an opinion, which is not subject to the rules of empirical investigation. Communities themselves engage in acts of believing, expressed symbolically in language, usually in rituals, texts or stories, which in turn produce experiences that the outsider presumes are similar, since they result from shared symbolic systems. Religious communities thus believe in and experience what, from the perspective of the scholar of religions, adherents merely postulate about alternate realities. Adherents themselves do more than postulate; they testify, bear witness, declare, affirm. For the scholar, the objects towards which these declarations of faith point remain entirely non-falsifiable and thus the declarations themselves cannot be credited scientifically with any higher status than that of postulations.

The identifiable communities postulate about something quite specific, what I call alternate realities. I am using this term quite deliberately, and not as it is often employed in everyday language as meaning 'alternative', such as might be implied in the phrase, 'alternate sources of oil'. Alternate, when used adjectivally, as I am employing it, literally has the meaning of switching between, or going from one to another, as in turns. The 'alternate' reality refers to another type of belief and experience from what we normally believe and experience in the world. Scholars writing from within the cognitive science of religion frequently refer to this as 'counter-intuitive'. For example, the Finnish scholar Ilkka Pyysiäinen argues that intuitive knowledge is universal since 'the material environment surrounding us is *to some* extent everywhere the same' and thus our way of thinking is also '*to some* extent similar' (2003: 19) (emphasis his). Intuitive knowledge is necessary for humans to survive in the natural environment. We know intuitively, for instance, that in the physical world we cannot 'go through' material objects, but in counter-intuitive ways of thinking, 'the boundaries of these domains are violated' (2003: 20). Counter-intuitively, people can pass through physical objects; they can leave their bodies as spirits or even rise from the dead or be re-incarnated. Pyysiäinen concludes that 'super-human agents' are 'counter-intuitive agents in the sense that in their case we are dealing with agents that typically lack some basic biological and physical properties, such as growth, aging or the need for food' (2003: 21).

I mean something similar, but not identical, to counter-intuitive when I use the term 'alternate realities'. When religious communities speak about their alternate realities, they refer to something like a spirit, a god, a power or force that, although clearly occurring in this world and within consciousness, refers to something quite identifiably different from ordinary experience and consciousness. When members of a group participate in a religious ritual, for example, they know that they are relating to what they postulate to be an entity or entities that operate in a time and space clearly differentiated from the time and space they experience normally outside the ritual context. In one sense, they switch their focus from the ordinary to the non-ordinary, or to an alternate reality. This is not best thought of as an *alternative* reality, as in another, contrasting reality, as implied in the term 'counter-intuitive', but as alternate in the sense that for believers the ordinary enters into and experiences the non-ordinary, moving in turns from the one and back to the other. The term 'realities' applies to the beliefs and practices shared by most communities, by referring to a multi-dimensional non-ordinary world. It can also refer to the fact that religious communities often experience what is alternate in different ways, and thus may switch between not just one alternate reality but numerous realities.

The scholar of religion, of course, cannot study the experiences themselves, nor the postulated alternate realities, but can only describe the observable social facts surrounding what communities do or say in response to that which they claim to be real. This is because beliefs about and experiences of postulated alternate realities are entirely non-falsifiable. Naturally, the fact of believing certain things or not believing them can be falsified, just as it is possible to falsify whether or not individuals in the community claim to have undergone extraordinary experiences. Analyses can proceed about the connections between belief and experience, and the ways these are expressed in mythic, ritual, legal, artistic or other symbolic ways. It is also possible to outline what types of experiences are most likely to be associated with particular belief systems. Yet, neither the objects of belief nor the alleged extramundane character of the experiences can be studied scientifically. This means that academic work is concerned with what communities postulate rather than the object or objects about which their postulations are made. This also suggests that when communities perform certain actions, affirm particular beliefs, organize social relations, endow particular individuals with positions of importance or engage in types of ritual behaviour, all in relation to their postulated non-falsifiable alternate realities, the scholar of religion describes these as accurately as possible and interprets them according to his or her declared theoretical positions. In this way, the process of scientific investigation proceeds based on empirical observations, which produce falsifiable conclusions in a fully transparent manner.

Religion as the Authoritative Transmission of Tradition

In several recent publications, I have sought to interpret a theory of religion as advanced by the French sociologist, Danièle Hervieu-Léger, by applying it to various contexts, including contemporary shamanistic revivals and the religious dimensions of land claims in Alaska and Zimbabwe (see Cox, 2003: 69–87; Cox, 2004a: 259–64; Cox, 2006: 239–43). My initial interest in Hervieu-Léger's model of religion was generated by her attempt to remove 'sacredness' from a definition of religion by insisting that religion must be understood as a social expression through its institutions and the authority they maintain over the communities which relate to them. In this way, I hoped to overcome the problem identified by Timothy Fitzgerald who argues that the category 'religion' must be dropped as a legitimate field in the social sciences since, as he has observed correctly, it hides within it a theological assumption that defines religion always in relation to a transcendental referent (2000: 17–18). In Hervieu-Léger's analysis I discovered a way to separate the 'sacred' from religion, while still retaining the category as a distinct field of study irreducible to theology. In the end, I wanted to drive a wedge between Fitzgerald's dilemma which forces the study of religion either into theology or into a field Fitzgerald regards as more amenable to scientific approaches he calls 'cultural studies' (2000: 227–34).

As I have argued throughout the chapters of this book, part of my aim still is to establish religion as a scientific category fully worthy of being included amongst academic disciplines. Yet, I regard Hervieu-Léger's insights as offering more than a means to ensure the survival of the term religion in scholarly language. Her approach contributes substantially in its own right to theoretical discussions within the academic study of religions. Clearly, I do not want simply to embrace the Hervieu-Léger thesis in its entirety, since I want to balance it with the definition I have just outlined where I describe religion as an identifiable community's beliefs and experiences of postulated non-falsifiable alternate realities. Yet, I want to do more than combine two definitions into a single formulation. I intend to analyse Hervieu-Léger's argument in depth as a further step towards arriving at a scientific definition of religion which serves the entirely utilitarian function of clarifying the field we call religion and, in the context of this book, making a study of religion amongst indigenous societies viable.

It is important to understand that Hervieu-Léger's concern is to discuss religion in the context of sociological theories of secularization, particularly in light of an idea maintained by scholars well into the 1960s that religion had entered into the last phases of an inevitable decline as society had come increasingly under the sway of scientific rationalism (Hervieu-Léger, 1993: 129). The reduction of church membership and affiliation to religious institutions in Western Europe was seen as a clear sign of the eroding influence of religion in modern society. By the 1980s, this interpretation was shown to have suffered from underlying anti-religious presuppositions and as having been quite limited in scope with relevance only to particular established religious institutions operating within Western Europe and North America (Hervieu-Léger, 2001: 114–16). Towards the end of the twentieth century, secularization theories seemed to have been proved wrong by contemporary events, such as the revival of religion in the West through charismatic Christianity and the upsurge in New Religious Movements, which on a global scale had parallels in the rapid intensification of religious activity and growth throughout Africa and South America (Lambert, 1999: 303–32). Hervieu-Léger's discussion of religion in terms of various themes, such as the originating place of emotion in religion, the boundaries of religion *vis-à-vis* widely perceived 'secular' collective activities and the place of tradition in religion must all be understood as part of the ongoing secularization debate. This debate does not define my main concern in this book, but the insights Hervieu-Léger offers about the boundaries between the religious and the non-religious add strength to my wider aim of developing a socially-embedded, non-theological definition of religion.

One of Hervieu-Léger's most explicit attempts to define religion is found in her contribution to the Platvoet and Molendijk volume in an article entitled 'Religion as Memory', in which she analyses what she calls the 'diverse surreptitious manifestations of religion in all profane and reputedly non-religious zones of human activity' (1999: 76). The diffusion of religion out of clearly demarcated institutional settings into nebulous, almost ubiquitous, contexts in contemporary Western society makes distinguishing the religious from the non-religious not only more difficult than in previous generations, but one that demands careful academic scrutiny. The modern context raises for Hervieu-Léger fundamental questions which scholars are forced to address when investigating the nature of religion in modernity. On the one hand, she asks, are scholars limited to studying the 'discrete' but clearly identifiable religious influences traditional or 'historic' religions like Christianity, Islam and Judaism exert outside their own institutional spheres? Or are they permitted to study the broad, but loosely defined, effects of religion over wide areas of social life, including political, economic, artistic and scientific interests? To answer these questions, Hervieu-Léger asserts, we must return to the question of defining religion (1999: 76).

The blurring of boundaries between what is religion and what is not has been exacerbated in modernity by the dispersal of religious beliefs outside the domains of the 'great religious systems' (1999: 78). Nowhere can this be seen more clearly than through the proliferation of new religious movements in contemporary Western society. This term covers a wide range of activities including 'cults and sects which have recently come to compete with the historical religions, ... syncretic groups with an oriental influence, revival movements within the organized religions', each of which aims at 'the self-development of the individual adherent' (1999: 79). The limits of such groups are fluid since they 'maintain ties with revues, publishers, and booksellers; they hold expositions, offer training courses, and arrange conferences' (1999: 79). In other words, it is possible, in light of such a wide array of loosely organized movements, for the individual to pick and choose from amongst them what at the moment suits his or her individual needs or tastes. Since this focus on 'interior fulfilment' represents an individualized and hence secular 'road to salvation', Hervieu-Léger asks if it amounts to 'a new modern religion'. Or, since many of them do not refer to transcendence at all, 'must one deny them all the qualification of "religiousness"'? (1999: 79).

Hervieu-Léger argues that recent efforts to address the problem of identifying the boundaries of such movements have become entangled in the old debate between substantive and functional definitions of religion, the former defining religion in terms of supernatural entities and hence in a restricted way, and the latter defining religion according to its function, such as providing meaning, and thus operating in an overly broad way. Substantive definitions render improper all scholarly efforts to comment on expressions of 'sacredness' in modern society, as evidenced, for example, in the ecstatic fervour expressed by fans at football matches. Functional definitions, on the other hand, stretch the limits so widely that religion can include almost anything that relates to questions of meaning in the world (1999: 78). Substantive definitions tend to restrict the study of religions to 'the historical religions' and thus 'condemn sociological thought to being the paradoxical guardian of the "authentic religion" which these historical religions intend to incarnate' (1999: 83). Functional definitions 'turn out to be incapable of mastering the unlimited expansion of the phenomena they try to account for' (1999: 83). It thus becomes clear on Hervieu-Léger's analysis why those who define religion substantively have stressed the decline of religion in the modern world, while those who maintain functional positions emphasize the dispersal of religious symbols in diverse ways through many avenues, previously considered secular, that reflect the atomization of life within contemporary Western culture.

Hervieu-Léger contends that the problem cannot be resolved by siding either with a substantive or functional approach to defining religion, but by turning the focus of defining religion towards a sociological perspective. She asserts that the concern of sociology is not 'knowing, once and for all, what religion is in itself' but of understanding the dynamic transformations that are occurring within society that affect religion. From this point of view, religion is not defined 'ontologically', but practically as a tool 'to aid the researcher in his attempt to think socio-religious change, as well as to think the modern mutation of the religious' (1999: 84). This implies that religion cannot be defined as a fixed entity, the parameters of which are demarcated clearly for all time. Nor can religion be defined in terms of the changing beliefs that come to characterize religious transformations. Rather, for Hervieu-Léger, religion must be understood precisely by analysing '*the mutating structures of believing*' (1999: 84) (emphasis hers). The term belief is central to Hervieu-Léger's position, which she prefers to cast in terms of action, as 'acts of believing', not dissimilar to my concept of 'postulating'. She explains: '"To believe" is belief in motion'; it incorporates 'the practices, languages, gestures and spontaneous automatisms in which these beliefs are themselves inscribed' (1999: 84). Again, in a way similar to the way I explained above, Hervieu-Léger notes that 'the actual act of believing … escapes experimental demonstration' but 'one can affirm its existence from the point of view of those who believe' (1999: 85).

   The act of believing outlines a relationship between the one who believes and the object of belief, whereby 'both individuals and groups submit themselves (consciously or unconsciously) to an exteriorly imposed order' (1999: 85). The act of believing in the modern world, of course, is quite different from believing in a pre-scientific era, but, Hervieu-Léger insists that humans still crave 'security', which remains 'at the heart of the quest for intelligibility' (1999: 85). For individuals, this is expressed in the face of death; for society, it results from the effort to avoid the threat of anomy, or a descent into disorder, chaos and lawlessness (1999: 86). These concerns with individual death and social disorder do not represent leftovers from a previous era; rather, they arise 'out of modernity itself' (1999: 86). Paradoxically, as modernity dissolves the old systems of certainty about the world and substitutes its own ways of maintaining order, 'it develops ... the social and psychological factors of incertitude' (1999: 86). This makes the scholar's task a complex one, where 'the modern act of believing' is analysed in terms of structures or modes of response to incertitude, since in modernity, a new situation has emerged: 'In the mobile, "fluid" universe ... all symbols are interchangeable, combinable and transposable into the other' (1999: 86). To define 'religion' in such a context requires the scholar to analyse not a fixed object, or reified thing, but to think of religion as 'a process, as motion' (1999: 87). This means that the content of religion can no longer be thought of as restricted to a certain way of believing, either excluding or including political, social and economic factors, as required both by substantive and functional definitions. 'Religious' believing is not delimited by content, but must be understood in 'an ideal-typical manner' as 'a particular modality of the organization and function of the act of believing' (1999: 87).

   If we follow Hervieu-Léger's train of thought to this point, we will see that the question confronting scholars is not, for example, could a modern spectator sport like football be considered a 'religion', any more than it asks if modern expressions of Christianity, Judaism or Islam can be regarded as religious. The important issue for a socially-embedded interpretation of religion depends on the question of legitimization. How is the act of believing legitimized? And here Hervieu-Léger reaches her own definition of religion as a mode or structure of the act of believing: 'There is no religion without the explicit, semi-explicit, or entirely implicit invocation of *the authority of a tradition*; an invocation which serves as support for the act of believing' (emphasis hers) (1999: 88). What makes something religious depends on whether or not the forms of believing invoke or 'justify themselves, first and foremost, upon the claim of their inscription within a *heritage of belief*' (emphasis hers) (1999: 87–8). The ensuing continuity of belief defines for any religious group who is included within or excluded from 'a spiritual community assembling past, present and future believers'. In this way, religion functions as a mode of 'social integration' and, at the same time, distinguishes insiders from outsiders by differentiating 'those who are not of the same heritage' (1999: 88). These considerations lead to Hervieu-Léger's 'definition' of religion 'as an ideological, practical and symbolic framework which constitutes, maintains, develops and controls the consciousness (individual or collective) of membership to a particular heritage of belief' (1999: 88). Hence, religious groups define themselves 'objectively and subjectively as *a chain of memory*, the continuity of which transcends history' (1999: 89) (emphasis hers). By relating to a chain of memory, religious communities collectively share in acts of remembrance of the past which give 'meaning to the present' and contain the future (1999: 89).

Distinguishing the Religious from the Non-Religious

Although Hervieu-Léger claims that her intention is not to demarcate strict boundaries between the religious and the non-religious following prior dichotomies between substantive or functional methods of defining religion, in so far as she is offering a 'definition', her analysis must help us distinguish 'religion' from 'non religion'. And, in fact, she is forced into making just such distinctions when she asserts that particular types of legitimizing authority in support of a religion's heritage indicate which modes of believing can be considered genuinely religious and those which cannot. The key indicators of a religious, as opposed to a non-religious legitimation of the heritage of believing are found in the words 'transmission' and 'authority'. The transmission of the tradition, she explains, is 'bound up within the processes of elaboration' of the chain of memory (1999: 90). As such, it entails much more than passing the tradition from generation to generation; 'transmission is the very movement itself whereby the religion constitutes itself in time as a religion' (1999: 90). Because by transmitting its tradition a religion is constituted, that which is transmitted must bear within it an overwhelming authority which establishes the community and makes it entirely distinctive from any other community. Hervieu-Léger most fully develops and explains these key ideas in her book, *Religion as a Chain of Memory* (2000).

In Chapter 5, entitled 'As our Fathers believed ...', the idea of authority is presented as being bound up with tradition, which 'confers transcendent authority on the past' (2000: 86). The transcendence of authority results from the impossibility of ever determining its origin, because 'it is fed only from itself' (2000: 87). Religious communities invoke the tradition's authority as they interpret and re-interpret its power over the living communities which are derived from the tradition. This means that for any group's present identification 'what comes from the past is only constituted as tradition insofar as anteriority constitutes a title of authority in the present' (2000: 87). The antiquity of the tradition is not what gives the tradition its authority, although it may give it 'an extra value' (2000: 87). Religious groups receive transmissions from the past, which they reprocess through a 'sifting' and 'shaping' of the tradition so that the heritage of the past becomes continually renewed as a 'norm for the present and future' (2000: 87). The reformulations of the past are not always performed by those who hold power within the community; sometimes, new leaders emerge as prophets who give fresh interpretations of the authoritative tradition and thus affect the way it is transmitted. Nonetheless, prophets or reformers still relate to the authoritative tradition and frequently justify their re-interpretation on the grounds that theirs represents the 'authentic' tradition (2000: 87).

The central point in this analysis for Hervieu-Léger is that religion must be understood as religion only insofar as groups identify themselves as belonging to a chain transmitting from generation to generation a tradition which maintains an overwhelming authority over the group. Hervieu-Léger stresses repeatedly that this does not describe religion in static terms, or as stuck in the past, since the transcendent authority of the past 'serves present interests' (2000: 86). This gives room for new religious movements, re-interpretations of the tradition and new forms of authority, but religion will always, on her accounting, claim an authority that derives from tradition, the transmission of which, although buried in myth, always conveys a transcendent power. The three fundamental components of a definition of religion thus must include: (1) expressions of believing; (2) the memory of continuity; and (3) the legitimating reference to an authorized version of tradition (2000: 97).

In order to clarify how this definition helps us distinguish what is religion from what is not, Hervieu-Léger returns to the question of sport as religion. We will be aware, of course, in the case of football, that huge crowds gather regularly to support a team. These supporters are united by common symbols acting as emblems of the team; they recite chants in unison, as in a ritual; they share beliefs about the superiority of their team, if not by winning, in an ethical sense, by asserting that their team somehow 'ought' to win. On Hervieu-Léger's criteria, therefore, football supporters express beliefs about their team, they carry a memory of great achievements of the past and they often tell the authorized version of the history of the team in order to inspire greater loyalty in the present. Yet, Hervieu-Léger refuses to accept that football supporters constitute a religion, although she admits that they may experience moments of euphoria or despair that coincide with many accounts of religious experience. The main point of differentiation is found in the fact that 'high-level competitive sport ... functions *in the moment*, in the immediacy of the gathering in a kind of corporate emotional awareness' (2000: 103) (emphasis hers). In this sense, football matches correspond to the 'instantaneous production of collective meaning' which characterizes the atomized, individualized and subjective 'systems of meaning' operating within contemporary Western society. In a football match, for example, 'of their own accord' supporters 'fulfil the expectations they arouse' (2000: 103). This means, for Hervieu-Léger, that such sporting events mirror the difference in modern society between 'sacredness', which indeed is a collective experience of a force transcending the individual that provides meaning, as in devotion to the team, its history and shared symbols, but it is not religion, which must have as its defining characteristic 'a ritualized remembering of a core lineage, in relation to which present experience constructs meaning' (2000: 103–4). The inevitable conclusion from this analysis is that sporting events, like mass rock concerts and political demonstrations 'offer in small pieces ... access to an experience of the sacred (an immediate, emotional realization of meaning) which *en masse* no longer functions in the religious mode' (2000: 104).

I regard the value of Hervieu-Léger's distinction at this point as resulting from her attempt to separate 'sacredness', understood as immediate gratification, individualized emotional meaning, subjective states and atomized spirituality, from religion, which always and everywhere follows from the transmission of an authoritatively binding tradition over the lives of individuals who identify themselves collectively in a group. This means that, in Western society, the process of atomization or intense individuality erodes the power of authoritative traditions and thus explains why such traditions have lost their hold over individuals, but, at the same time, it helps us separate religion as a social phenomenon from theological assumptions. If there is a transcendental referent in Hervieu-Léger's thinking, it is precisely the historical transmission of tradition, interpreted and re-interpreted by communities, as binding on the group. This is far different from defining religion in terms of divinities, spiritual entities or a supernatural realm. The 'pick and choose' approach towards individual self-fulfilment in modern Western society, whereby traditions are divested of their authority and overtaken by matters of taste suited to the particular needs or interests of individuals, distinguishes experiences of the 'sacred' from religion. Even in great sporting events, the immediate gratification of the individual is evident and is lost in the emotional satisfaction or despair conveyed in the transience of a result on any given day.

If we push this analysis very far, we will soon discover that Hervieu-Léger is open to the criticism that her distinction between the religious and the non-religious points to a difference of degree rather than of substance. The transmitted authority must in some sense be overwhelming and not moderate; the emotional effect must be lasting and not transient; the power over life must be total and not split between many competing interests; the allegiance of the individual must reside in the group and not depend on personal needs. When such intense commitments fade and other interests become more consuming, we see individuals seeking experiences of 'sacredness', which confer existential meaning, but, for Hervieu-Léger, this cannot be religion, since these experiences lack the overwhelming authoritative power of a tradition that has been transmitted, according to the community's myths, from ancient times. If the dividing line between religion and experiences of sacredness is simply one of degree, the arguments about the constitutive factors within religion are not resolved. Indeed, to continue with the example of sport, the Scottish football clubs, Celtic and Rangers, with their historic roots in sectarian allegiances, may engender something much stronger than transient emotional fulfilment for their respective supporters when one team triumphs over the other (Giulianotti and Robertson, 2006: 171–98; Giulianotti and Gerrard, 2001: 23–42). This explains why I find unconvincing Hervieu-Léger's submission that 'there is every justification for treating the celebration of the Olympic Games as a religion in the full meaning of the term' (2000: 104). There seems only a relative difference between the Olympic Games, which in Hervieu-Léger's words, 'convey meaning and legitimacy to the rites and celebrations' (2000: 104) and football matches, where supporters may well trace their team's traditions to collective struggles for independence and identity. The Hervieu-Léger definition, in my view, although extremely useful for embedding religion in socio-cultural contexts, cannot stand on its own, and requires the first part of my two-sided definition to indicate unambiguously what we mean by the academic category 'religion'.

A Delimited Socio-Cultural Definition of Religion

By incorporating my earlier discussion of religion as outlined in the Platvoet and Molendijk volume into the one developed by Danièle Hervieu-Léger, I am able to create a definition which I contend is empirical, socio-cultural, non-theological and non-essentialist. It is embedded in a sociological perspective, but avoids Hervieu-Léger's lack of clarity when distinguishing the religious from the non-religious on sociological grounds alone. I thus offer the following definition as one that promises to break new ground in the way we conceive and study religion:

> Religion refers to identifiable communities that base their beliefs and experiences of postulated non-falsifiable realities on a tradition that is transmitted authoritatively from generation to generation.

The emphasis in my own earlier definition of religion on an identifiable community is fully consistent with Hervieu-Léger's assertion that there is no religion without the transmission of an authoritative tradition amongst social groups. The problem Hervieu-Léger encounters when trying to separate the religious from the non-religious is overcome by inserting into her account a limitation that contends that communities are acting religiously only in so far as the traditions they are transmitting derive their authority from postulated non-falsifiable alternate realities. On this definition, no degree of emotional attachment is necessary before experiences within identifiable communities can be regarded as religious. The components of religion are entirely objective and include an identifiable community, its beliefs about and experiences of postulated non-falsifiable alternate realities, and its traditions that are derived from and centred around an authority that is passed on from generation to generation.

On this account, football is not religion, simply because its referent is neither non-falsifiable nor an alternate reality, even if its traditions are transmitted with such a hold over the supporters that they adhere to the team's authority and undergo intense emotional experiences as a result. On the other hand, Marxism might be regarded as a religion, since, not only do adherents follow an authority that is transmitted, but the reality envisaged is alternate, in the sense that it is eschatological and involves a non-falsifiable claim that history will achieve an inevitable utopian conclusion. Of course, this interpretation of Marxism could be challenged on grounds that what it postulates can be falsified by history, and, for some, already has been (Morris, 1987: 41–43: 320–4). Nonetheless, in so far as Marxism attracts adherents whose beliefs and experiences relate to a faith in an ideal world, I would contend that this fits my definition of religion, since the forces that create the inevitability of history's end are entirely non-falsifiable. At the same time, we could argue that Marxism contains the key elements of the Hervieu-Léger definition: groups identify and organize themselves in response to a tradition that is transmitted authoritatively, but in the process of transmission they revise their beliefs in light of present circumstances.

If Marxism is included within this two-pronged definition of religion, but sport is not, it is clear that a religion is not a religion unless the identifiable community postulates beliefs about and experiences of a non-falsifiable alternate reality. Equally, a group does not qualify as a religion if it does not transmit its tradition authoritatively. For this reason, the development of individualistic spirituality in Western society does not meet the definition. Self-help groups, for example, whose members come and go at will, shifting between one meeting and another, although reflecting personal quests for meaning, do not meet the criteria for a religion (Bruce, 2002: 75–105). As I will discuss in the final chapter of this book, even contemporary neo-shamanistic groups with their appeals to ancient traditions do not constitute religious communities, but instead illustrate the atomized condition of contemporary Western society, where individuals try out various ways to achieve meaning without ever attaching themselves to an identifiable community that traces its existence to the transmission of an authoritative tradition (Jakobsen, 1999: 147–207). This same argument could be applied to other contemporary Western movements, such as neo-paganism or esoteric religions, many of which are listed in recent volumes on New Religious Movements (Partridge, 2004: 267–302, 303–56; Chryssides, 1999: Sutcliffe and Bowman, 2000). Many of these new groups, on Hervieu-Léger's analysis, have been fostered by the disintegration of the collective memory in the West rather than from the assertion of religious continuity extending from generation to generation. She explains:

> The growth of secularization and the loss of total memory in societies without a history and without a past coincide completely; the dislocation of the structures of religion's plausibility in the modern world works in parallel with the advance of rationalization and successive stages in the crumbling of collective memory (2000: 127).

My argument follows that many recent movements, including self-help groups, associations founded by neo-shamanistic practitioners and contemporary Western paganism, fit better into Hervieu-Léger's model as individualistic responses to the crumbling of a collective memory than they do as bona fide new religions.

The Definition in the World Religions Paradigm

I have argued that a genuinely revolutionary definition of religion must challenge the essentialist assumptions buried within the world religions paradigm, which conceives religions as discrete, self-contained systems that express a common or universal religious core. It could be argued that the definition I have created falls into the same trap as other substantive definitions by limiting religion to a belief in gods or supernatural entities, which although understood differently in various cultural contexts, reflects the same essential focus. This could even be extended to the charge that my definition veils theological assumptions, since it is restricted in one part by insisting that religions focus on alternate realities. These points need to be addressed if I hope to maintain that my new definition actually provides a major innovation or breakthrough in the ways we conceptualize religion.

As we have seen, the world religions paradigm insists that major religions can be identified and classified according to a shared history, frequently presented in geographical terms, and organized according to common beliefs and practices. Very few scholars these days would argue that the major traditions do not comprise wide variations in belief and practice, but, as I noted in Chapter 2, many books on the world religions maintain that religious traditions can be considered as discrete units because they refer to a shared history and commonly held elemental beliefs. Insofar as this approach depends on historical evidence, it remains entirely consistent with the definition I have developed which stresses identifiable communities and their authoritative transmission of tradition. The common problem with the world religions model is that it tends inevitably to minimize differences among the communities to which the religious label is attached and thus creates the impression that the distinctive major religions are far more internally congruous than they actually are. For this reason, my definition that stresses 'identifiable communities' tends to localize the discussion and at the same time insists on arriving at conclusions derived from specific historical research and ethnographic descriptions. The term 'discrete' in this sense applies to the identifiable communities, and only within a very limited frame of reference, can this be extended to similar communities that share elements of a common heritage. This make books on the world religions particularly suspect because necessarily they must minimize differences in favour of generalizations, which may serve little purpose even at the most basic levels of teaching.

This, however, is not the major argument that could be put against my definition. It is clear that I have employed a modified version of a substantive definition of religion by insisting that religions everywhere must refer to non-falsifiable alternate realities. This sounds very similar to those who argue that for a religion to be defined as a religion, it must direct its primary attention towards supernatural entities or divinities. I have tried to show that I am not restricting the definition to supernatural entities, but to experiences in time and space that clearly are distinguished by adherents from their ordinary experiences in time and space. These can include ritual contexts or reverence paid to special objects or landmarks, but something other than the ordinary is associated with the attention paid by devotees within such times and to such places. Without such a focus, I am arguing we do not have religion, but something else that is quite identifiable in other terms, such as a political order, an economic system, a psychological reaction or a social construct. Religion, of course, is interwoven into each of these elements, and only artificially extracted from them for scholarly analyses. This is not a practice restricted to religious studies, but occurs in all academic disciplines. The political scientist examines how decisions are legitimated; the economist studies means of exchange and market forces that affect them; the psychologist analyses individual reactions to external stimuli; the sociologist outlines structures that influence community behaviour. The scholar of religion describes and interprets how communities relate to non-falsifiable alternate realities. The focus in the study of religion, as I argued above, is not on the alternate realities, which cannot be studied, but on the communities that do the postulating, and thus follows an entirely empirical methodology.

This is essentialist only in the sense that every academic discipline must define what it means by its field of study. It is not essentialist in a theological way. This is because the study of religion concentrates precisely on what identifiable communities postulate about non-falsifiable alternate realities, not on what the scholar postulates about them. As a student of religion, I do not define the focus towards which people direct their attention when they act religiously; I simply define what I mean by actions that I regard as religious. That identifiable communities organize many of their activities around what they postulate to be alternate realities is incontrovertible. They tell stories about them, perform rituals to them, communicate directly with them, appeal to them in times of crisis or at moments of significance in the life of the community. The communities act in these ways according to their own declarations about their non-falsifiable alternate realties. In other words, they do the postulating; the scholar describes, classifies and interprets, but does not postulate about non-falsifiable alternate realities unless the scholar is a theologian. The scientist of religion remains focused entirely on empirical facts and on observable behaviours.

World religions on such a definition are not integral to the study of religion as such. If identifiable communities form part of a global network and if they share fundamental beliefs, practices and attitudes in common, their international characteristics form part of the descriptions provided by the scholar, but they do not constitute a necessary part of the definition of the category religion. Identifiable, small-scale, localized communities equally comprise legitimate subjects for the study of religion. And, certainly, the interaction between small-scale, localized communities and global religions outlines much of the most creative work being done today by researchers. A world religions paradigm, where religion is understood as six or seven major, but discrete units that can be described as a whole for purposes of comparison, oftentimes to identify an essence shared by each in common, is foreign to the definition I have suggested. In this sense, I am offering a non-theological, non-essentialist descriptive definition that, in Molendijk's words, stipulates what we mean by religion in order that the process of research in this distinctive field can proceed pragmatically.

Another objection to my revised definition could employ the charge that it favours the historical religions, precisely because it emphasizes authoritative tradition and its cross-generational transmission. This might even seem to be restricting the study of religions to institutions, and thus placing out of bounds the new forms of spirituality that are becoming extremely popular in Western society. In this sense, somewhat by the back door, the world religions would gain precedence over loosely organized movements in the academic study of religions. As I argued above, my definition restricts itself to identifiable communities, but this does not refer exclusively to the historic or world religions. As I will show in my case studies, this definition can be utilized quite pragmatically in the study of indigenous societies. By insisting that religion must be defined in relation to authoritative traditions, I am suggesting that the identity of religious communities is constrained by their association with the traditions they have inherited and by the authority these exert over them. In other words, religion is not about individual tastes, preferences, choices or needs unless these are connected directly into a community that legitimates its authority by reference to a tradition that constitutes its heritage. This does not exclude religions outside those conventionally designated as the world's historical religions, such as Indigenous Religions, but, as we have seen, it excludes transient, popular, individualistic movements.

Finally, an objection could be made that by excluding numerous examples of contemporary individualistic quests for meaning, an entire field of interest to contemporary scholars of religion by definition has been placed outside religious studies. In the first instance, I would reiterate, with Hervieu-Léger, that this definition does not exclude new religious movements from the academic study of religions. As Hervieu-Léger argues, when a prophet arises, or reform movements develop, or an individual claims to be the vessel of a personal revelation, in each case these can be defined as religious to the extent that the claims behind such new movements are 'rendered immutable by becoming the starting point for a new heritage of belief', one that normally is related, either in a real or invented way, 'to an authentic tradition' or to 'an aspect of a deepened understanding of the tradition itself'. In all cases, for innovations to fit into the category 'religion' there must exist 'the imperative of continuity, which … expresses the founding of the religious and social bond' (Hervieu-Léger, 1999: 88–9). This part of the definition limits the study of religion to 'social facts', just as the first part insists that the study of religion, properly constituted, extracts out of the many actions of identifiable communities those that refer to non-falsifiable alternate realities.

The Significance of this Approach to the Study of Indigenous Religions

I am now ready to suggest how my reformulated definition of religion clarifies in what ways the category 'Indigenous Religions' constitutes a legitimate field for academic enquiry. I have argued already that the term indigenous must be restricted to location and to kinship, that is, it is limited to groups that construct their identity as belonging to a place and to a particular lineage. If we add to this the definition of religion I have just suggested, we will delineate the study of Indigenous Religions as those identifiable communities whose traditions relate to the place to which they belong and whose authority is derived from the chain of memory traceable to ancestors. The beliefs and experiences of these identifiable communities refer to postulated non-falsifiable alternate realities, which are connected to the locality to which the people belong and are related integrally to ancestral traditions. The study of the religions of indigenous societies, unlike other religions, is restricted by definition to authoritative traditions about non-falsifiable alternate realities connected specifically to particular locations and kinship lines, but it also includes the ways such religions have changed under the forces of colonialism and globalization, which have forced them to accommodate to competing world views.

That which justifies the study of Indigenous Religions as a discrete subject thus is not derived from an essence that belongs universally to each, since the variations within localized, kinship religions are vast and their responses to outside forces diverse. What binds them into a category quite simply is the restricted definition I have imposed on both terms, indigenous and religion. The study proceeds necessarily case by case, since such religions are local and kinship based, and their authoritative traditions are transmitted in quite specific ways. Thus, one is not an expert on 'Indigenous Religions', but can only acquire specializations in the religions of particular indigenous societies. This differs only in degree from the study of other religious traditions. I would contend that a scholar is not an expert in 'Hinduism', but in some aspect, such as the history, philosophy, texts or ritual practices of the religions of India or the Indian diaspora. The same could be said for Islam, in the sense that a scholar specializes in various features of Islam, either historical periods, texts, doctrines, laws, philosophy, art, contemporary movements, mystic elements and so forth. In so far as Hinduism and Islam can be regarded as extending beyond locality and kinship, of course, they do not belong to the category Indigenous Religions; nonetheless, a legitimate study in what are labelled Hinduism and Islam must be reduced in scope from what we normally find in books on world religions to consider the beliefs and practices of specific communities. In this sense, even the so-called major religions must be studied as cases operating within a complex arrangement of relationships.

This contention raises numerous epistemological problems, including the legitimate place for generalizations about Indigenous Religions, other religions, or religion in general on the basis of comparative studies. We are thus brought back to the issue I raised when I discussed methodological problems exhibited by the approach of the *New Lion Handbook of World Religions*, where eleven case studies of Indigenous Religions are presented following Graham Harvey's general introduction to the theme. I suggested that this approach appears to start with a pre-conceived notion of what is indigenous, as an essential category, and then fits the cases into the theory as expressions of the essence. If I am right that what we can say about indigeneity is severely restricted to locality and kinship, rather than focusing on essential characteristics, I seem to be confining the study of Indigenous Religions to case studies, which can be multiplied beyond any manageable limit. In other words, if my critique of prior approaches to the study of religions stands and no universally applicable inferences are permitted, seemingly we would require whole libraries to contain our case studies without being able to make any meaningful comparisons or reach any general conclusions, however tentative. Clearly, this is not what I mean, but it is important to raise the warning that we must be extremely cautious about claims that seem to imply that essential components exist in all localized, kinship-based religions. To compare Indigenous Religions in parts of Africa with those in Australia or China without giving priority to the specific traditions entailed in each too readily leads to facile and superficial conclusions. It is far better to provide details of just one society than it is to entertain meaningless comparisons. This same principle applies to the study of religions everywhere.

It will be clear from these comments why I have chosen to designate the category for this study in the plural, 'Indigenous Religions', as opposed to the singular form, 'Indigenous Religion'. Since my definitions are pragmatic and intended, as heuristic tools, to avoid the problems found in many prior books that define religion as a unitary essence with diverse manifestations, I am insisting that we distinguish between the plural and singular uses when classifying the objects of our research. For this reason, the case studies I present in the next two chapters focus primarily on two identifiable ethnic groups, the Yupiit of southwest Alaska and the Korekore of northern Zimbabwe. I thus refer to the Indigenous Religions of Alaska but endorse the nomenclature Yupiit Indigenous Religion. Likewise, I contend that it is preferable to refer to the Indigenous Religions of Zimbabwe, since various groupings with different practices are found in this wide area, but it is correct to speak about Korekore Indigenous Religion. Although close similarities in religious thought and practice converge, for example, between the Yupiit and Inupiat in Alaska or between the Korekore and the Zezuru in Zimbabwe, my definition of indigenous as belonging to a place and as kinship-based requires that terminological precision be maintained. We will see that as the boundaries between groups become blurred and, particularly in the case of Zimbabwe, where the foundational myths connecting various communities have become entangled with contemporary nationalist rhetoric and political action, distinctively local characteristics are more difficult to maintain. Nonetheless, in general, I am using the plural to designate variations within the broad category Indigenous Religions, and the singular form when describing specific and localised cases.

This suggests that comparisons, when properly distinguished in this way, prove useful for developing carefully constructed theories and analytical categories. Indeed, a strong defence can be made for using a case study approach to clarify specific theoretical problems or questions. Sometimes the case studies themselves generate the theoretical problems; sometimes they are used to clarify or resolve them. All research begins in this sense with a problem. The researcher is puzzled by certain incongruities either in fact or theory, or more commonly in both. This leads to a series of questions that drive the investigation, often entailing studies of specific situations in order to resolve the questions, or, as I indicated earlier, to falsify or modify a particular theory. If the study of religions begins within a framework that raises research questions or addresses particular theoretical problems, then the argument for drawing conclusions from specific studies can be justified. This applies to global religions just as it does to Indigenous Religions, and aims at building up knowledge on the basis of carefully constructed investigations into fact and theory. This is where insights from the sociology of knowledge become important. Our theories about religion cannot be said to be derived from nowhere. They are social and personal constructs, or as Roger Trigg (2003: 100) puts it, 'science … is itself a social and cultural construction'. This means, again in Trigg's words, that 'what is to count as a fact, and which facts are relevant, are typical questions that cannot be addressed without presuppositions arising from one's theory' (2003: 100). This is why I emphasized earlier that the researcher begins by making transparent his or her own theoretical presuppositions and, by acknowledging these, indicates how theory will be used in the process of interpreting religious data.

This does not mean that we approach the study of religions using a different method from the other sciences, nor that we seek insight using a different type of rationality. The process remains fully scientific. We devise research questions in accordance with transparent theoretical considerations, study specific situations related to them that may provide insight into the questions posed or at least raise further more pertinent questions, all in order to arrive at conclusions that are fully testable, and capable of falsification. Following Jeppe Jensen on this point, I would argue that the problem of acquiring knowledge operates no differently in the study of religions than it does in other disciplines. Jensen (2003: 129) asserts:

> We are (still) able to say that there are no principled grounds for considering 'objectivity' (as an ideal) to be less relevant in the study of religion than in any other study of human

affairs and that our studies do not *per se* rely on logical canons or forms of rationality different from those of other fields of science.

If the problem of building knowledge based on concrete observations that are fitted into certain pre-existing theoretical frameworks dogs any of the sciences, in an entirely similar way, it will provide challenges within like-minded scientific studies of religion.

The study of Indigenous Religions on this line of thinking belongs in university departments of religious studies, as a theoretical problem for the study of religions, as instances of specific, localized kinship-based religions, as ways in which globalized religions influence and have been influenced by local religions, and as cases that address and illuminate rationally, empirically and specifically pre-formulated research questions. If studies in Indigenous Religions, and indeed of religions generally in universities, are to proceed by eventually dismantling the world religions paradigm, this theoretically guided empirical approach must be implemented. Indigenous Religions in this way will be treated like every other religion, not by arguing, on ethical grounds, that they deserve a place in the world religions paradigm alongside other traditions, but by insisting that every religion must be studied similarly with due respect to particular contexts and transparent theoretical objectives. Only in this way, can the study of religions obtain an academic credibility that separates it from A-Level or similar pre-university courses in religion and establishes it as an equal partner with other scientific disciplines operating in universities and research institutions.

Concluding Remarks

In the first four chapters of this book, I have sought to make a case for the study of Indigenous Religions largely by re-formulating the way we think about the two categories, indigenous and religion. I have demonstrated how the study Indigenous Religions developed out of late nineteenth century thinking, how it evolved in the work of Geoffrey Parrinder and Andrew Walls and how in recent times it has become a competitor amongst the other world religions for study in university departments of religious studies. I have drawn attention to what I regard as the fatal flaw of theological essentialism at the root of the world religions paradigm and suggested that by re-defining the terms indigenous and religion we can promote a study that is socially embedded, fully empirical, non-theological and non-essentialist. At the end of this chapter I suggested that the revision of the term religion, when applied to the study of Indigenous Religions, directly impacts on the study of religions generally by shifting comparative studies away from facile generalizations towards responses to carefully constructed theoretical questions. In this sense, the study of religions inescapably employs a case study approach by focusing on identifiable communities, but with the aim of distinguishing, clarifying, raising or resolving the theoretical concerns which drive research into religions.

In the next two chapters, I test my own theories about Indigenous Religions through two quite detailed case studies, based in part on regions of the world in which I have conducted research or on topics about which I have written previously. My guiding questions are dictated by my decision to designate indigenous as a term referring in a quite limited way to locality and kinship and to my definition of religion as focusing on non-falsifiable alternate realities that are postulated by and legitimated within identifiable communities through the transmission of an authoritative tradition. I do not intend through the case studies to confirm the correctness of my definitions, or their 'truth', since I have already asserted these in a preliminary way, but rather my aim is to test their utility as pragmatic tools for promoting scientific studies in Indigenous Religions. I will also use the case studies to lay the foundation for the theoretical problem surrounding 'primitivism' and the current debates it has spawned, which I address in the final chapter of this book.

Chapter 5

The Yupiit of Alaska: The 'Real People'

In this chapter, I analyse Indigenous Religions in Alaska by concentrating on one group of indigenous people, the Yupiit. I will draw substantially from the extensive work of the independent Alaskan anthropologist, Ann Fienup-Riordan, whose books on the Yupiit provide some of the most comprehensive accounts of the people as they understand themselves today and as they remember their past traditions (Fienup-Riordan, 1990, 1994, 1996, 2000). I will also consult the work of the earlier anthropologist, Wendell Oswalt, who wrote extensively about the Yupiit, beginning with a detailed description of the encounters between the Moravian missionaries and the Yupiit living in the Kuskokwim Valley region during the late nineteenth century (Oswalt, 1963). The first Moravian missionary accounts were supplemented by the journals of Ferdinand Drebert, who for forty-two years, beginning in 1912, worked as a Moravian missionary along the Lower Kuskokwim River and the Bering Coast. Drebert has recorded his experiences in a collection published in 1959, in which vivid descriptions are provided of his encounters with Yupiit religious beliefs and practices. Other important sources are available, particularly the writings of the late nineteenth-century ethnographer, E.W. Nelson, whose works are housed in the Smithsonian Institute in Washington D.C., and partially reproduced in a landmark study of change amongst the indigenous peoples of Alaska conducted in the early 1930s by two researchers from Stanford University, H. Dewey Anderson and Walter Crosby Eells (1935). Anderson and Eels documented how 'Eskimo' life had been organized at the onset of the systematic 'Americanization' of indigenous societies begun in the 1880s through a joint venture conducted between the American Protestant churches and the United States government. They then outlined how traditional cultural patterns, such as housing, education, economy, language, stories and religion, had altered radically by 1930, just fifty years after the United States began its sustained attack on indigenous ways of life under the overall direction of the Presbyterian minister and United States Agent for Education, Sheldon Jackson. I have written about this in detail in another publication, which I do not re-produce here (Cox, 1991), but I draw attention to this at the outset to indicate that at the very least the indigenous peoples of Alaska have been in various states of transition imposed by numerous US government initiatives since America acquired the territory from Russia in 1867.

Because this chapter comprises a case study dealing with Indigenous Religions as I have defined them, I will restrict my descriptions of Yupiit culture to three main areas: (1) an analysis of how the Yupiit traditionally understood locality and kinship, including the central ideas of 'naming' and 'personhood'; (2) a description of beliefs and experiences related to postulated non-falsifiable alternate realities, particularly by noting the traditional importance of the men's community house or *qasgiq*, the place of shamans as mediators and the importance of masks and dances in community festivals; (3) an examination of tradition and authority, with significant attention being paid to the strictly enforced rules and boundaries circumscribing relations amongst members of the society and with animals, natural objects and spirits. It is

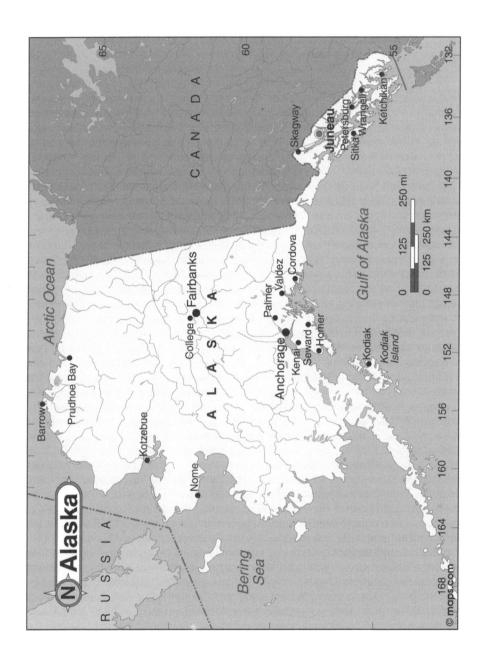

important to note that conversion to Christianity throughout Alaska after 1900 was almost universal, at least on the surface, with traditional practices surviving only in a Christian guise or through attempts by contemporary Yupiit leaders to reconstruct past traditions and revive the values associated with elders. These developments underscore what I have indicated earlier that the study of Indigenous Religions cannot be relegated simply to a period of 'pre-history' or even refer exclusively to 'pre-contact' reconstructions. Indigenous Religions everywhere engage dynamically with forces of modernity and globalization. Nonetheless, as we will see in the case of the Yupiit, the fundamental symbols associated with indigenous expressions of religion disappeared under the onslaught of missionary education. This has forced me to rely on reports written largely prior to 1940, although some contemporary commentators also shed light on what are now for all practical purposes extinct practices. In light of these complex factors, at the conclusion of this chapter, I will indicate if, and in what ways, my prior definitions of 'indigenous' and 'religion' are useful for constructing a field, applied in this case, to Yupiit Indigenous Religion in south-western Alaska.

Setting the Context

Before beginning my analysis, I need to identify the context about which I am writing and define some basic terms. It should be noted that Alaska extends over 533 000 square miles crossing nearly 20 degrees of latitude (see map of Alaska on p. 96). Within this wide area, numerous indigenous peoples reside including the Aleuts, who inhabit the chain of islands extending into the Pacific Ocean in the direction of Asia, the Alutiiq or Pacific Eskimos who are found along the Gulf of Alaska, the Yupiit, who comprise the Yup'ik speakers in southwest and central Alaska (often referred to simply as the Yup'ik Eskimos), the Inupiat whom Ernest Burch (1998: 3) calls the 'Inuit-Eskimo speaking inhabitants of the northern part of Alaska and extreme north western Canada', the Athabascans, an Indian group living in the interior regions, and the Southeast Coastal Indians, primarily the Haida and Tlingit. The anthropologist Steve Langdon (2002: 4) explains that 'these groupings are based on broad cultural and linguistic similarities', but in a strict sense they 'do not represent political or tribal units'.

Since terminology can be confusing, in my case study, I will use the term Yupiit (plural form of Yup'ik), following Langdon (2002: 48), but it should be noted that this term often is designated, as has been done by Oswalt (1999: 5), under the broad general category Yuit. Oswalt's basic classifications denote the connections between the Alaskan Yupiit and Siberian Yup'ik speakers, and he also draws attention to the links between the Inupiat and Inuit groups stretching from northern Alaska across Canada and into Greenland, all of whom speak similar dialects of Inupiaq. The Yup'ik and Inupiaq languages have common roots, but they are likened by Langdon (2002: 11) to the differences between German and English and thus they are mutually unintelligible. The terms 'Yuit' and 'Inuit', or their derivatives, translate into English as 'the real people' or as Burch (1998: 3) suggests, 'authentic' or 'special' human beings. Scholars today persist in lumping Yupiit, Inupiat and Alutiik Alaskan indigenous peoples under the generic term 'Eskimo', which Oswalt (1999: 5) contends originally had a derogatory meaning since it was derived from the Algonkian-speaking Indians of Eastern Canada who referred to the Canadian Inuit as 'eaters of raw flesh'. I should add, moreover, that the term Native (note with an upper case N) is used widely today by all indigenous peoples of Alaska to designate themselves collectively, particularly in the context of land claims and indigenous rights.

Ann Fienup-Riordan explains that the Yupiit and Inupiat peoples are members of the larger family of Inuit cultures that extend from Prince William Sound on the Pacific Coast of Alaska to the Siberian and Alaskan sides of the Bering Sea and from there thousands of miles north and east along Canada's Arctic coast and into Labrador and Greenland. The Yupiit and Inupiat of Alaska thus claim a common ancestry with the other Inuit peoples in Eastern Siberia and Asia, who probably appeared on the west coast of Alaska in relatively recent times, perhaps just over 2400 years ago (Fienup-Riordan, 2000: 9). According to Oswalt (1999: 6), the Yupiit and Inupiat were characterized by the manufacture of 'harpoons, tailor-made skin clothing, oil-burning lamps, and skin-covered boats known as kayaks or *umiaks*'. They became sea-mammal hunters along the coasts of the Bering and Chukchi Seas, or in more inland regions, they hunted caribou or fished the rivers and streams. Despite their common origins with other Inuit peoples, the Yupiit and Inupiat of Alaska varied in significant ways from related groups, particularly those living in Canada and Greenland. Oswalt (1999: 203) notes that the economies of the Alaskan Inuits were more diversified than their Canadian, Greenlandic or Polar counterparts since they 'did not base their livelihood on hunting seals at breathing holes' as those in Canada did nor did they 'concentrate on open-water sealing' as was done in East Greenland. Snowhouses were rarely constructed in Alaska, but instead semi-underground dwellings insulated with sod were built. Moreover, unlike Inuits living in Canada or Greenland, the Yupiit and Inupiat of Alaska developed well established centres for trading which were accompanied by elaborate ceremonies aimed at re-enforcing relationships with neighbouring groups. Numerous complex rituals were observed at various levels in which, according to Oswalt (1999: 203), 'all the members of a village participated and great wealth might be redistributed'. Often the rituals included dramatic dancing which was enhanced by the use of masks symbolizing the spirits of animals, birds or sea mammals.

Patterns of life amongst the Yupiit and Inupiat traditionally have centred on subsistence activities. A Canadian judge, Thomas Berger, who in the early 1980s conducted an extensive survey of Alaskan Natives on behalf of the Inuit Circumpolar Conference, quotes a woman who testified at one of the over sixty village meetings he conducted as saying, 'To us, subsistence is our inherent right because that is how we have always been and, I believe, that is how we will always be' (1985: 65). Another woman called subsistence 'our spiritual way of life, our culture' (1985: no page indicated, directly after p. 47). Berger explains these comments by referring to the tradition of whale hunting in north and northeast Alaska: 'For thousands of years, Inupiat Eskimos have lived and taken bowhead whales.... The Inupiat believe that these great whales give themselves to their hunters, if they have been hunted by Inupiat rules that govern the relationship between the people and the whales' (Berger, 1985: 48). Berger notes that throughout Alaska the traditional economy is based on similar activities to those he found amongst whaling communities. Success in hunting and fishing depended on observing rules in relation to the natural environment. Berger (1985: 51) calls these 'cultural values', which include 'mutual respect, sharing, resourcefulness, and an understanding that is both conscious and mystical of the intricate interrelationships that link humans, animals, and the environment'. Further south along the coast of the Bering Sea, where the Yupiit live, the waters are too shallow for hunting bowhead whale. Instead, the people traditionally hunted seals, beluga whales, and sea lions. The region stretching inland from the sea is crossed by numerous streams and rivers that yield abundant supplies of salmon, trout, northern pike, several species of whitefish, burbot, blackfish and stickleback. In addition to sea mammals and fish, a variety of birds, including geese, ducks and swans supplement food sources (Fienup-Riordan, 1990: 8–9). Amongst both Yupiit and Inupiat peoples, Caribou herds were hunted, as they moved through the inland mountain passes to the coasts. In addition, mountain sheep, polar bears, grizzly bears and moose provided sources of food for those living in inland areas. Various types of berries, which are also abundant throughout Alaska, were harvested annually. In some regions, these were mixed with seal fat and preserved.

Despite the abundance of natural resources available to the Yupiit and Inupiat, due to the extreme climate and, in many places, the barrenness of the land, a certain fragile relationship with nature existed. The people had little control over the environment and depended on their own skill and ingenuity in hunting and fishing to ensure adequate supplies of food and materials needed for survival. This tenuous relationship to the land explains why in the traditional world view life, spirit or soul (*inua* in Inupiaq or *yua* in Yup'ik, translated literally as 'personhood') was attributed to the animals and fish which provided the primary sources for sustenance (Dupre, 1975: 207). Spirits were thought also to inhabit the instruments used in hunting and fishing, and to be connected to the weather, particularly the winds blowing from the cardinal directions which brought quite distinct climatic conditions (Fienup-Riordan, 1994: 317). The spirits, which were necessary for survival, could be influenced in rituals, or even controlled by shamans, but mostly they could be counted on to respond favourably to the needs of the people if the rules of the society were followed.

Yupiit Traditions: the Central place of the *Qasgiq*

With this background in mind, I now consider the main features of the Yupiit way of life in line with my earlier definitions of Indigenous Religions. I begin by describing the *qasgiq*, or men's communal house (variously referred to as *kashgee* or *kashim* in earlier ethnographic literature), which before the sustained attack on indigenous culture conducted by the US government's missionary teachers after 1880, constituted the central place for Yupiit social, religious and ceremonial activities. Its importance has been underscored by Oswalt (1963: 51) who calls the *qasgiq* 'the focal point of all community life' and 'by far the largest and most complex structure in every village'. Traditional rituals, festivals, dances and shamanic séances took place in this building, as well as informal gatherings for the men, and it also served as a place where the men could repair their kayaks or prepare in other ways for hunting and fishing. The building was located near the centre of the village, and often was situated on the highest place so it could be seen from any vantage point. Oswalt writes: 'On a pleasant summer's day the men often sat on the roof of the *kashgee* and scanned the river for useful logs that might drift by, or watched for jumping salmon' (1963: 51).

Since the *qasgiq* was a partly underground structure, it looked from the outside, in Oswalt's words, 'like a high mound of grass-covered earth' (1963: 51). E.W. Nelson (cited by Anderson and Eells, 1935: 35–6) described a typical *qasgiq* as being about 30 feet by 30 feet on the floor and 20 feet high where a smoke hole opened to the sky. He reported that the walls were made of split logs placed vertically, and the floor was made of hewed planks. The men placed logs around the room around three feet from the walls, on which they placed their heads when they slept with their feet pointed towards the centre. Nearer the wall, benches were built for seating. The entrance passage differed from summer to winter. In the summer it was 'high and roomy, opening directly into the kashim above ground by means of a round hole in front of the wall'. In winter, the men entered 'through a hole in the floor of the entrance passage' and through an underground tunnel to 'an exit hole' (Nelson, cited by Anderson and Eells, 1935: 36). Some larger villages might have two or even three *qasgit* (plural), and, Nelson reports that in some cases the dimensions were larger than the one he described. The *qasgiq* was strictly a men's house, into which women were allowed only on specific occasions, during prescribed ceremonies or during winter festivals. Fienup-Riordan indicates that all men and boys older than five years ate and slept in the structure. She describes how the men would rise at three or four in the morning, leave to do their work and return at sunset. The men's daughters or wives would bring them their meals, and, in Fienup-Riordan's words, would wait 'demurely by their sides while each man emptied his own personal bowl' (1994: 35–6). The men also took their sweat bath in the *qasgiq* by opening the smoke hole and feeding the fire until it became extremely hot inside. Fienup-Riordan indicates that they would then rub their bodies with urine 'aged in wooden buckets' which produced an ammonia that 'worked to cut the grease and, combined with a rinse of fresh water, effectively cleansed the bathers' (1994: 36). Each *qasgiq* was surrounded by a number of sod houses in which the women and children lived, with between four and twelve inhabitants in each.

The *qasgiq* reflected social ranking in the community with distinctions made, according to Fienup-Riordan, 'between young and old, married and unmarried, and host and guest' (1994: 36). Oswalt (1963: 53) notes that 'an individual's place changed as his standing in the village increased or decreased'. As a man grew older, he sat nearer to the tunnel entrance, and, if he lived to a very old age, 'he would finally die upon the portion of the bench near the tunnel opening' (1963: 53). Anderson and Eells report that the society was governed by 'established custom'. In the *qasgiq*, 'the affairs of village importance were discussed' and 'old men ... gave their weighty judgment' (Anderson and Eells, 1935: 49). Nelson notes that there were no chiefs among the Yupiit, but, in the words of Anderson and Eells, respect was given to 'the old men, who had accumulated a store of experience of the hunt, who knew the folklore of the people and who were wise in the rites, ceremonies and customs' (1935: 49). Fienup-Riordan indicates that amongst the Yupiit, an important figure was the *nukalpiaq*, or 'good provider', who was a successful hunter and who could 'contribute wood for the communal sweat bath and oil to keep the lamps lit'. He also 'figured prominently in midwinter ceremonial distributions'. This meant in the end that 'social status and power accrued to those who could afford to give' (Fienup-Riordan, 1994: 37). The power of the *nukalpiaq* was tempered by the elders, who 'advised when to harvest' and determined 'when distribution was appropriate'. Disputes were settled indirectly and informally, often by 'gossip and avoidance' (Fienup-Riordan, 1994: 37). Anderson and Eells (1935: 49) refer to frequent misunderstandings of this social structure by early white whalers and traders who mistook the *nukalpiaq* for a chief, when in fact he was acting as a village spokesman in dealings with outsiders.

Village life varied with the seasons. During the winter, the villages were occupied fully, with the *qasgiq* providing the location for important festivals and social occasions. During the spring and summer, the men established seasonal camps near to rivers or the sea to fish or hunt. Sometimes, the families would accompany the men to the seasonal camps, as Fienup-Riordan (1994: 37) explains, living together 'in multiroomed dwellings' with passageways connecting 'a large central compartment to smaller sleeping and storage chambers'. Even during the seasonal camps when families accompanied the men, the duties between men and women were strictly demarcated and observed. During the months between November and February, Nelson reports that five major rituals were observed in the *qasgiq*. These were what he called the asking feast (held annually in the middle or latter part of November), the feast of the dead (annually in November or December), the bladder feast (annually from the end of December into January), repetition of the feast of the dead (after the bladder feast and before the spring fishing season) and the great feast of the dead (at intervals, sometimes with ten year gaps) (cited by Anderson and Eells, 1935: 69). Oswalt indicates that at the community of Napaskiak, which is seven miles downriver from Bethel, the annual round of festivals, typical for the region, included the 'woman's dance' held in early February, followed by the 'boy's dance' later in the month, the 'inviting-in feast' which was held during the summer when the men were not fishing for salmon, the 'sending a messenger ceremony' in September or a bit later, after the salmon fishing season had ended. He adds that 'every four to ten years, a "Great Ceremony for the Dead" was held, which was more elaborate than any in the normal yearly round' (1963: 58–9). Certain discrepancies in the literature are found concerning the annual cycles, partly because definite regional variations existed, and because the accounts of missionaries like Weinland and Kilbuck refer to all ceremonies as 'plays' without discriminating between their purposes or cultural meanings. Langdon indicates that the ceremonial season amongst the Yupiit consisted of at least eight separate events, two of the most important being the messenger feast and the bladder festival (Langdon, 2002: 59–61). Nelson, Oswalt and Fienup-Riordan each confirm that the annual and great feasts for the dead comprised another important series of rituals within Yupiit life.

The Messenger Feast

The Messenger Feast (*Kevgiq*) is important partly because it indicates how social relationships were constructed in typical Yupiit communities and how neighbouring villages related to one another. The Messenger Feast was described in the journal of the Moravian missionary Romig in 1888, and is recounted in great detail by Ann Fienup-Riordan, who devotes a chapter to it in her book, *Boundaries and Passages*, noting how the event has persisted in modified forms even in the years after the *qasgiq* has been destroyed as a centre of village life, with regional social gatherings being held now in the bingo hall or the school gymnasium. Romig's early description seems to have confused the Messenger Feast with Feasts of the Dead, probably due to the lack of familiarity missionaries in the early days had with the separate customs practised by the Yupiit. Nonetheless, portions of his account are repeated in other literature and seem to reflect the basic structure of the feast as it occurred near the end of the nineteenth century.

Romig (cited by Oswalt, 1963: 62–4) indicates that members of the community would store up valuable items for many years, ready to bring as gifts when they were invited to a Messenger Feast. The term 'messenger' refers to the way the announcement concerning its timing was made and the invitation issued to neighbouring villages. Two young men were selected to deliver the message, which involved carrying a 'small stick', staff or 'wand' on which members of the village carved marks indicating whom they were inviting to the feast and what they requested from those they were inviting (Romig, cited by Oswalt, 1963: 63). The gifts that the hosts solicited from those they had invited, as Fienup-Riordan explains, were ones that 'the guests could supply only with difficulty' (1994: 327), such as walrus meat or reindeer skins. If those invited could pool their resources and meet the requests of their hosts, 'their village acquired the reputation of a place in which people worked together' (Fienup-Riordan, 1994: 327). The messengers were required to memorize the requests that were being made from those they invited. The requests were made known in ceremonies called 'songs of solicitation', which took place in the *qasgiq*.

The stick or wand was planted in the centre of the *qasgiq* before the messengers left, and the songs of solicitation were recited and memorized by the messengers. Romig (cited by Oswalt, 1963: 63) explains that the messengers would then travel to the intended village, would arrive without saying anything, and only would speak after they had been 'generously fed'. The stick, which had been wrapped in moose skin or fur, was then unwrapped, placed in the centre of the *qasgiq* of the invited villagers, followed by an explanation from the messengers of all the signs that had been carved on it. If the requests seemed too difficult to fulfil, those who had been invited could decline to attend, but, as Fienup-Riordan notes, this would be 'tantamount to a humiliating defeat' (1994: 327). Romig adds that after the invitation had been received 'the bustle of preparation for the trip keeps the village in excitement for some days, during which the messengers remain in the place and are treated as honoured guests' (cited by Oswalt, 1963: 63). The messengers were then told by the elders precisely what gifts their village expected from their hosts, what they wanted to eat and how they were to be honoured when they arrived at the host village. These requests were then carved on another stick, which the messengers carried back to their homes, placed in the centre of their own *qasgiq* and interpreted for the elders of their home village. Placing the stick in the centre of the *qasgiq* had symbolic meaning in both cases, since it opened the way for the movement of people from one place to another, in a manner that corresponded to movements within the spirit world, such as when the dead travelled to the land of the living and when a shaman moved from one state of consciousness to another. Fienup-Riordan suggests that the manner by which the messenger conveyed invitations and requests between villages indicated a passageway between communities that normally were kept apart (1994: 328).

It is clear that the Messenger Feast was anticipated by differing villages and that preparations went on for many months, or even longer. Communication between the villages occurred during this time, so that the actual delivery of the stick represented a formal invitation in a ritualized format. When the visitors arrived, they were encircled by the hosts, in a counterclockwise direction, in order to obviate any bad influences coming from strangers (Fienup-Riordan, 1994: 333). During the feast itself, which went on for many days, numerous rituals took place, one of the most important of which Fienup-Riordan calls the 'songs of indigestion'. These were intended to ridicule the hosts, who in turn sought to embarrass the guests by conjuring up severe accusations against them. Fienup-Riordan explains that 'the challenge to the guests was to remain calm and controlled during this onslaught' (1994: 334) The purpose of the 'songs of indigestion' and the accusations hurled by the hosts at the guests was intended to defuse and resolve conflicts within what Fienup-Riordan calls 'a safe context' (1994: 335). Various other dances and elaborate ceremonies accompanied the exchange of gifts, often with quite role specific obligations outlined. For example, men and women took turns on different nights performing 'asking songs', a ritual that included total gender reversal, with men wearing women's clothes' (Fienup-Riordan, 1994: 345). This type of boundary-crossing, just like the songs of ridicule and accusation, allowed the release of social tensions within controlled situations.

The Messenger Feast concluded with the distribution of the gifts from the guests to the hosts and from the hosts to the guests. Romig reports that 'they are usually articles of real worth, which have cost much to gather and store away for years'. He adds that after the goods have been distributed, the 'guests return informally to their homes' (cited by Oswalt, 1963: 64). The functions of the Messenger Feast in traditional society, as I just noted, included relieving social tensions, or in Fienup-Riordan's words, it allowed an 'outlet to people's aggressive emotions' and thus 'helped to keep the peace' (1994: 345). It also provided an occasion where the values of the society could be displayed ritually, showing the practical rewards of hard work and cooperation, with the added advantage that age-old traditions could be passed on to the next generation through dances and games. By inviting guests from neighbouring villages to one's own village, marriages could be negotiated and those who had come of age could be recognized and noted by outsiders (Fienup-Riordan, 1994: 345). Fienup-Riordan stresses that what went on in the Messenger Feast also points towards the deeply held conviction within society that generosity was highly valued, and that hoarding and stinginess were regarded as vices. This fundamental attitude towards society was mirrored by the spirits of animals and fish, who, according to tradition, gave themselves up in the hunt willingly to those who were generous, but would not return to those who refused to share their harvest freely. Fienup-Riordan (1994: 347) concludes: 'Not only were generous gifting and ample feasting during Kevgiq required for good relations in the human world, they were essential demonstrations to the animals that people were worthy of their generosity.'

The Bladder Festival (*Nakaciuq*)

Oswalt calls the Bladder Festival, which was performed by the Yupiit annually in December, a ceremony rarely matched in 'drama, pageantry, staging, and community-wide involvement' (1999: 254). He claims that the purpose of the festival was to 'appease the souls' or *inua* (*yua*) of the animals that had been killed during the previous hunting season by entertaining them with songs and dances, feeding them and honouring them. He explains that the people believed that the *inua* of the animals resided in their bladders, and thus each year the bladders of all the animals that had been killed were kept, and when it was time for the festival to begin, they were inflated, painted and hung in the *qasgiq* (1999: 254). A series of rituals were performed over a period of six or seven days, culminating in the return of the bladders to the sea through an ice hole and a fire ceremony aimed at purifying the community.

E.W. Nelson has written a detailed description of a Bladder Festival he observed in St Michael during the time he was stationed there between 1877 and 1881, which he included in his ethnographic report of 1899, and which has been re-printed in an abbreviated form by Anderson and Eells (Nelson, cited by Anderson and Eells, 1935: 452–3). Nelson describes the events surrounding the festival over a six-day period, which he says at St Michael normally occurred at the full moon nearest the winter equinox, usually between 10 and 20 December. It should be noted that the length of the festival and the exact timing of it varied throughout the region, but it always occurred during the darkest part of the winter when no hunting took place, and usually lasted between five and fifteen days. Nelson describes the first two days of the festival he attended as entailing elaborate preparations beginning with a thorough cleaning of the *qasgiq*, including the fire pit. After the cleaning was completed, all the men, women and children of the village gathered on the roof of the *qasgiq*, where an old man began beating a drum while the people sang a song to the wild celery plants, 'the stalks of which are standing ungathered on the distant hillsides'. On the second day, Nelson relates that four men gathered the stalks of the wild celery, which they placed on the top of the semi-underground entrance hole to the *qasgiq*. At nightfall, the bundles were taken inside and little boys rolled over them and wrestled with one another on them, presumably to make it possible to separate them. They stalks were then opened and spread on the floor. Each man took one stalk in his hand and sat at his appointed place in the *qasgiq* according to his social status, while together the men sang a song asking the celery to become dry.

On the third day, with the preparations completed, the inflated bladders of the seals, whales, walruses and white bears that had been killed during the previous hunting cycle were brought into the *qasgiq*, and the central part of the ritual was ready to begin. Each man tied his bladders in a bunch using the stalks from the wild celery, and hung them up on a spear stuck in the wall in a row six or eight feet above the floor at the back of the room. Food was then brought into the *qasgiq* with small bits thrown on the floor in front of the bladders along with a little water. On the morning of the fourth day, each hunter removed his bunch of bladders and marked each with dots of paint made from charcoal and oil. In the evening, each hunter took small torches, lit from the celery stalks, ran around the room, leaping and waving his torch around the bladders, so as to 'bathe them slightly in the fire and smoke'. The fifth day was the day of the full moon, and Nelson notes that no one was permitted to do any work. That night, at the first sign of the waning of the moon, the men went out of the *qasgiq* to the frozen sea and made a hole in the ice about a quarter of a mile from the shore. After this, the hunters ran two-by-two out to the hole in the ice with spears, which they dipped into the water and ran back to the *qasgiq*, where they waved their spears around the bladders in a stirring motion, which was intended to encourage the spirits of the animals to return to the sea. The rest of the village was then invited into the *qasgiq* to participate in singing and dancing.

On the sixth day, the ritual reached its dramatic conclusion with every hunter taking the spear on which his bladders had been hanging, formed a long line and ran as fast as possible to the ice hole. Some accounts indicate that the bladders were pushed up through the smoke hole in the ceiling of the *qasgiq* (see Fienup-Riordan, 1994: 292). When they reached the ice hole, each hunter knelt down holding animal bladders, thrust them through the hole in the ice and pushed them into the water. In the meantime, the elders took the remaining bundles of celery stalks, placed them on the ice in front of the village facing the sea, and set them on fire, causing a high flame. As the hunters returned from the ice hole, each one jumped through the flame, uttering a resounding shriek while the remainder of the village made loud shouts and cries. After all the men had finished jumping through the fire, the women and children rushed towards it and stamped it out with their feet. The villagers then formed two lines and walked around the village in single file going in opposite directions. After this, a fire was built in the *qasgiq* and the men enjoyed a sweat bath. The men, still nude after bathing, then formed a circle with two boys placed in the middle of the ring. They moved in a circular motion around the boys four times, in Nelson's words, 'from left to right (with the sun)'. After the fourth circuit was completed, the young men competed in deeds of strength by lifting themselves from handles tied to the roof of the *qasgiq*. The festival ended with such activities and feats of strength, but, Nelson adds, no work was done in the village for another four days.

Ann Fienup-Riordan's research indicates that the bladder festival was connected closely to the relationship of the spirits of the animals and the well-being of the community. She refers to a number of rules that were 'strictly enforced', for example, so long as the bladders were hanging in the *qasgiq*, people must always be present and a light must remain burning at all times. Otherwise, 'the bladders might become offended and return to their home, taking the village with them' (Fienup-Riordan, 1994: 283). In addition, the men sang constantly while the bladders were hanging in the *qasgiq*, which had the effect of holding the 'reluctant spirits' so they did not escape back to the sea too early. One of Fienup-Riordan's informants, Billy Lincoln, explained that the men kept singing so long as the bladders remained hanging in the *qasgiq*, usually for five days (Fienup-Riordan, 1994: 283). The songs included ones sung during warfare, other traditional songs of the village and new ones that had been composed for the festival itself. Fienup-Riordan (1994: 284) notes: 'Many traditional tales recall the power of singing and drumming to effect the action or transformation of a person or a spirit'. Other rules included a prohibition against pubescent girls entering the *qasgiq* during the festival. Sexual activity also was encouraged, Fienup-Riordan explains, since 'the parallel between people's sexuality and their ability to attract animals was an important theme in Yup'ik moral discourse' (1994: 285).

In Fienup-Riordan's view, the Bladder Festival was aimed at constantly renewing life. She argues that the intention of the festival extended beyond returning the spirits of the animals to the sea, so that having been honoured, they would return the next year to give themselves up to the hunters. The festival's primary purpose was to maintain a continuity 'between living humans and the shades of their dead, as well as helping spirits and other natural elements that participants "fed" and otherwise honored' (Fienup-Riordan, 1994: 297). The symbols of the cosmic cycle were present in the ritual, with circles being formed to represent the natural rhythms of nature, and the counter-clockwise movements symbolizing acts that cross boundaries or that go against the way of the universe (1994: 298). It is clear throughout the Bladder Festival that openings between the worlds played an important part, with the *qasgiq* representing the contained and circumscribed life of the village and the opening to the sea reflecting the dependency the people felt towards nature. By bringing the bladders into the *qasgiq* and then symbolically releasing them back to the sea in order to ensure their return, in the words of Fienup-Riordan, the people were able 'to control the cosmological cycle on which they were modeled' (1994: 297). In this context, it is important to underscore that the annual cycles for the Yupiit did not follow on one from the other automatically; rather, humans and spirits 'actively participated in the annual regeneration of the seasons' (1994: 298). To accomplish this, people had to 'clear the passages between the worlds' and at the same time protect themselves from being taken over by the spirits (1994: 298). For this reason, they performed rituals that included the men becoming naked when they circled around the boys in the *qasgiq*. They also they drew paintings on the bladders and disguised themselves by wearing the garments of the other sex. Fienup-Riordan concludes: 'The many reversals enacted during the Bladder Festival were part of this elaborate attempt to remake the world' (1994: 298).

From the accounts of the Messenger Feast and the Bladder Festival, a picture of the Yupiit social and cosmological order emerges. The passage of one community to another through rituals of invitation, gift-giving and cooperation as shown in the

Messenger Feast found parallels in the passage between the worlds inhabited by the spirits of animals and the human community in the Bladder Festival. We have seen that central to both of these was the *qasgiq*, which functioned not simply as a space for social gatherings and ritual performances, but itself constituted a place of passage, of openings for the inward and outward movement of people, which were governed by strict social rules, and the movement of spirits, often upward and downward through the smoke hole opening from and towards the sky. The Messenger Feast and Bladder Festival have shown the significance of and the close relationships between the social and spiritual worlds, both of which affected the survival and well-being of the people. The annual Feast of the Dead and the periodic Great Feast of the Dead provide further insight into the Yupiit understanding of the spirit world and the relationship the community maintained with ancestral traditions.

The Yupiit Understanding of Personhood and Death

Amongst the Yupiit, annual festivals for the dead were held, and intra-regional festivals or great feasts for the dead were conducted every six to ten years. In order to understand the significance of these ceremonies, it is important first to describe the Yupiit understanding of personhood and the namesake. We have seen already that the term '*yua*' (*inua*) translates as a 'real' or 'authentic' person, but in Yupiit thinking this applied to more than human characteristics. For example, the seals that were returned to the water in the bladder festival possessed *yua*, which resided in the seal's bladder, and was re-born in a new seal after the festival was completed. Human beings similarly possessed *yua*, which on death needed to be cared for in anticipation of being re-born in one's namesake. Fienup-Riordan notes that other qualities also made up a human being, such as 'breath', 'felt presence', 'lifeline', 'warmth' and 'mind', but without a name, a human being was not a real person. She explains that 'a nameless person was a contradiction in terms' (1994: 213). A name conveyed potency; it represented re-birth or a passage from the condition of being a dead person to a living one. This does not correspond precisely to a belief in re-incarnation, since essential parts of a person were thought to inhabit a namesake. When a person died, a feature of the individual was re-born in his or her namesake, such as mind, lifeline, breath, felt presence or warmth, and thus a deceased person could have more than one namesake and individuals could possess more than one name. In addition, more than one individual could be named after the same deceased person, depending on kinship relations or on the influence the person held in the community when alive.

When a newborn child was given a name, it was believed that a part of a deceased person after whom the child was named entered the baby. The child was usually named for a relative who had died recently or for someone particularly respected in the community. The name-giving ritual involved dropping water at four corners around the child's head, but not on the head itself (Fienup-Riordan, 1994: 244). The power of a name is attested by the way families regarded the giving of a name. Sometimes, a child would become ill, which would be interpreted as a sign that a deceased person wanted that child as a namesake. Fienup-Riordan reports that parents would not punish a child for fear that this would offend the deceased's spirit, who might leave the child causing illness or death (1994: 244). If the match between the namesake and the deceased person was not appropriate, that is, if the personality or characteristics of the child proved alien to the person after whom the child was named, the spirit of the deceased might depart the namesake, again resulting in illness or death. Each human being was also accompanied through life by a *tarneq* (Fienup-Riordan, 1994: 212), a term corresponding to what Nelson called a 'shade', which was like a shadow extending from a human's body (Anderson and Eells, 1935: 66). Fienup-Riordan (1994: 212) explains that every *tarneq* was 'destined for a future life', perhaps as an animal or as a shaman's helper, called a *tuunraq*. Illness was attributed to the temporary absence of the *tarneq*, which, if it returned, resulted in healing. If the *tarneq* left for good, the person would die. The *tarneq* could be stolen by malicious spirits, indicating why one of the shaman's chief duties was to travel in trance states out of the body to retrieve a stolen *tarneq* and return it to its owner (Jakobsen, 1999: 81–5).

The passage between the living and the dead was ensured within the community by giving a name to the deceased's namesake, but the community also clearly drew a line separating the condition of those who had died from the living. The relationship between life and death was ambiguous; the dead were necessary for life to persist but at the same time, they could be dangerous to the living. Fienup-Riordan admits that various accounts of the Yupiit understanding of the human being appear contradictory or confusing, partly as a result of the suppression of traditional beliefs by the missionaries and teachers. Nonetheless, she notes, it is clear that 'there was no single correct term for a person's soul as distinct from the physical body. Rather people believed that aspects of their being … possessed properties essential for life, both in the present and the future' (Fienup-Riordan, 1994: 213). The attitudes of the Yupiit towards life and death, and towards the importance of the namesake are shown clearly in the performance of death rituals.

The annual feast for the dead (known as *Merr'aq* on Nelson Island and along the lower Bering Sea coast) induced spirits who had not yet been recognized in the Great Feast of the Dead (*Elriq*) back into the community so they could be fed and clothed for another year (Fienup-Riordan, 1994: 299). E.W. Nelson (cited by Anderson and Eells, 1935: 451–2) provided a detailed account of an annual ceremony held at St Michael. He indicates that the ritual, called the *Ihl'-u-gi'* by the Yupiit at St Michael, normally was held two days after the Bladder Festival and was 'given for the sole purpose of making offerings of food, water, and clothing to the shades of those recently deceased, and of offerings to the dead who have not yet been honoured by one of the great festivals' (1935: 451). He adds that those who prepared the ritual were the nearest relatives of those who had died within the past year, and those members of the community who still were awaiting the Great Feast of the Dead for their relatives. The ritual began by the nearest relative going to the above-ground grave of the deceased, which was typical of the area, and placing a stake with a seal spear on it in front of the grave. If the deceased was a woman, a wooden dish was placed in front of the grave. These symbols could vary, with other instruments, such as a model of a kayak paddle, substituted for the seal spear. Sometimes a totemic animal was carved on the stake. The purpose of placing the objects by the grave was to notify the spirit to come from the land of the dead to the grave, where it was supposed to wait until invited into the *qasgiq* by the singing of those assembled inside.

In the *qasgiq*, those who had relatives to honour, lit an oil lamp and placed it around the room on specially constructed supports around two feet high. In the case of a man, they placed the lamp directly in front of the bench where the deceased normally sat when he was alive. The lamps remained lit throughout the entire ritual. The relatives of all those to be honoured then began the song of invitation, which

Nelson describes as quite long, and as containing the refrain: 'Dead ones, come here; sealskins for a tent you will get. Come here, do; reindeer skins for a bed you will get. Come here, do' (1935: 452). When they heard the songs of invitation, the spirits moved from their graves, entered the *qasgiq* and assembled in the fire pit, under the floor. During the ritual, the spirits ascended from beneath the floor, in Nelson's words, 'entering and possessing the bodies of their namesakes' (1935: 451). In this way, they were fed and clothed vicariously through those they had possessed. Variations of this practice apparently occurred even within the same ceremony, since Nelson also reports that small portions of food were placed on the floor and water was poured from ladles through the cracks of the floor, as if the spirits were being nourished directly. Fienup-Riordan confirms Nelson's earlier description noting that 'living relatives provided for the shades of the human dead through the feeding and clothing of the namesakes with whom they were identified', but she adds that after the namesakes had eaten, they 'threw portions of their food into the fire pit, where the dead received them as whole stores' (Fienup-Riordan, 1994: 299, 300). The Moravian missionary Drebert observed that in some cases the spirits were 'incarnated ... in those who were named after them'. He added that some of the younger namesakes were treated in the festival as 'special guests of honor and received gifts of new clothing' (Drebert, 1959: 68).

These accounts would suggest that when Nelson used the term 'possessed', he did not mean that the namesakes literally were taken over by and assumed the actual personality of the deceased in a trance, but that they were being nourished and clothed through their namesakes. This interpretation is supported by Nelson's further comment: 'In this way they believe that the spiritual essence of the entire quantity of food and water from which the small portions are offered goes to the shade' (Anderson and Eells, 1935: 451). Nelson concludes that after the spirits had been nourished, through the feeding of their namesakes and through libations, the people then distributed the remainder of the food amongst themselves, which they followed by singing and dancing. After all the offerings had been made and the festivities were nearing an end, the men stamped their feet on the floor, signalling that the spirits should leave and return to the land of the dead for another year.

Nelson observed that strict prohibitions surrounded the festival for the dead. No work was to be done around the village, and no sharp-edged object or any pointed tool was allowed 'for fear that some shade may be about, and, being injured, become angry and do harm to the people' (1935: 451). He added that it was essential for the relatives of the deceased to conduct this ritual so that, in proportion to the 'generosity exercised on these occasions the shade is made happy and comfortable' (1935: 451). Anyone who did not have children would adopt a child, so that when that person died, someone would survive to ensure that rituals were conducted in his or her honour. Nelson notes that 'people who have no one to make offerings for them are supposed to suffer great destitution in the other world' (1935: 451). Fienup-Riordan (1994: 249) draws attention to the reversal of roles represented by both the Bladder Festival and the Annual Feast for the Dead, where in each case those on whom the community depended for its well-being, the seals for nourishment and the spirits of the dead for protection, were themselves hosted, honoured and cared for. This delicate relationship between the spirit world and the living community indicates why strict rules surrounded the ways humans conducted rituals of honour and why clearly delineated prohibitions and rules of respect were observed whenever any contact between the worlds was anticipated.

The Great Feast for the Dead (*Elriq*)

The Great Feast for the Dead (called *Elriq* on Nelson Island and along the Bering Sea coast) was held in a particular village every five to ten years, although, because as an intra-regional event people were invited to the ceremony from other villages, some families might attend a different one every year (Fienup-Riordan, 1994: 302). The preparations for the *Elriq* were elaborate and costly. Fienup-Riordan asserts that 'it required years to acquire and prepare the tremendous supply of goods necessary to play the part of host' (1994: 302). Sometimes, people came from large distances to participate. The Moravian missionary Henry Weinland indicated that 'every one from far and near' was welcome to attend a regional feast for the Dead. He described its main feature as 'the distribution of gifts', since it is important for the host village to make its gifts 'as numerous and as valuable as possible' (cited by Oswalt, 1963: 65). Sometimes, in order to make the gift-giving even more widespread and valuable, people from surrounding villages were invited to contribute to the collection. Weinland (cited by Oswalt, 1963: 65–7) describes in substantial detail a Great Feast for the Dead he attended in 1887 in the village of Nepaskiamute (present-day Napaskiak), on the lower Kuskowim, indicating that at the beginning of the event the hosts brought into the *qasgiq* 48 bags of frozen fish, each bag weighing 60 pounds, thus producing a total of 2880 pounds of fish to be distributed to the guests later in the evening. In addition, 14 large dishes of 'ice cream' were brought into the *qasgiq*, each dish containing 'about six quarts'. The 'ice cream' was made from 'snow, salmon berries, seal oil and deer tallow'. Weinland counted the number of visitors attending at 580, swelling the normal population of the village from 125 to 706, which he says, meant the *qasgiq* was 'packed with men' and the other huts equally jammed. He notes that individuals also brought gifts to the festival, lowering them through the hole in the roof of the *qasgiq*. One woman, whom he described as 'doubled nearly to a right angle by old age and disease' contributed gifts consisting of '27 pairs [of] fish skin boots with [a] pair [of] straw socks with each, 21 fish skin coats and fish skin bag for each, 20 fish skin bags, 23 grass baskets, 21 grass fish bags, 40 tin dippers, 20 small wooden buckets' (67). Weinland interpreted the ceremonies primarily to be about gift-giving, and thus reported 'nothing immoral in them'.

Oswalt describes the purpose of the Great Feast of the Dead as having much deeper religious significance than Weinland recognized, calling it a ritual 'to free the souls of the deceased from the earth forever' (1967: 228). Similarities existed between the Annual and Great Feasts of the Dead, with both ceremonies beginning with drumming and singing to awaken the dead. Fienup-Riordan (1994: 302–3) explains that the songs were comprised of 'ancestral songs' that people performed year after year at the annual festivals, and some that had been composed that year. After the spirits had been awakened and called to the feast, the host's guests were invited to join in the feast, but at this point the spirits of the dead had not yet entered the *qasgiq*. Fienup-Riordan indicates that on the first day, each guest received a gift from their hosts. On the second day, another feast was held, which was accompanied by rituals in which dances were performed by namesakes in new clothing, according to the gender of the deceased, as a preparation and anticipation of the climax of the ceremonies on the fourth and fifth days. It should be noted that names in Yup'ik do not indicate gender, and thus a male could be the namesake for a female or a female for a male. Fienup-Riordan (1994: 303) reports that 'it was not unusual to see young men dressed as women and, alternately, young women dressed as men'. On the third day, the hosts danced, but this time in old clothing or 'gut parkas', symbolizing that the spirits had not yet been transformed by the final ritual for the dead. The spirits of the dead were then invited into the *qasgiq*, through the smoke-hole opening on the roof (Drebert, 1959: 68). This is important, since, when the person died, his or her body had been lifted out of the *qasgiq* through the same opening and transported to the grave. Just as in the Annual Feasts for the Dead, the ceremonies that followed after the spirits had entered the *qasgiq* included feeding the namesakes and dropping small portions of food and water on the floor over the fire pit.

Fienup-Riordan (1994: 303) reports that on the fourth and fifth days of the ceremony 'major distributions' took place 'when first the women and then the men ritually clothed the living namesakes according to the sex of their deceased relatives'. Just as the spirits had entered through the smoke-hole the previous day, so the new clothing was lowered into the *qasgiq* through the same opening in the roof. The namesakes then would ask for a wide range of gifts 'from a small wooden bowl to a sled or a kayak', but always food, clothing and water were included amongst the requests, which they received on behalf of the deceased whose name they bore (Fienup-Riordan, 1994: 303). When the ceremonies surrounding the new clothing were completed, the elders instructed the spirits to depart out of the *qasgiq*, go back to their graves for the last time and travel to the land of the dead. On their way to the grave, the spirits circled the village in a counter-clockwise direction, according the Fienup-Riordan (1994: 304), to 'open the pathways … out of the human world' and at the same time 'to bound off their entryway so that members of the human world could not follow them'. The distribution of gifts on the fourth and fifth days corresponded to the Yupiit belief that the spirit of a deceased person requires four or five days to step finally into the underworld (Fienup-Riordan, 1990: 61). By putting on new clothes on the fourth or fifth day, the namesake thus signalled a transformation from death to life. The spirit of the deceased left its human community once and for all to reside with all other spirits who had been honoured similarly over the generations in a Great Feast. At the same time, the spirit of the deceased continued to live in the community through his or her namesake. In this way, the spirits were conceived, without contradiction, as remaining forever in an underworld land of the dead while at the same time continuing to exercise a lasting influence over the living.

Ceremonial Masks and the Role of the Shaman

Thus far in my descriptions of Yupiit rituals, I have not referred to the central importance of masks as conveyors of symbols, nor have I discussed the role of the shaman (*angalkuk*) in facilitating communication between the community and the worlds of spirits. These two dimensions within Yupiit ritual life need to be explained before I can draw conclusions about the religion of the people indigenous to the southwest region of Alaska. A close connection between masks and the shaman has been noted in the anthropological studies conducted by Wendell Oswalt and Ann Fienup-Riordan and confirmed in a recent book entitled 'Our Way of Making Prayer' (1996), which comprises a series of commentaries by Yupiit elders on an exhibit of traditional masks displayed in Alaska and other parts of the United States between 1993 and 1995. Fienup-Riordan (1996: 17) asserts that the book represents 'the first time anywhere in the world that an exhibit of Alaska Native material has been accompanied by a book written, essentially, by Native elders'.

Comments from contemporary elders on the traditional mask exhibit underscore the connection between masks and the role of the shaman. For example, Paul John, a Yupiit elder and member of the 'Our Way of Making Prayer' steering committee, explained that the masks he remembers as a young person often represented animals, like a fox or a sea mammal 'that were desirable to acquire … in the hunt' (Fienup-Riordan, 1996: 21). Mary Mike, observed: 'It appears to me that they [masks] would reveal [the shaman's] helping spirits' (Fienup-Riordan, 1996: 21). Justina Mike elaborated on this explaining that during rituals, performers 'would dance using the masks representing desired things while they would beseech the spirits for animal and plant productivity' (Fienup-Riordan, 1996: 27). Paul John called shamans 'the scientists of our ancestors', since they would use their helpers (*tuunrat*) 'to assist them in performing rituals that would remove all obstacles from the path the fish were going to use while coming up during the summer' (Fienup-Riordan, 1996: 27). In both functions, as representing animals in a subsistence economy and as shamanic symbols, in the words of Paul John, masks conveyed 'the ways of our ancestors' that have been 'passed down to us … since time immemorial' (Fienup-Riordan, 1996: 11).

Fienup-Riordan draws attention to the suppression of the use of ceremonial masks in rituals by the Moravian missionaries, but notes that traditionally 'masked dances were a central element in the Yup'ik representation to themselves of their world, both spiritual and material' (1990: 49–50). The eyes on Yupiit masks typically were decorated with circles and dots, symbolizing spiritual awareness, called in Yup'ik, 'the eye of awareness' (*eelam iinga*) (Fienup-Riordan, 1990: 52). Circles and dots implied more than vision, since they depicted the interconnected parts of the body, including the joints and muscles which bind the body together. Symbols of the body clearly referred to the shaman who, as 'the one who sees', possessed vision extending beyond ordinary human perception. In typical shamanic initiation ceremonies, the shaman's body was torn apart or dismembered only to be reassembled when the person obtained full shamanic power (Eliade, 1989: 35–7). Masks related in other ways to the shaman, since they often portrayed images of birds, which have the ability to see from great heights and at distances denied to human beings. The concept of vision translates also to cultural situations, for example, even today when young people meet an elder, they must turn their eyes in a downward direction, out of respect. Culturally, the ability to see clearly and from afar comes with age, and in the fullest sense of seeing into areas hidden to others, this power traditionally remained the prerogative of the shaman. With such cosmological dimensions communicated through ceremonial masks, it becomes evident why the missionaries made such concerted efforts to uproot the use of masks in rituals and why they tried at every opportunity to discredit shamanic practices.

Wendell Oswalt's research indicates that face masks in traditional rituals set the performers apart from the audience (1967: 229). Ceremonial masks, which were carved out of wood, were used only once, and burned after each use, since, Oswalt (1999: 259) explains, 'artistic forms were made for specific purposes … most often to convey a visual image about the deeds of ancestors or the realm of supernatural'. Masks frequently were made under the supervision of a shaman and had two principal purposes: (1) to influence the *yua* of animals to cooperate in the next round of hunting and fishing by giving themselves up freely to sustain the human community; (2) to assist the shaman in contacting the spirit world. In the first instance, the mask contained an image representing the *yua* of a particular animal or bird, usually with one half of the mask symbolizing the human and the other half the animal, the line of division usually running directly down the middle. Variations of this occurred, but in each case the mask, in Oswalt's (1967: 230) words, 'conveyed the meaning that animals were capable of assuming human forms'. In the case of the shaman, in addition to an animal's *yua* being painted on the mask, the shaman's spirit helper, the *tuunraq* (singular), frequently was represented as 'a distorted human face' (Oswalt, 1967: 230).

The Bladder Festival in particular, as we have seen, was conducted to ensure that the spirits of seals and other animals that had been killed during the past hunting season made themselves available for capture during the next hunting season. During the Bladder Festival, masked dancers entertained the inflated bladders containing the *yua* of the animals so they would be pleased at having been honoured and respected. Some masks employed in the ritual dances were quite elaborate, so that an animal's image appeared on the outside of the mask, but a dancer could pull a string and a human face appeared on the inside, demonstrating, in Oswalt's (1999: 262) view, that 'everything, animate and inanimate alike, had a human essence that could be revealed'. Fienup-Riordan (1994: 288) reports that 'young men entertained the bladders daily' through dances that 'depicted particular helping spirits'. She quotes Billy Lincoln, one of her Yupiit informants, who explained that 'before they danced, they decorated themselves with *qaraliit* [designs] and hanging things' (1994: 288). At other times, teenaged boys sat on the floor of the *qasgiq* imitating the sounds of birds and the movements of animals (1994: 288). Although the role of the shaman in the Bladder Festival seems to have been limited, Fienup-Riordan indicates that on the final day, when the seals' bladders were pushed back under the ice, the shaman, as the conduit between the human and spirit worlds, would leave his or her body and accompany the spirits of the seals through the hole in the ice into the sea to ensure that their passageway was clear and their way back to the community during the next hunt remained free of any obstructions (1994: 289).

The ritual most associated with masks and shamans amongst the Yupiit was called *Kelek*. Unlike the Bladder Festival, which honoured the animals that had already given themselves up in the previous hunting season, *Kelek* was performed, according to Fienup-Riordan (1994: 304), 'to please the spirits of game yet to be taken to supply the needs of the living'. As such, *Kelek* was the final ritual performed in the annual ceremonial year. The ritual, to a much greater extent than other ceremonies, emphasized masks and thus was referred to in some of the literature as the 'Masquerade' (Fienup-Riordan, 1994: 304). It also placed the shaman in the centre of the ritual performances, causing the Moravian missionary, John Kilbuck to conclude that the 'festival was probably instituted by shamans' (cited by Fienup-Riordan, 1994: 304–5). Another explanation of the central role of the shaman in *Kelek* relates to its future orientation. The shaman, as a prognosticator, could see into the future and as a diagnostician, was able to influence the game to give themselves to the hunters and could direct the hunters towards the most productive places to capture their prey (Oquilluk, 1981: 116–17). Fienup-Riordan (1994: 305) explains that due to their supernatural vision, shamans had 'the ability to travel to the skyland, the undersea home of the seals and the underground land of the dead, where they could communicate with and pacify the forces of nature'. As we have seen, they were assisted by invisible helpers, the *tuunrat*, who in much literature on the subject, are described as having been overpowered by shamans in fierce struggles and harnessed into their service (see for example, Firth, 1967: 296; Firth, 1996: 175; Eliade, 1989: 6).

During the *Kelek* ceremonies, the spirits of animals and *tuunrat*, which normally were invisible to all but the shaman, were invited into the *qasgiq* and appeared to the community through the masks. Preparations for *Kelek* were directed by the shaman, who instructed wood carvers how to make the sometimes quite elaborate images that were engraved on the masks. According to Fienup-Riordan, the shaman was integral to this process, since the masks represented what the shaman alone was able to see and sometimes resulted directly from visions the shaman had experienced in trance states (1994: 316). The masks possessed power, and thus 'were dangerous and had to be handled carefully at all times' (1994: 316). After they were completed, they were hidden until they were used in the ceremony and afterwards they were always destroyed. During the ritual, these prohibitions were lifted, because the person who put on the mask could see what otherwise was invisible and those who looked at the masked dancer had revealed to them a vision into worlds that normally could not be perceived. During the *Kelek* festival, just as they had done during the Bladder Festival and the Feasts for the Dead, the people sang traditional songs and other songs composed specifically for the event held that year. The people also imitated animals by making motions and sounds, and in dances acted out the mannerisms of animals. One of Fienup-Riordan's interviewees, Theresa Moses, explained: 'Every living thing dances ... even ducks and geese' (1994: 321). Fienup-Riordan (1994: 316) concludes: 'The use of masks during Kelek provided a concrete image of the contrast between restricted vision and powerful supernatural sight.'

The shaman acted also in situations outside communal rituals, often working as a healer or as one who could predict forthcoming events. Although these often affected individuals, the shaman's activities were performed and validated within carefully constructed social rules. The shaman's cataleptic trances, in which he appeared to have died only to be revived, demonstrated, in Fienup-Riordan's (1994: 309) words, that 'the shaman derived power from his paradoxical position as a person who had experienced death but could not die'. In his early journals written in 1916, the Moravian missionary Ferdinand Drebert (1959: 41) described his first encounters with shamans, or what he called 'witch doctors', as a mighty struggle between good and evil for power and influence over the people. He reports that one shaman had warned the people against carrying a corpse across the river where the Moravians had constructed their church and cemetery, because 'it would offend the spirit of the fish and there would be no more fish caught in the river' (1959: 41). Drebert also describes a healing session he attended in the *qasgiq*. On entering, he observed the patient sitting on the floor and behind him, squatting, was the shaman, who was drumming and singing, invoking the help of his *tuunraq*. Drebert describes how the shaman entered into a trance: 'He worked himself into a frenzy, frothing from the mouth and oblivious to all surroundings' (1959: 42). The shaman then picked up various objects including animal heads, crow feathers and smooth stones. A seal gut parka was also waved over the patient, since it made a noise intended, in Drebert's interpretation, 'to blow the spirit away' (1959: 43). Drebert notes that when the shaman came out of his trance he looked 'exhausted', but gradually regained consciousness of his surroundings (1959: 43).

Drebert reported that shamans not only had the power to heal, but they could also cause harm, which they would threaten to do if the patient did not provide the requisite gift in payment for a consultation or if strict rules and prohibitions were not observed. To illustrate this negative power, Drebert recounted the story of a man whose two sons had died quite recently:

He blamed himself, because the year previous he had refused to give the shaman a phonograph that had been demanded of him. 'So now' he said, 'I am reaping his wrath. He has killed two of my sons and my third and only remaining son is sick' (1959: 43).

Communities often sought to destroy such malevolent or selfish shamans, but because they were impossible to kill, they always revived or in some cases were re-born in unusual circumstances. Fienup-Riordan (1994: 309) describes how a particularly evil shaman on Nelson Island was attacked by members of the community, who stole his eyes, seemingly to take away the special vision only he possessed. They then killed the shaman by cutting his body into pieces, in a way resembling the shaman's initiation ordeals. They hid his eyes so that he would be unable to see to put his body parts back together. Although he was blind, the spirit of the shaman travelled to a neighbouring island where he was reborn from a woman who had never before been able to conceive. Fienup-Riordan observes: 'Nelson Islanders knew this was so because they had heard the child sing the shaman's songs.'

In traditional beliefs, the shaman often visited the moon to request the spirit of the moon literally to give birth to the animals which would populate the earth. Some reports indicate that the shaman copulated with the moon-spirit, in Fienup-Riordan's words, 'to release the game and insure a rich harvest season for the coming year' (1994: 307). Paul John describes how when the *angalkut* decided to travel to the moon, the men and boys were told to assemble in the *qasgiq* and the women and small children were ordered into their houses. 'Then when [the shaman] was going to go, he would have someone warn them not to go outside until he came back [or the shaman would not find his way back]' (cited by Fienup-Riordan, 1994: 310). Drebert (1959: 44) reports a similar incident confirming that the entire community believed that shamans 'could fly to the moon'. Drebert's account describes events surrounding an eclipse of the moon, which the people interpreted as meaning that the moon-spirit had died. The shaman had to travel to the moon to heal the moon-spirit so that its light would return to the earth. Drebert recounts how the shaman, wrapped in a seal skin parka, went out through the semi-underground winter opening of the *qasgiq*. From Paul John's statement, we can assume that the men and boys were gathered in the *qasgiq* and the woman and children were huddled inside their houses. Drebert says that the shaman was gone around 30 minutes. When he returned, 'he related ... how he came to the moon, and found him very sad and sick, sitting there with a dish of food before him but unable to eat it' (1959: 45). Drebert does not explain what methods the shaman used to heal the moon-spirit, but he indicates that 'he and another shaman from the next village had worked over him and cured him'. The shaman predicted that as a result of the moon's illness an epidemic would occur among the people who live 'on the other side of Kuskokwim Bay' (1959: 45).

The ceremonial masks and the central role of the shaman in community life, expressed in the various rituals and festivals, confirm the overall relationship of the Yupiit to nature that derived from their dependence on animals and fish for survival. *Kelek*, just like the Bladder Festival, was aimed at giving the people a feeling of control over events that directly affected their continued existence. Particularly in the *Kelek* rituals, because they were seeing through the eyes of the shaman into the worlds of the spirits, the community was assured that, so long as they respected the animals and followed the guidance of the shaman, they would achieve a bountiful harvest and survive throughout the long, dark winter. Throughout the entire ceremonial season, culminating with *Kelek*, this interconnection between the spirit world and the human community was at once opened and closed; the boundaries became transparent, but they were then shut and obscured. This applied to the movement of neighbouring communities from the periphery to the centre and back to the periphery in the Messenger Feast and equally to the interchange between the spirits of animals, the spirits of the dead, shamanic spirit helpers and members of the living community as evidenced in the Bladder Festival, the Feasts for the Dead and *Kelek*. The perceived connection between the seen and the unseen was necessary for the maintenance of community well-being, but at all times the relationship was tentative and dangerous, and thus subject to strict ceremonial and social rules. For this reason, the shaman was a central figure in the entire process, as one who could see into the spirit world, who could travel to the sky, underworld or the sea, who could heal or harm, and, perhaps most significantly, who died repeatedly but persistently was brought back to life. Fienup-Riordan (1994: 322) concludes that Yupiit rituals, exemplified in ceremonial dances and centred on the power of the shaman, accomplished the 'movement of the spirits from the edge of the human community to its center and finally back out of the human world'.

Yupiit Traditions as Indigenous Religion

The descriptions I have provided of Yupiit traditions in this chapter relate largely to the period between 1880 and 1940. During this time, the United States government, in collusion with missionary teachers, embarked on a project aimed at eradicating Yupiit patterns of life. As a result, the *qasgiq* long ago disappeared; many of the traditional stories have been lost; the ceremonies for the dead are no longer performed; the shaman has been vanquished. Subsistence economies have receded in the light of capitalist ventures, most notably expressed in the Native Corporations, which were created as part of the Alaska Native Claims Settlement Act (ANCSA), first enacted in 1971, and amended several times over the next thirty years (Mitchell, 2001; Case and Voluck, 1984). Villages today look very different from those the first American missionaries encountered over 100 years ago. Young people frequently leave their homes seeking jobs in larger cities like Anchorage, Fairbanks, Bethel or Juneau, and for many of those who stay, village life has been plagued by problems of alcohol and suicide (Fienup-Riordan, 2000: 20–23). Educational reforms have occurred over the years from the heyday of regional boarding schools in the 1960s to the building of modern schools in every major village from the mid-1970s onward (Cox, 1991: 149–61; Fienup-Riordan, 2000: 16). Fienup-Riordan (2000: 16–17) writes that now in south-western Alaska 'the most significant feature of village economy ... is its dependence on government'. She adds: 'As much as 90 per cent flows through the village economies from the public sector.' As such, a hunter today measures his success in 'harvesting animals' by 'his ability to harvest cash'. The ramifications for Indigenous Religions of such changes in contemporary Alaska are overwhelming, so much so that today a researcher can find only vestiges of former religious traditions, operating usually beneath the surface or in adaptations to Christianity, although many of the longstanding cultural patterns and social attitudes remain intact.

In this chapter, I could not consider such enormous changes affecting Yupiit traditions, although the Mask Exhibit of the mid-1990s described by Fienup-Riordan and its accompanying commentary by elders such as Paul John, provide evidence that strenuous efforts are underway to recover and preserve many of the ancient ways. My aim in this chapter has been to study the Yupiit as a case study in the practical application of my formal, preliminary working definition of an Indigenous

Religion. This has meant examining the Yupiit in terms of their localized, kinship-based communities with strong ancestral traditions to determine in the process how and in what ways they postulated beliefs and experiences about non-falsifiable alternate realities by appeals to an authoritative tradition that was passed on from generation to generation. The case study has clarified the nature of Yupiit indigeneity and it has delineated the patterns according to which 'religion' functions within this particular indigenous society. My definition did not prescribe the content of Yupiit Indigenous Religion by appeals to an essential core, but it functioned throughout as a paradigm into which specific content has been inserted. Yupiit Indigenous Religion in this sense has been shown to be strictly Yupiit and nothing else. It does not refer to a disconnected essence that somehow manifests itself around the world in various ways. By placing limits around the study, nonetheless, my preliminary definition has enabled us to understand in what ways the Yupiit traditionally understood their locality, how they interpreted the meaning of belonging to a place and in what manner their ancestral traditions dictated acceptable patterns of social behaviour.

As the 'real people', the Yupiit of south-western Alaska operated from a position at the centre, symbolized principally by the *qasgiq*, where various ceremonies were performed either annually or periodically, and from which the shaman made excursions to far off and dangerous places only to return back to the centre. In this sense, the Yupiit as a people clearly emphasized belonging to a particular place; they were defined by it and derived their meaning from it. As a localized people, they traced their identity to ancestors, who, like the shaman, died only to be re-born, in their namesakes. Although the spirits of the dead resided ultimately in an underground world and did not directly affect the community after they had been settled in the land of the dead through the Great Festival, they retained a lasting influence on the living through those who bore their names. Numerous other spirits populated the Yupiit universe; many, like the animal and moon spirits were necessary for their survival, but others posed a threat to well-being unless they could be mastered and used for good by the shaman. A study in Yupiit traditional society thus fills out and provides content to the broad category, indigenous, since the Yupiit, represent, even to this day, a people of locality, who define themselves in relation to their place, to the traditions associated with it, and increasingly through the re-invention of their ancient ways of life, to their ancestors.

The case of the Yupiit also adds substantive content to the category religion. Yupiit groups clearly represent identifiable communities, which continue into the twenty-first century to be bound together by traditions and kinship. Certainly, prior to extensive contact with Moravian missionaries and well into the twentieth century, they maintained numerous beliefs about non-falsifiable alternate realities, chiefly the spiritual extension of 'personhood' or *yua* virtually to everything, but particularly to those forces of nature which most affected their subsistence needs. Their ceremonial life persistently invited the *yua* of animals, objects and unseen spirits into the central ritual space, to communicate with them, to entertain them and to honour them. Through masks, dances, sounds and gestures, the people visualized and imitated the spirits, but when they needed to see directly into that which otherwise was hidden, they employed the eyes of the shaman. By going into trances, the shaman encountered alternate realities, overcame threats to well-being and returned to the community to provide healing, to predict the future and to advise on how best to ensure the necessary requirements for survival. The traditional beliefs of the Yupiit are shown in this way to have been active and experiential: how they related to the spirit world affected the well-being of everyone in the village; in ritual contexts and through shamanic trances, they experienced directly the power and reality of the spirit world.

Fienup-Riordan's research emphasizes that Yupiit traditions were constrained by boundaries and rules, the authority of which was attained by the power attributed to spirits and re-enforced by social convention. Since the Yupiit had no chiefs, authority was vested in elders and those most respected in the community. In the *qasgiq*, stories were told about the origin of the 'real people' and ceremonies were performed both for entertainment and for purposes of effecting control over a harsh environment. Social relationships between neighbouring villages and amongst those living in the community were cemented through elaborate and expensive feasts. The long tradition of elders passed on from generation to generation and re-enforced by namesakes ensured that the proper balance between social and spiritual needs was maintained, particularly between the human community and the animals on which the community depended for its survival. Passages from outside the *qasgiq* into its centre, either through the semi-underground entrance or through the smoke-hole to the sky, and then out again, were prepared and executed following strictly prescribed rituals and social regulations. The transmission of the tradition in Yupiit society as a result, although not coercive, was nonetheless fully authoritative.

From these general conclusions, it becomes apparent that the case of the Yupiit demonstrates the way my definition of Indigenous Religions works in practice by establishing parameters around the category without positing a universal content for what fits into the classification. We will see in my next case study on the Shona in Zimbabwe that locality, beliefs and experiences of non-falsifiable alternate realities and the manner whereby the authoritative tradition is transmitted operate very differently from the Yupiit of Alaska. My definition, because it is a working, pragmatic and non-essentialist one, is not discredited by such differences, but is shown to be a useful heuristic instrument for ascertaining what constitutes an Indigenous Religion.

Chapter 6

The Adaptive Nature of Indigenous Religions in Zimbabwe

In this chapter I consider Indigenous Religions in Zimbabwe as a second case study. I have chosen this topic because I have written about it extensively in previous publications (see Cox, 2000a: 190–207; 2000b: 230–242; 1998a; 1996b: 87–107; 1995: 339–55), have worked in the country and have conducted fieldwork there, most recently in 2004. In addition to my personal reasons for using this region to discuss Indigenous Religions, it serves as a highly useful contrast to the case of the Yupiit of Alaska. Quite obviously, Zimbabwe provides sharp geographical, cultural and historical variations from Alaska, and thus, when religious practices in the two areas are compared as instances of the same category called Indigenous Religions, the problem of essentialism re-surfaces. I consider this issue briefly in the concluding section of this chapter, but return to it in detail in the discussions of Chapter 7. The case of Zimbabwe is important for other reasons. Unlike the Alaskan situation, Indigenous Religions in Zimbabwe persist to this day. Traditional rituals can be observed in virtually every part of the country and appeals to ancestors and various other spirits remain a part of everyday life. We have seen that such active participation in traditional rituals in Alaska ended within 50 years of intensive Protestant missionary activity in the region, and that today we are limited largely to observing reconstructions of past traditions by indigenous leaders who are trying to restore respect for the customs of prior generations. In Zimbabwe, although traditions have adapted to changing historical situations, indigenous beliefs and rituals remain ubiquitous throughout the country.

The current population of Zimbabwe is nearly 13 million, although the growth rate at .051 per cent falls far below the international average, largely due to the high infection rate in the population of HIV-AIDS.[1] The average life expectancy is now around 37 years, whereas just after Independence in 1980 it stood at 57 years (Berens, 1988: 40). The two main ethnic groups in Zimbabwe are the Shona and the Ndebele, terms that refer to the languages spoken by each group, both of which form part of the extensive Bantu linguistic family, and to their distinctive cultural identities. The Shona comprise the majority of Zimbabwe's population (around 80%), but they are broken into various groupings distributed largely throughout the northern, eastern and central regions of the country, including the Korekore in the far north, the Zezuru in the north central region around the capital, Harare, the Manyika and Ndau in the eastern regions and the Karanga in the south-central portion of the country. The other main Shona-speaking group is the Kalanga, located in the extreme south western area along the border with Botswana. Today, these groupings are referred to collectively as the Shona, but Bourdillon suggests that its general application to all those speaking a similar dialect was introduced by the British

---

[1]   www.indexmundi.com/Zimbabwe.

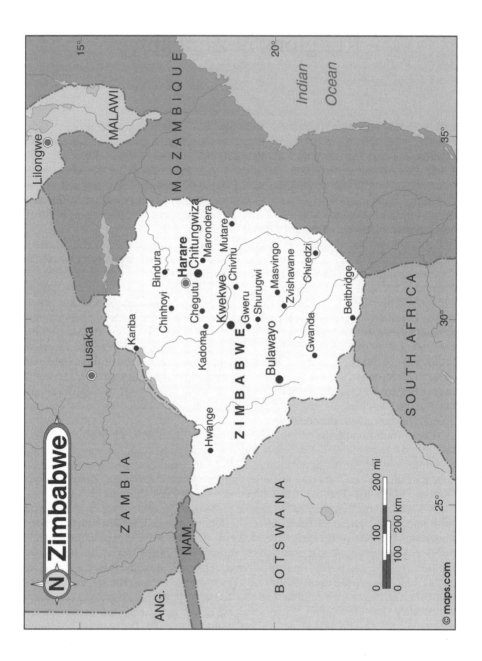

during colonial rule (Bourdillon, 1997: 17). The majority of the people in the south western region, called Matabeleland, speak Ndebele, which is an Nguni language closely linked to the Zulu spoken in South Africa, with its characteristic 'clicking' sounds. Other ethnic groups in Zimbabwe include the Tonga in the far northwest near Lake Kariba and along the Zambezi River, and the Sotho, Venda and Hlengwe living near the south western and southern borders with Botswana and South Africa (Berens, 1988: 40–1) (see map of Zimbabwe).

In this chapter, after outlining how society traditionally is structured in a hierarchical way that almost exactly corresponds to the ordering of authority in the spirit world, I explain why Indigenous Religions played such a critical role in the Zimbabwean wars of liberation against colonialism and why they persist as potent forces motivating the current land resettlement project. At the conclusion of the chapter, I will suggest how my prior definitions of 'indigenous' and 'religion' have served as important pragmatic devices for guiding my discussions and for disclosing the basic elements of Indigenous Religions in Zimbabwe. I am aware that any study of religion in Zimbabwe is subject to the error of oversimplification, since quite fundamental variations occur throughout the country, depending on whether the research focuses primarily on regional or local religious performances, and to what extent either is interwoven into Christian ideas. The complexity of religion in Zimbabwe is increased further by important differences amongst regional cults. Scholars such as Richard Werbner (1977: 179–218), Leslie Nthoi (1998: 63–93; 2006), Terence Ranger (1999) and Martinus Daneel (1970; 1998: 94–125) have written widely about the High God or Mwari shrines in southwest Zimbabwe, which provide a focus for religious activity in regions as widespread as north eastern Botswana and northern parts of South Africa, as well as across the southern third of Zimbabwe. In the north and north-eastern parts of the Zimbabwe, the Mwari cult does not exist, but instead regional religious attention is directed towards *mhondoro*, or territorial spirits, who are appealed to when the people are faced with major threats such as drought, pestilence and warfare (Bourdillon, 1997: 279). When Indigenous Religions are restricted to local situations, people are seen to be concerned with matters of health, community stability, rituals of birth, marriage and death, and relationships with neighbouring villages. In these cases, the variations of belief and practice become less pronounced than those amongst regional cults.

In order to make sense of such complex arrangements, I have chosen to restrict my analyses to traditional *mhondoro* cults and their relationship to village and family social structures as practised primarily amongst the Korekore ethnic group. It will be necessary also to describe how Korekore ideas about founding and chthonic spirits have fused with similar beliefs amongst the neighbouring Zezuru people to create the basis for a more widespread national myth that played an important role in Zimbabwe's wars of liberation. Throughout this chapter, I will draw from research conducted by anthropologists who have worked amongst the Korekore over the past thirty years, including Michael Bourdillon (1997), David Lan (1985), Kingsley Garbett (1977: 55–92), and most recently Marja Spierenburg (2004). I also refer to the preliminary findings of my own pilot study conducted in a Korekore region near the town of Mount Darwin in 2004, in which I sought to identify the religious dimensions operating beneath the Zimbabwean government's current land redistribution programme (Cox: 2005: 35–48). I discovered that beliefs in ancestor spirits have contributed significantly to the current political and economic policies of the government, demonstrating the remarkable ability of Indigenous Religions in Zimbabwe to adapt to current events. Such adaptations, however, cannot be understood without knowledge of the social structures through which they persist today, particularly in rural areas.

The Korekore, the *Mhondoro* Tradition and Chthonic Spirits

Amongst the Korekore, two types of regional spirit cults operate side by side and interpenetrate one another. One is territorial, hierarchical and ancestral, and follows a pattern characteristic of the social organization within chieftaincies. The other is not restricted to one territory, the spirits of which are chthonic, literally from the ground, hence ancient, known only in myths, whose traditions precede ancestors or may not even be known (Garbett, 1977: 56–7). The spirits of both are referred to by Bourdillon (1997: 253) as 'lion spirits', although the territorial spirits, the *mhondoro* (translated 'lion' in Shona) are more commonly designated in this way. Garbett (1977: 57) refers to the chthonic spirits as 'local' in order to distinguish them from those operating within one geographical region, although he admits there is much crossing over between the two, and at times, the spirits of one are transformed in the minds of the practitioners into the other type. I will consider each in turn before showing how a spirit, like Nehanda, who was so important in the Zimbabwean wars of liberation, is subject to numerous interpretations, including being treated as a founding ancestor, and hence as a *mhondoro*, and as a local spirit with multiple mediums and without territorial restriction.

Bourdillon (1997: 253) explains that the *mhondoro* refers to the 'belief that certain powerful spirits, particularly the spirits of departed chiefs, take the form of or take possession of young lions' and later either grow into or take possession of 'a young maneless lion that wanders about in the bush until it decides to enter a medium'. The *mhondoro* thus refers both to the spirit of the chief and to the medium that the spirit possesses, which explains why the medium is often reported to be heard roaring like a lion. The concern of the *mhondoro*, like that of any living chief, is with the general welfare of the territory over which the spirit is responsible, rather than with problems of individuals or families. This is why Bourdillon differentiates sharply between the medium of a *mhondoro* and a *n'anga* or traditional healer, calling the latter the person to whom people turn in cases of individual or family affliction, although he admits that in some regions of Zimbabwe a medium for a *mhondoro* may also operate within the community as a *n'anga* (Bourdillon, 1997: 256). Bourdillon also draws attention to regional differences regarding *mhondoro* spirits. Amongst the Korekore, for example, *mhondoro* mediums almost never act as mediums for family ancestor spirits, while further south in Karanga regions, the term *mhondoro* seldom is used to refer to the spirits of departed chiefs at all (Bourdillon, 1997: 254). Moreover, amongst the Korekore, a hierarchy amongst *mhondoro* spirits exists, with senior territorial spirits being traced ultimately to the founder of the chief's lineage, and in the case of the most important, all the way back to Mutota, the quasi-legendary founder of the people (Garbett, 1977: 58–62). Ritual attention directed at the *mhondoro* thus is not defined strictly along kinship lines, since, like any chief, the spirit concerns itself with the needs of all those who fall within its territorial jurisdiction.

The traditional organization of chieftaincies, with their hierarchy extending from paramount chiefs through sub-chiefs to headmen mirrors a corresponding hierarchy in the spirit world. The pre-colonial Shona states would have placed the king at the top of the pyramid. Aided by his ancestor spirits, he assumed broad responsibility for the welfare of the whole state. Lesser chiefs followed the same pattern, concerning themselves with more restricted territories, until finally the hierarchical structure reached families, with elders and subordinates being ordered according to seniority. In every case, the world of ancestor spirits followed a similar hierarchical pattern from those of the paramount chief (senior *mhondoro* spirits) down to the level of the family ancestor spirits (*midzimu*). Clearly the destruction of the great Shona states during a period culminating in the nineteenth century has reduced the scope of chiefs, and their roles have become intertwined with various colonial and government administrations over the years. Nonetheless, the basic pattern correlating social to spiritual hierarchies persists to this day, as noted recently by Marja Spierenburg (2004: 33), who calls the *mhondoro* a spirit of 'royal ancestors' and claims that 'all present-day chiefs claim to descend from one of the *Mhondoro*'. This explains why *mhondoro* spirits have been linked to the Zimbabwean liberation struggle. As descendants of the founding ancestors, they were responsible for protecting the land or for re-claiming it from outsiders who had appropriated it for themselves. Spirit mediums (*svikiro*) of principal spirits thus came to play important roles as voices for those who claimed a prior right to the land.

David Lan, whose work amongst the Korekore closely links the role of *mhondoro* spirits to the wars of liberation, has outlined how the hierarchical structure works within the spirit world. Lan illustrates this by drawing attention to the persistent need throughout the area for regular and reliable rainfall, although in reality the rains often are sporadic and undependable resulting in frequent droughts. Since this problem affects a wide area, it defines a central concern of territorial spirits. This means that in many regions amongst the Korekore, the *mhondoro* is associated with bringing the annual rains, or, if for some reason the *mhondoro* is offended, is credited with preventing rain until the particular grievance has been identified and rectified. Lan discovered that although annual rituals for rain are made at the shrine of each *mhondoro*, the appeals for rain within each chieftaincy are conveyed by the territorial spirit upwards until eventually it reaches the founding ancestors. 'The request must be sent up a chain of *mhondoro* until it reaches the most senior, the *mhondoro* which is in charge of the realm as a whole' (Lan, 1985: 74). The link to past dynasties in this case appears incontrovertible, since as Lan notes, requests for rain are sent through 'the genealogy of the chieftaincy which links the present chief to his most distant ancestors' (Lan, 1985: 74).

Kingsley Garbett (1977: 61), who conducted research in northern Zimbabwe during the 1960s, claims that the Korekore conceptualize regions 'as autonomous ritual territories' that are sub-divided according to 'ancient and immutable' boundaries. The boundaries are regarded as ancient and immutable because they have been established and recounted in the people's myths of origin. Garbett (1977: 66) cites one version of the myth, which describes how the Korekore, under the leadership of the sons of the founding ancestor, Mutota, conquered the Tavara people living in the land surrounding the Dande region along the Zambezi River. According to the legend, Mutota had travelled in search of salt from an undefined land in the north called Guuruswa (land of high grass) towards the Zambezi valley. As he was approaching the edge of the escarpment, he was prevented from knowing he had reached his destination by his sons, a secret which placed him in 'mystical danger', finally resulting in his death. Just as he was dying, he forbade that his body should be buried unless one of his sons had sexual intercourse with his daughter, Nehanda. His son, Nebedza, slept with his sister, Nehanda, an act of incest which caused the ground to open miraculously to receive Mutota's body. Garbett discovered at the time of his search that the ritual territories were named after the early founders of the Korekore, such as Nehanda and Nebedza, thereby linking care for the people's welfare directly to the royal ancestral line (Garbett, 1977: 62). David Lan's (1985: 76) version of the founding myth is similar to the one recounted by Garbett, although he adds that each son of Mutota, except Nebedza, refused 'to perform this forbidden act', and for this reason Nebedza, the youngest, inherited 'his father's position as head of the lineage'.

Garbett explains further that, according to oral tradition, when Nebedza and the rest of the Mutota clan arrived in the Zambezi Valley, the region was under the control of Tavara chiefs, whose ritual authority was legitimated by 'powerful chthonic beings, among them Dzivaguru and his sons Karuva and Musumua Nyamukokoko and the latter's guardian, Chimombe' (Garbett, 1977: 66). These stories clearly identify the Korekore as invaders and thus portray Mutota and Nebedza as founding ancestors of the Korekore in the land of Tavara. In this sense, as Lan (1985: 19) notes, the descendants of Mutota 'own the land' as conquerors, not as 'autochthons, the first people ever to have lived there'. Beach (1980: 64) confirms that, since the story of migrations from a land called 'Guruuswa' are widespread, there must be some historical truth behind the oral traditions that refer to the movements of peoples into the land. He adds that there still exist some survivors of the Mutapa State, who are Shona-speakers known as Tavara and who claim to have preceded the local 'Guruuswa' groups. He concludes: 'There is little doubt that they [the Tavara] predate the Mutapa dynasty, which gives them a very long history indeed' (Beach, 1980: 64). In Korekore mythology, what Garbett refers to as 'chthonic beings' for this reason are distinguished from ordinary Tavara chiefs. The chiefs were conquered and could be killed by ordinary means, but the chthonic beings either had to be subdued by mystical powers or placated by offerings aimed at re-directing their powers towards protecting the invaders. Over time, ritual activities in honour of the chthonic beings were either minimized or absorbed into the ancestral traditions dominated by the *mhondoro* spirits. Garbett (1977: 67) speculates, for example, that the decline of the chthonic Dzivaguru cult was accompanied by the rise of the Mutota cult, to the point that by the end of the nineteenth century 'chiefly ancestors came to be accorded the powers of chthonic beings, and the mediums who represented them became associated with fixed territories'.

Bourdillon (1997: 258) defines Korekore autochthonous spirits, like Dzivaguru and Karuva, as 'spirits of an ancient dynasty defeated by the invading Korekore centuries ago'. As such, their lineage is not known in the same way that the Korekore claim to relate to their own founding ancestor, Mutota. Their main function is to bring rain (the word Dzivaguru in Shona means 'great pool'), and thus at their shrines, representatives from chieftaincies covering a wide area travel to influence the chthonic spirits to release the annual rains. Bourdillon (1997: 258) notes that normally only *mhondoro* spirits would be consulted within a chief's region on matters of territorial concern, but during times of severe drought 'delegations from chiefdoms over a hundred kilometres away come occasionally to the sacred grove to request from Dzivaguru and Karuva alleviation of drought at home'. Beyond their power to produce rain, however, these spirits have little influence amongst the Korekore, and are regarded as less significant than the *mhondoro*, since, in Bourdillon's (1997: 259) words, they are like 'a woman who fetches water for her husband'. Much more important are the ancestor spirits of the conquering nation, since 'it is the invaders who now own the land'. This may reflect what Garbett observed about the decline in the nineteenth century of shrines devoted to the autochthonous spirits, or to their being absorbed into the legends about founding ancestors.

Some senior *mhondoro* spirits are deemed to be so important that they cross over territorial boundaries. Often, in pre-colonial times, these were the ancestors of a paramount chief, but even today, they may refer to alleged common ancestors between neighbouring chieftaincies, which Bourdillon (1997: 272) asserts, 'may involve some form of kinship, an ancient marriage between the two chiefly families or simply friendship'. In the case of the founding ancestors, the senior *mhondoro* unites numerous chieftaincies, each of which traces its lineage to the same original founder. Mutota serves this function for the Korekore, as Bourdillon (1997: 273) notes, since 'many chiefdoms claim to have some connection with him, whether because in the legends they travelled with Mutota or he gave them their land, or through some (probably fictional) kinship link'. Amongst the Zezuru in central Shona regions, Chaminuka is depicted in some versions of oral history as a founding ancestor, and thus plays the same role as Mutota by uniting people from many territories. Bourdillon (1997: 273) explains that in these cases, the people 'believe in a common spiritual power that cares for all and controls their well-being'.

The Zimbabwean historian and novelist, Simon Mutswairo (1996: 20–21), claims that in Zezuru oral tradition, the first ancestor of the Shona, Mumbiri (Mbire), migrated from the north to the south, coming either from southern Sudan or Ethiopia to the east of Lake Tanganyika (Guruuswa). In that location, Mumbiri began a lineage extending through his son, Tovera, through Tovera's son, Murenga, and finally to Murenga's most important son, Chaminuka. From this clan, the people migrated further south, led by the three sons of Chaminuka. Mutswairo (1996: 21) writes: 'They subdued the riverine Tonga, the Tavara, and the Chikunda in the Zambezi valley.' A similar version of the story has been told by the historian A.S. Chigwedere (1980), and confirmed by interviews conducted by T. Chiura in 1989 with Chief Svosve (1991). D.N. Beach (1980: 315), however, argues that the nineteenth-century cult devoted to Chaminuka, which became highly significant amongst some Shona groups in the twentieth century as reflected in Chigwedere's and Chiura's research, 'does not appear to have been the ancestry of any modern dynasty' and thus his shrines and spirit mediums, although seeming to fit into an ancestral tradition like that of Mutota, probably correspond more closely to Garbett's local cult associated with autochthonous spirits whose genealogy is not known. Bourdillon (1997: 259) concludes that powerful Zezuru spirits, like Chaminuka, have 'become so well known that they form a clear apex to the spiritual hierarchy of a number of subject peoples'. It is in the context of autochthonous spirits that we meet the Zezuru account of Nehanda, whom Bourdillon (1997: 274) describes as 'a female spirit renowned throughout central Shona country and on a par with Chaminuka'. As we will see, the Korekore and Zezuru versions of Nehanda merged in popular perceptions during the 1970s to form part of the Zimbabwean national myth.

The Central Place of *Midzimu* in Local Zimbabwean Religion

We have already noted that the chief has overall responsibility for a defined region. Before the colonial period, during the times of the Shona states, paramount chiefs were responsible for wide areas, with junior chiefs caring for a more restricted territory. Today, a similar social order operates, but there are no paramount chiefs. Below the chief, nonetheless, at the village level, a hierarchical social order is maintained in various forms depending on the size of the village and the number of extended families living within it. Very strictly defined rules govern relations between and among families living in the village. A village head, followed by heads of extended families and other members of the family are ranked according to their seniority and social position. In addition, parallel or corresponding worlds operate between the spirits of the departed and the living community. The most important local spirits are those of ancestors, called *midzimu* (*mudzimu*, singular), who perform functions in the spirit world that generally are comparable to the responsibilities they fulfilled when they were alive. In this way, we see the same pattern prevailing at the local stratum as at the level of *mhondoro* spirits.

Bourdillon (1997: 57) explains that the English word 'village' is misleading, since it implies a fixed, stable location. In traditional Shona society, the word *musha*, which is usually translated as 'village', refers to a group of extended families that cluster around a headman. A *musha* thus primarily is relational rather than being physically tied to one location and the buildings that comprise it. Of course, territory is occupied by the members of the *musha*, who tend the fields around the homesteads that encompass it, but social relationships prescribe how a *musha* is organized. According to typical Shona social patterns, each *musha* is led by a headman who founded it or is the patrilineal descendant of the founder. Those living in the *musha* consist of the headman's descendants, and, especially in Korekoreland, at least until recent times, a number of men who were working in their wives' village as a way of paying the bride price, rather than in the traditional manner by offering the bride's father an agreed number of cattle in exchange for the woman moving to the homestead of the husband's family (Lan, 1985: 21). Bourdillon (1997: 57–8) notes also that large villages usually include families that are unrelated to the headman, many of whom joined the village on the basis of friendship with the headman's families. In the past, villages tended to split up more than they do today, often because they became too large for the land to support all the inhabitants. Other reasons for such divisions in a headman's territory include succession disputes or the general loss of confidence in the ability of the headman to perform his duties. Although since colonial rule (and also after Independence) the mobility of village heads has been restricted due to the imposition of Western ideas of land ownership, the basic structure of the *musha* persists to this day in rural areas.

The headman is responsible for the welfare of the *musha* as a whole. He must ensure that those living in the village have enough food, that land is distributed fairly, that social harmony prevails and that any disputes between families are resolved properly. In some cases, according to Bourdillon (1997: 60), the headman may organize rain rituals, but in most instances, this duty falls to the chief. The headman may need to take disputes to the chief, and when these involve problems between different villages in the chief's domain, the headman will represent the concerns of his own *musha* at the chief's court. Within the Korekore villages in the Dande region, Lan (1985: 60–62) describes how a triangular system operates between the *mhondoro* spirit, the *mutapi*, a well-respected family man in charge of a shrine dedicated to the *mhondoro*, and the medium of the *mhondoro*. The *mutapi* originates from the territory of the *mhondoro* and remains there throughout his life, whereas a medium may come from the outside and may not always remain within the territory. Nevertheless, the medium is possessed by the *mhondoro* during rituals and conveys important information the current chief needs in order to make important decisions. Lan explains:

The legitimacy of the chief rests on the fact that he was selected by the *mhondoro* from all other possible candidates and … before a medium can establish his authenticity he requires a *mutapi* to lend him the authority of his position. Chief depends on *mhondoro* and *mhondoro* depends on *mutapi*. The circle is completed by the fact that the authority of the *mutapi* ultimately derives from the chief. Almost invariably the *mutapi* is also the headman of the village in which he lives (Lan, 1985: 61–2).

In these ways, headmen act as intermediaries between the chief and the village, serving the chief and the chief's ancestor spirits, while at the same time representing the interests of the particular village over which they have responsibility. This means that headmen carry greater and more extensive responsibilities, particularly when they are also *vatapi* (pl. of *mutapi*), than the heads of the extended families that comprise the headman's village.

An extended family consists of what Bourdillon (1985: 27) describes as a 'patrilineage of three to five generations of the descendants of one man', a system called *chizvarwa* in Shona. Bourdillon (1985: 26) explains that it is the ambition of a man 'to gather around him a growing lineage of descendants and dependants who … act as a corporate body for economic purposes'. This unit also acts together in cases of disputes with neighbouring homesteads and forms the basic entity for marriage negotiations. Seen from the perspective of the eldest son in an extended family, Bourdillon (1997: 27) describes how the system operated traditionally, although he notes that the means of subsistence have been affected by Western education and commerce and by migrations to large urban centres from rural areas. In traditional society, the son would grow up in a homestead with paternal grandparents, his own parents, his father's brothers and their wives, his own brothers and sisters and his patrilineal cousins. When his father died, he would normally inherit his father's name and position, although sometimes this passed to his father's younger brother. Bourdillon (1997: 27) explains that many factors affect whether or not a family stays together after the father's death, such as 'the size of the group and on the relationships between the sons of the family head'. The eldest son also maintains a number of important other relationships in the extended family. For example, he will refer to his father's brothers also as father (*baba*). The term brother similarly has a broader meaning than in typical Western households. In Shona extended families, the eldest son will regard his father's brother's son as his brother, and not as a cousin as in Western families. All the women in the patrilineage are regarded as aunts (*vatete*), regardless of how distant they may be from the eldest son's own father's sisters. When the eldest son's sister is married, it is the father's sister who is responsible for instructing her in how to be a good wife, including sexual duties, and not the actual mother of the girl (Gelfand, 1979: 18–20). Finally, it is important to note, according to Bourdillon, that the son's mother, although not from the same clan as the father, holds a special relationship with her son. This is reflected by the fact that the mother's brothers are referred to as *sekuru*, usually translated as grandfather (Bourdillon, 1997: 31–5).

For each of these figures from the village head to members of the extended family, there are corresponding ancestor spirits. Quite clearly, the head of the family holds an important place in the ancestral world for each extended family, since he was responsible for caring for the general needs of the members of his family when he was alive. In this sense, his concerns had to do with more immediate problems than that of either the village head or the chief. As a sign of respect, the ancestor of the deceased father of the family usually has a bull dedicated to him that will be slaughtered in his honour in regular rituals of remembrance (Bourdillon, 1997: 27–8; for a ritual description of the bull sacrifice, see Cox, 1998a: 209–11). Other members of the family also become ancestors and relate to various members of the extended family in ways similar to how they functioned in life. For example, the mother's spirit maintains a nurturing role with respect to her children so much so that, in Bourdillon's (1997: 32) words, it is believed that 'nothing harmful can happen to a person without the consent of the maternal spirits'. It is understandable in this social structure that the ancestor spirits or *midzimu* receive the majority of ritual attention in Shona religious life (Cox, 1995; 339–55). The village head is one step removed and thus his spirit is concerned with matters relating to a number of extended families, and the chief's spirit is even further removed from everyday matters. Just as it was in life, when the main needs of a person were met within the extended family, so is it in the spirit world. It is for this reason, as I have noted in previous publications when I collated descriptions of rituals described by my students in the University of Zimbabwe, that the great majority of student accounts consisted either of rituals honouring family ancestor spirits (*bira*) (Cox, 1998a: 199–212) or were rituals conducted to bring an ancestor home (*kurova guva*) about one year after death to take up his or her ancestral duties protecting, guarding and guiding family members (Cox, 1998a: 232–45).

Just as the chief's spirits need mediums (*svkiro*) to communicate directly with the chief, so too do family ancestors need mediums to receive the requests of family members and to respond with messages the people need to hear to rectify a problem or to ensure well-being. In the case of *midzimu*, the most recently departed are addressed ritually, and they carry messages to their seniors up to three or four generations by name, who continue the chain of communication to those who are no longer remembered by name. In this way the hierarchical structure that exists in the social world is replicated amongst the spirits, until eventually at the apex are the most important ancestors who brought the people into the land. Of course, the *midzimu* have other indirect ways of communicating, just as the *mhondoro* spirit does, for example, when the *mhondoro* withholds rain or allows other regional disasters to occur to gain the attention of the people or to indicate strong disapproval for some misdeeds. In the case of the *midzimu*, frequently a series of afflictions are allowed to plague the family, such as illnesses and deaths, failure of a woman to conceive or bear children or successful attacks against the family by witches. In contemporary society, the *mudzimu* may inflict economic problems in a family or even cause the failure of a child at school or university. These misfortunes indicate that something has gone wrong, and that the people need to establish contact with the ancestor who either is causing the problems or is allowing them to occur. Frequently, a *n'anga*, or traditional healer, is consulted, who may use a number of means to determine that the misfortunes have occurred, for example, because the ancestor has been forgotten and needs a ritual of honour, or because some social rule has been transgressed by a member or members of the family. Sometimes, the *mudzimu* causes a person to become so ill that no treatment from any source can succeed until the sick person learns, usually in a ritual context, that the ancestor spirit wants the person to become his or her medium. In these cases, the sick person appears to be nearing death at the beginning of the ritual, but, after becoming possessed by the spirit of the ancestor, recovers almost instantaneously (Cox, 2000a: 190–207).

Finally, although much more could be said about *midzimu*, it is important to note that it is the aim of every person to become an ancestor spirit. This means that all people want descendants who will honour and remember them after death. As a result, the failure to have children is regarded as a great affliction. Only those who are considered socially unfit fail to be made an ancestor through the performance of a bringing home, or *kurova guva*, ritual. The most common social misfit is a witch, but other causes can make a person unsuitable for becoming an ancestor, such as committing suicide. Normally, to be brought home as an ancestor is a sign that the person has lived an honourable life, has followed social norms and has performed his or her functions while alive in an admirable manner. It is widely believed that after death, a person's spirit wanders around in the bush in an unsettled state and thus is potentially dangerous to the living. When the bringing home ritual is completed, the spirit is settled back into the homestead and assumes the role of a guardian and protector of the family. If someone does not receive a burial according to customary practice and thus is not brought back home, that spirit will cause havoc in the family leading to a series of misfortunes and deaths. The role of a *mudzimu* in the family thus largely is beneficent, but if the spirit is not treated according to traditional ways, it becomes malevolent or at least extremely disruptive to normal family life.

We have seen from the above discussion how myths of origin have been intertwined in traditional religious perspectives with a system of corresponding social and spiritual worlds. The founding ancestors are remembered and are linked to the present through the *mhondoro* spirits who communicate directly to the chief and who carry the chief's concerns to the appropriate level in the spiritual hierarchy. The *mhondoro* spirits also relate to the headman, who, as Lan (1985: 61–2) has shown, often maintains the shrine at which the *mhondoro* communicates with the chief through his medium. The headman also has ancestor spirits who relate to the concerns of the extended families living within his village. We have seen finally that the extended family defines the most common and direct place for communication between the living and their ancestors. Throughout the entire system, connections are maintained in the hierarchy between the extended family, the village headman and the chief, with each exercising authority over well-defined customary matters. The spirits of each are also inter-connected and respond to those needs that are appropriate for their level of seniority. For this reason, if family problems develop, they are resolved according to the relationships within the family and are not brought to the village head or to the chief. In the spirit world, the same applies. Only those matters that concern the territory as a whole come to the *mhondoro*; all others fall under the purview of the *midzimu* of either the headman or family members.

Indigenous Religions in Zimbabwe's Wars of Liberation

The socio-cultural background I have presented thus far in this chapter helps to explain why Indigenous Religions have played such a decisive role in the history of the Zimbabwean resistance movements throughout the twentieth century. Much of this history has been well documented by David Lan, which I will not repeat in detail here. My point is to relate these events to what I have defined previously as an indigenous religion. It will be important in this regard to draw attention to the role of spirit mediums, particularly those possessed by Nehanda, in what is referred to generally as the First Chimurenga, or first war of liberation, which occurred in a series of uprisings amongst Ndebele and Shona peoples against the white settlers in 1896–97, and in the Second Chimurenga, which is the term widely applied to the armed struggle that was conducted during the 1970s and which eventually resulted in Zimbabwe gaining independence in 1980. As we have seen, Nehanda features significantly in Korekore and Zezuru mythology. During both wars of liberation, mediums for Nehanda, and other spirits, became the 'voices' for *mhondoro*, and thus embodied a tradition that claimed an authoritative right to ownership of the land.

The Zezuru Nehanda should be distinguished from the daughter of Mutota in the Korekore tradition, but the two often are closely associated, so much so that some Korekore legends describe the head of Nehanda as residing along the Zambezi River and her feet as planted in the land of the Zezuru (Bourdillon, 1997: 274). This widespread belief enabled the medium Charwe, who claimed to be possessed by the spirit of Nehanda during the 1896–97 Shona uprising, in Bourdillon's (1997: 274) words, to receive 'the allegiance of a number of chiefs' and so 'to co-ordinate their resistance to European settlers'. Beach attempts to separate written historical accounts drawn largely from reports of Portuguese traders and explorers, from oral legends about Nehanda, which he maintains were intended to reinforce the king's authority in the Mutapa State. For example, he asserts that the story of the incestuous act between Nbedza and his sister Nehanda was told to justify the custom whereby the king's principal wife was always his own full-blooded sister (Beach, 1980: 96). Although incest was strictly forbidden in the society as a whole, this myth allowed the king to contravene normal cultural traditions thereby, in Beach's words, demonstrating his 'special status' (Beach, 1980: 96). Beach notes further that the name 'Nehanda' has been traced to a wide geographical area beyond that of the Mutapa State and thus may suggest a 'common source far back in the Shona past' (Beach, 1980: 314). This may explain, in part at least, why Charwe claimed to be possessed by the spirit of Nehanda. At any rate, it is clear that the Korekore version of the myth of Nehanda as a powerful ancestor spirit concerned with issues of land is connected to socio-historical circumstances surrounding the Mutapa kings in the seventeenth and eighteenth centuries. The Korekore account either spread as the geographical limits of the state expanded or, what is more likely, eventually merged with Zezuru legends about Nehanda, both traditions having derived from a more ancient source.

Little is known about Charwe, although Berens (1988: 293) speculates that she may originally have come from Dande, which would suggest why she adopted Nehanda as the *mhondoro* spirit who possessed her. Lan (1985: 6) argues that Charwe was from Mazoe, north of the current capital Harare, and thus was fully associated with the Zezuru tradition. We know that she first appeared in Zezuru regions near Mazoe, but Berens (1988: 293) says she may be linked to the present-day city of Chitungwiza, near Harare, which is the legendary home of the great spirit Chaminuka. Although precise details about her background are not known, there is little doubt that in popular opinion Charwe combined in her person the two strands of legends about Nehanda, the Korekore version of an original ancestor and the Zezuru account of an ancient, autochthonous ancestor, whose genealogy is conveyed in myths. In this way, she could draw on indigenous traditions to motivate resistance to the white settlers who were appropriating African lands for themselves. Charwe was executed by the colonial authorities in 1897, along with another medium, who claimed to be possessed of a spirit called Kagubi, about which very little is known (Bourdillon, 1997: 274). Before she was put to death, Charwe famously prophesied that her bones would rise again, a phrase which inspired another important medium of Nehanda during the Second Chimurenga (Lan, 1985: 6).

Lan claims that as the nationalist movement developed strength during the middle part of the twentieth century, the Korekore and Zezuru myths about Nehanda merged: 'In songs, in verse and in myth, Nehanda came to represent the inevitable but so-long awaited victory of the Shona over their oppressors.' As the two Shona traditions moved together, Nehanda became associated with Chaminuka, and eventually was described as the sister of the 'royal ancestor of the Zezuru peoples' (Lan, 1985: 6). Lan also notes that novelists, poets and political activists extolled Nehanda, along with Chaminuka, transforming them into symbols of a unified Shona history. Lan cites a poem first written in 1957 by Solomon Mutswairo, which contains the phrase: 'Where is our freedom, Nehanda? Won't you come down to help us?' Lan also refers to a poem written in 1958 by the nationalist leader, Herbert Chitepo, which asks tellingly: 'Where are our heroes of old? Where is Chaminuka and Nehanda? Where are our tribal spirits? (Lan, 1985: 6–7).[2] By the late 1960s, therefore, a tradition about Nehanda had been re-invented by Zimbabwean nationalists who used her story to create a unified tradition in support of the ancient authority of Shona founding ancestors.[3]

During the Second Chimurenga, guerrilla training camps were situated across the Zimbabwean border in Mozambique. The freedom fighters called one of the sectors in north eastern Zimbabwe in the Korekore region by the name Nehanda (For a description of the military operations in the area, see Turner, 1998: 21–5). In 1972, they discovered in that region an old woman claiming to be a medium of Nehanda, who formed part of a series of mediums in the area that were exercising a powerful influence over the people. Lan (1985: 147) reports that the fighters, at first for quite pragmatic reasons, used the mediums to assist in recruiting soldiers and to ensure the support of the people in the struggle. Bourdillon (1997: 276) adds that after the guerrillas had begun surreptitious activities in Dande, it became apparent to their leaders 'that the cult of lion spirits had been influential in rallying support' for their cause and that the mediums were assisting them by encouraging the people to 'keep a veil of strict secrecy over their operations'. Throughout the fighting, the mediums played important roles in facilitating communication between the people and the soldiers. In the meantime, the fighters themselves began to consult the mediums to seek their assistance in guiding troop movements and in providing protection against the enemy. One of T. Chiura's informants, a former freedom fighter, is reported as saying, 'spirit mediums helped fighting units of the guerrillas to be integrated into the fabric of society' which had the practical effect of enlisting the support of the

---

[2]   In 1961, the Zimbabwe African People's Union (ZAPU) was created under the leadership of Joshua Nkomo. In 1962, it was banned by the government and went underground. Divisions in the leadership over the appropriate strategy of opposition to the white government's increasingly oppressive measures developed within ZAPU resulting in the creation of another more militant movement, which took the name Zimbabwe African National Union (ZANU), amongst whose leaders included Herbert Chitepo, Ndabaningi Sithole and Robert Mugabe.

[3]   The beginning of the Second Chimurenga, or second war of liberation, officially is traced to a ZANU attack on white farms and electricity sources on 29 April 1969, near the town of Sinoia (present-day Chinhoyi). The beginning of the war in earnest, however, occurred when the military wing of ZANU, called the Zimbabwe African National Liberation Army (ZANLA) led an attack on the white-owned Altena Farm, located 150 kilometres north of Salisbury. At the same time, the army of ZAPU, the Zimbabwe People's Revolutionary Army (ZIPRA) was operating in the western regions of the country. ZANU and ZAPU formed an alliance, called the Patriotic Front, which pursued political and military objectives aimed at securing an independent majority government. Throughout the 1970s armed resistance increased, with many ZANLA forces operating from across the border with Mozambique, which had obtained independence in 1974 after a military coup had overthrown the Portuguese government in Lisbon.

people in providing basic requirements like food, clothing and blankets (Chiura, 1991: 97–8). Throughout this period, the importance of Nehanda, and her new medium, increased. Although she was too frail to become involved directly in the fighting, in order to protect her, the freedom fighters carried her from her home near Musengezi in the north-east to a camp called Chifombo, along the border between Mozambique and Zambia. From there, according to Berens (1988: 294), she inspired 'the new generation of freedom fighters'. She died at Chifombo in 1973, but her remains were returned to Zimbabwe for reburial after the war concluded.

The medium for Nehanda operating from Chifombo, of course, was just one among many mediums that were important in the liberation struggle of the 1970s, but her significance derived in part from the role Charwe had played as the first medium of Nehanda in the emerging national myth. Charwe's death and her promise to return meant that the medium for Nehanda during the Second Chimurenga had a kind of double authority. She could be regarded in one sense as the persistent voice of the *mhondoro* associated with the Korekore tradition, who in an evolving tradition had become merged into the Chaminuka myth as his sister. At the same time, the new spirit medium of Nehanda became linked in popular perception with Charwe, who promised that her bones would rise. This added a mysterious element to the Nehanda myth, and made the new Nehanda medium a voice that united the traditions of original ancestors directly with the first liberation struggle against the colonial invaders. For this reason, Nehanda not only inspired the guerrillas, but convinced them that their cause carried the full authority of Shona ancestral traditions and justified their armed resistance against the foreign invaders. That this was the case was confirmed by a song sung by the ZANU-PF Ideological Choir, which was broadcast over the Zimbabwean Broadcasting Corporation on the day independence was granted, 17 April 1980, and cited by Lan. The song begins: 'Grandmother Nehanda, you prophesied, Nehanda's bones resurrected, ZANU's spear caught their fire which was transformed into ZANU's gun, the gun which liberated our land' (Lan, 1985: 217).

After Independence, the attitude of the new ZANU government towards Indigenous Religions changed, as Marja Spierenburg (2004: 37) notes: 'The government tried to end the *Mhondoro*'s political role' (37). This view has been supported by Ngwabi Bhebe and Terence Ranger (1995: 24) and has been confirmed in my own field studies, about which I have written previously, conducted amongst the Karanga in 1992 in the region of Chief Chingoma, near Mberengwa (Cox, 1996b: 160–63). The chief's spirit medium complained to me in an interview that decisions rightfully belonging to the chief, such as where to build roads or authorization for new mines, were being usurped by representatives of ZANU-PF. My informant indicated that the severe drought of 1991–92 was a direct result of the anger of the chief's ancestor spirits at the government's disregard for traditional authority. No issue over the last century has been more closely linked to such authority as that of land, which is precisely why I was told that the chief, not political party appointees, needed to have final approval over where to build roads or establish mines. Although there are many reasons the Mugabe government moved slowly on land-related issues after 1990, including foreign economic and political influence (Palmer 1990: 177–9), it was the failure to act decisively on land resettlement that led the war veterans to take events into their own hands in what now is widely dubbed the 'Third Chimurenga', described by many as the culmination of over one hundred years of fighting to regain indigenous land rights. It is here too that we find the longstanding influence of Indigenous Religions re-surfacing in post-independence Zimbabwe.

Indigenous Religions in the Third Chimurenga⁴

The current political and economic crises confronting Zimbabwe, which have been reported widely by the Western media and have resulted in the suspension of Zimbabwe from the Commonwealth, can be traced to the decision of President Robert Mugabe in late 1997 to accede to the demands of the National Liberation War Veterans' Association for financial compensation and tracts of land (Harold-Barry, 2004: 271). The government allocated to all war veterans a one-off cash payment and began monthly pension payments, while at the same time promising them a large share of land recently acquired for resettlement. According to Hammar and Raftopoulos (2003: 7), 'these commitments placed an unsustainable burden on the economy, while giving clear signals as to the regime's strategic preferences'. During 1998 and 1999, the economy declined dramatically producing mass anti-government strikes in urban areas. At the same time, the war veterans, buoyed by their success at lobbying the government and presumably frustrated by the slow pace of land redistribution, embarked on a series of spontaneous invasions of white-owned commercial farms. Political momentum for a more democratic constitution also accelerated in 1998 under the influence of the National Constitutional Assembly, described by Hammar and Raftopoulos (2003: 9) as 'a popular and powerful alliance of some 96 civil society organizations including church groups, trades unions, human rights organizations, and student and intellectual groups'. In response, the government held a referendum in February 2000 on its version of a new constitution, which was denounced by the NCA and the opposition party it and the Zimbabwean Confederation of Trades Unions (ZCTU) had spawned, the Movement for Democratic Change (MDC), which claimed that the government's version was a smokescreen aimed at inhibiting democratic reforms rather than enabling them.

When the voters in the referendum rejected the government's new constitution, Mugabe's rule was threatened seriously for the first time since independence in 1980. With a parliamentary election due in June 2000, ZANU-PF faced a realistic prospect of defeat by the opposition MDC. What followed is well documented: white-owned commercial farms suffered systematic invasions by war veterans, who, with tacit approval from the government and the police, committed acts of violence against white farmers and their black farm workers (Alexander, 2003: 100–101). As the election approached, the violence spread beyond farms to include 'widespread attacks on actual or suspected members of the opposition MDC' (Hammar and Raftopoulos, 2003: 11). ZANU-PF narrowly won the elections, claiming 62 seats to 57 for the MDC. Citing a report compiled shortly after the election, Eldred Masunungure (2004: 180) notes that in general there was an urban-rural split with 'most of the opposition to the ruling party' coming 'from the working and middle-classes in the urban areas while its support was largely from the poorer and less educated rural electorate'. Serious doubt, nevertheless, was cast by the international community concerning the fairness of the elections in the light of reports of murder, torture, rape and intimidation of voters (Raftopoulos, 2003: 232; Raftopoulos, 2004: 13). The MDC launched court appeals contesting the results in 37 constituencies in which ZANU-PF had been declared the winner. As David Harold-Barry notes (2004: 269): 'Without the 30 unelected seats [guaranteed by the constitution to the winning party] ZANU PF would have found it almost impossible to govern.'

---

⁴   This section contains portions, in a slightly revised form, of my previously published article on the question of religious intolerance in Zimbabwe (Cox, 2005a: 35–48).

The history of traditional rights to the land and its expropriation by white settlers during the colonial period formed the background for a great deal of the rhetoric during the election, and explains to some extent why the rural population continued to support the Mugabe government. The relevance of Indigenous Religions to these series of events has been expressed forcefully by Emmanuel Manzungu (2004: 66) of the University of Zimbabwe, who argues that the land resettlement programme since 2000 (under the government's 'Fast Track' Programme) 'has tended to claim the endorsement of black ancestral spirits, with reference to the heroes and heroines of the First and Second Chimurengas'. He adds: 'This explains why the programme was dubbed the Third Chimurenga.' Hammar and Raftopoulos note (2003: 18): 'The colonial heritage of often violent land appropriations and dispossessions, and resistance to them, has engraved itself deeply into Zimbabwe's inter-related physical, political and psychic landscapes.' When the government came under intense pressure between 1998 and 2000, by focusing on the longstanding problem of land resettlement, the war veterans revived the anti-colonial and patriotic fervour which had motivated the liberation war of the 1970s. It also drew into the picture once again the spirit mediums, who claimed to be possessed by the spirits of those killed during the liberation struggle of the 1970s, but who had never been buried according to customary practices.

I learned first-hand about the growing number of spirit possessions by the war dead during field visits I conducted in Zimbabwe in July and August 2004. I was hosted by a headmaster of a secondary school, in a rural region approximately 25 kilometres from the centre of the town of Mount Darwin and approximately 60 kilometres from the border with Mozambique. This is an important area, since, as we have seen, during the liberation struggle ZANLA forces, which were based in the Tete region of Mozambique, engaged Rhodesian Front troops in armed combat. In 1977, Rhodesian troops crossed the border in the notorious battle of Chimoio in which up to 1000 young Zimbabwean trainees were killed. During my visit I interviewed the headmaster and his brother, a businessman from Harare, both of whom had witnessed possession rituals quite recently in the region.[5] The businessman informed me that spirit mediums were becoming possessed by spirits of war veterans who had not yet received a traditional burial, such as the victims of the Chimoio massacre. He noted that recently mass graves had been discovered in the Mount Darwin region. Spirit mediums under possession would go to the graves, identify the bones of a particular person killed in the fighting, name the person, indicate the home area of the person and while still under possession accompany the bones home until they were buried according to tradition at the homestead. The headmaster explained that when a spirit medium becomes possessed by the spirit of a fighter killed in the war, the spirit identifies his own bones, which sometimes have been buried in a mass grave. He said that the medium picks this bone and that bone and then puts them together. He described a ritual that he had observed where eight mediums were possessed at the same time. They referred to each other by their military ranks. Orders were given as if in a battalion. He asserted that the spirits of those killed in the war were rising up because the aims of the war to return the land to the people had not yet been achieved. The war was still ongoing until the spirits of the war dead had been settled and the land belonging to their ancestors had been returned. He claimed that the war veterans, many of whom had themselves become mediums for the spirits of the dead

---

[5]   The interview took place on 31 July 2004 in Mount Darwin. I have chosen not to use the names of those I interviewed due to the current political situation in Zimbabwe.

liberators, were very powerful and that the government had no choice but to listen to them.

Later, still in the same region, I interviewed a war veteran, who explained to me the process whereby the remains of the war dead are identified and authenticated.[6] He said that a member of a family somewhere in Zimbabwe, who knows that a soldier from his family was killed in the fighting in northeast Zimbabwe or Mozambique, becomes possessed by the spirit of the dead soldier. The medium is led by the spirit to Mount Darwin where he or she meets with the mediums in charge of identifying the bones found in mass graves. The medium of the dead soldier becomes possessed and then is accompanied by local mediums to the site of the burials, where he identifies his own bones. A possessed person may go to sites other than the mass graves because many of the fighters were killed and buried throughout the region in shallow graves. Under possession, the medium identifies his bones, puts them together and then brings them back to Mount Darwin where they are held in the local police station. A local identification committee then certifies that these are the correct bones of the person identified by the medium. Once certified, they are carried back to the homestead of the deceased, while the person is still possessed, and then buried properly. In this way, the deceased takes his place as an ancestor who can be appealed to by his descendants for protection and guidance. I was told by another war veteran during the same interview that the mediums in Mount Darwin become possessed by the leaders or officers in the regiments. These coax the spirits of the dead to come out and possess a family member somewhere in Zimbabwe. He explained that the war had been fought for land. Up until 2000, very little progress had been made in land resettlement. The spirits of the dead war heroes were becoming impatient. The war, he claimed, had not been finished. The war would continue until the land was reclaimed and the dead settled.

The events referred to during my interviews in the Mount Darwin region have only recently come to light. The *Herald*, Zimbabwe's daily state-supported newspaper, reported on 16 July 2004 that 'the Ministry of Home Affairs will soon send officials to investigate the discovery of more than 19 mass graves containing remains of those who were massacred by Rhodesian special forces in Mount Darwin during the Second Chimurenga'. The article noted that the mass graves, which contain the remains of over 5000 people, were discovered in September 2003. The writer of the article adds that the Mount Darwin community wants 'the Government to consult spirit mediums and conduct ceremonies to appease the spirits of the fallen heroes'.[7] The decision of the Minister to investigate the situation in Mount Darwin followed a report that appeared in *The Herald* a few days earlier on 10 July 2004 under the headline: 'Remains of Liberation War Fighter Exhumed'. The article, written by Tsitsi Matope, outlines her experience of entering a 30 metre deep mine where remains of a liberation war fighter were exhumed by a spirit medium and a village elder. The bones had been identified by the medium as a freedom fighter from Murewa who 'is suspected to have been thrown into the pit alive'.[8] The mine, which is situated around 28 kilometres from Mount Darwin centre, is reported by Tsitsi Matope as containing hundreds of bodies 'suspected to be of freedom fighters and war collaborators'.

---

6 This interview occurred on 14 August 2004 in Mount Darwin.
7 *The Herald* (Harare), 16 July 2004. 'State to Probe Discovery of Mass Graves'.
8 *The Herald* (Harare), 10 July 2004. 'Remains of Liberation War Fighter Exhumed'.

The reporter recounts her experience of accompanying five people into the mine shaft, including the spirit medium and the village elder. When she finally descended to the mine floor, she could see human skeletons near the wall. 'It appeared scores of bodies had been piled on that section, which was another wing off the main tunnel, judging by the huge amount of remains.' They proceeded further into the mine and eventually came to the remains of the freedom fighter believed to be from Murewa. The reporter then recounts what occurred:

> The six people stood close to the pile of remains while the spirit medium carefully collected the bones for about 20 minutes. He then went into a trance while he conducted some rituals to inform the deceased that he had come to take him for a proper burial. He then instructed those accompanying him not to disturb a spirit (*mudzimu*) which was lying on another dark section of the tunnel where some unusual sounds could be heard. Someone whispered that the sounds resembled that of a big snake.

After a rather tortuous ascent out of the mine with bats flying towards the light and the sound of the snake reverberating, the group was met at the entrance to the mine by 'people possessed by the spirits of the fallen heroes asking to be exhumed from the pits so as to receive a decent burial'. When they saw the remains of the freedom fighter from Murewa, 'they burst into liberation war songs while some cried out loud'. One of those possessed was a 14-year-old girl who claimed the previous month to have identified the bones of her brother who had been killed during the war. The reporter saw her going through drills, marching like a soldier and smoking *mbanje* (cannabis). One of the possessed, a woman of around twenty years, called herself by her dead brother's name. The possessed, who were singing and dancing around the remains of the exhumed body, imitated a freedom fighter holding a gun. Later, one of those possessed, calling himself the commander, 'ordered them to be quiet and be disciplined since the body of their colleague had been retrieved'. The article quotes another spirit medium as declaring:

> The fallen heroes were not informed that the war was over. As far as they are concerned, the war is not yet over as no ceremonies were conducted when the war ended. The problem is no one is taking this seriously and as long as the spirits are not appeased and brought back home there will not be any peace in this country.

It has become clear from these recent events that a direct connection can be drawn between Indigenous Religions in Zimbabwe, in the form of spirit mediums, *mhondoro* spirits and *midzimu*, and the land resettlement programme. These relationships, which were crucial in the first two Zimbabwean struggles for independence, have now been reclaimed by the ZANU-PF government to coincide with the aims of the war veterans. This application of legendary ancestral authority, which was used by the guerrillas to motivate the armed resistance to colonial rule during the 1970s, now has been combined with the ancient and deeply embedded local custom of settling the dead on their ancestral lands. As we have seen, so long as the dead lie buried in mass graves, their spirits remain restless and troublesome. When this is combined with the government's failure to fulfil the aim of the armed struggle to win back the land, in traditional belief, the unsettled spirits pose an extraordinary threat to social stability throughout Zimbabwe. Initially, this religiously inspired interpretation of current events was seized upon by war veterans to apply pressure on the government to implement its longstanding commitment to land redistribution, but subsequently it has been adopted into the government's own political rhetoric. The role of Indigenous Religions in the Third Chimurenga thus testifies to their lasting significance in the lives of ordinary Zimbabweans, and at the same time demonstrates how they continue to exercise a powerful influence within the government's emerging political and economic policies.

Conclusions about Indigenous Religions in Zimbabwe

We have seen in this chapter that Indigenous Religion amongst the Korekore corresponds to traditional ways of relating to the land and the life that the land, fertilized by seasonal rains, sustain. We have also seen that the tradition depends on an authority, rooted in hierarchical and patriarchal systems, which the people acknowledge by respecting socially constructed boundaries and rules, and which they experience through the oral transmission of stories, ritual performances and particularly through spirit mediums of territorial and local ancestors, who facilitate communication between the seen and the unseen worlds. It is clear from the history I have outlined in this chapter that the people continue to pass on their traditions and customs authoritatively from generation to generation, and adhere to them closely in order to ensure communal well-being and to avoid calamities and misfortunes. What is most significant, particularly as we have seen in the cases of both the Korekore and Zezuru, is that the transmission of authoritative tradition does not mean Indigenous Religions are somehow stuck in the past without continued relevance to contemporary events. On the contrary, the imaginative ways that so many parties to the struggles to regain the land since 1896 have responded to various political and economic events provide evidence of the astounding adaptability of Indigenous Religions throughout Zimbabwe.

Factors consistent with my prior definition of an indigenous religion emerge from the details of this chapter. The first relates to the idea that to be indigenous is to belong to a place. We have seen from the outset that land has been central to the meaning of being indigenous in Zimbabwe. This has not meant that the people claim in every case to be autochthonous, although the importance of the chthonic spirits has been demonstrated in various cases cited amongst the Korekore and Zezuru, whose notable ancestors now seem to have merged with original ancestors into quasi-legendary founding figures. Still, most Shona traditions acknowledge a migration story, which suggests that according to tradition the land was conquered, and thus their ancestors first occupied the land before they came to own it. Traditional ownership of the land does not correspond to Western capitalist notions of a tract of land belonging to one principal person, but, as Bourdillon has noted, has relational connotations to the chief, village head or head of the family, and thus in each case to ancestors. It is for this reason, that in traditional Shona society, the whole community is intended to prosper, not just individuals, and if one individual appears to attain an advantage at the expense of others, witchcraft or other nefarious methods are suspected. To own the land, in this sense, means that the people who live on it share in its productivity and adhere to the authority of the person around whom they have clustered, including, and perhaps primarily, that person's ancestor spirits.

Kinship obviously plays a central role in the entire socio-religious order I have described. This is not contradicted by the hierarchical system whereby the chief governs over a wide territory, including those who are not part of his extended family. As the descendant of royal ancestors, the chief represents an ancestral tradition bound by his own kin, who exercises authority on the basis of that inheritance. The village head also leads various extended families, some of whom are not part of his own clan but, again, he occupies a place in the hierarchy following a lineage system. At the level of the extended family, the immediate kinship relations prevail, but, of course, ancestors play incontestable roles at every stage from the chief downwards. In this sense, we find in Zimbabwe kinship dictating location and relationship, both of which depend critically on sustaining proper ritual contact with ancestors. This is not strictly a local expression of religion, since today the *mhondoro* shrines are fully regional cults, with people coming from the whole chiefdom to consult the territorial ancestors. We have seen also that some shrines are devoted to chthonic spirits that, in extreme cases of drought, attract representatives from various chieftaincies covering a wide area. Yet, despite the regional nature within the interconnected hierarchical system, the focus is entirely local in that the concerns relate to a chief who traditionally owns the land and to those who live on the land, extending mythically to the founding ancestors. One is never converted into such a religion, since it is achieved as a matter of birth and by connection to the ancestral traditions.

Contemporary events might suggest that the various forms of Indigenous Religions in Zimbabwe have become globalized by engaging with complex economic markets and by transforming themselves to accommodate international pressure towards democratic governance. Of course, the creation of a state called Zimbabwe resulted from widespread international involvement both within Africa and beyond, particularly because of the British colonial heritage. The association of spirits like Nehanda and Chaminuka with the modern state of Zimbabwe implies a certain manipulation of the tradition to fit an invented national myth. In this sense, the new Zimbabwean state might be likened to any nation which celebrates its heroes and has developed inspirational stories about its founders. I would argue, nonetheless, that the roots of the story revert to widespread and genuine beliefs held throughout the population that connect their most local ancestors to the traditions of the founding ancestors in a chain of communication that is re-enforced ritually throughout the country to this day. Quasi-historical legends and ancestral traditions thus may have proved useful for many purposes, but their various applications in modern Zimbabwe do not contradict the fact that they have been conceived and nurtured through longstanding indigenous ways of life.

I conclude, therefore, that what I have described in this chapter refers to what I have defined as indigenous. It is a very short step from this to add that I have also been describing what is also quite evidently a religion, since the entire system is based on tradition and authority, both of which are passed on from generation to generation through story and ritual, and confirmed by the deeply held beliefs that dictate how communities are organized and how their customary rules are enforced. The authority of ancestors, with the age-old traditions they represent, from chiefs to family heads, thus lends itself very closely to Hervieu-Léger's definition of religion. We also find quite central to religion in Zimbabwe postulated beliefs in and experiences of non-falsifiable alternate realities in the form of numerous spirits that interact with and influence community life. The spirits are alternate in the sense that I have used the word as interactive with the ordinary, not as alternative to ordinary experience. The spirits move in and out of ordinary experience in a mutual interchange between the two. This does not mean that an indigenous believer in Zimbabwe does not know the difference between one type of experience, a religious one, and other types of experience which are quite ordinary. Otherwise, rituals would not involve such intricate preparations to set them off from other types of experience, nor would mediums operate as quite normal human beings in most aspects of life but become quite other when possessed by a spirit, including wearing ritual items, such as a black cloth or headgear made of eagle feathers. Ancestors also clearly live in an alternate state in that they no longer have a body, nor can it be said precisely where they reside. Moreover, their powers, although corresponding to responsibilities they held in life, are magnified, and they now have the capacity to do what they could not do in life, such as bringing rain, inflicting illness or warding off the invasion of witches. The ancestor world thus is alternate, but not different from the intentions or concerns of those who bear similar responsibilities in ordinary life.

Preliminary Conclusions from the Alaskan and Zimbabwean Case Studies

Quite obviously, numerous differences between the Indigenous Religion of the Korekore in Zimbabwe and that of the Yupiit in Alaska can be noted, evidenced in the first instance by the fact that traditional Yupiit society was never structured according to a hierarchical system nor did Yupiit ancestors intervene in daily life once they had been transported ritually to the land of the dead. Sharp differences between the environments on which each group depended for survival also affected religious beliefs and practices, with the Yupiit traditionally being semi-nomadic hunters and fishermen while the Korekore largely worked as agriculturalists and pastoralists. The alternate realities in both cases were seen by the people as responding to subsistence needs, indicating why the Yupiit had intricate rituals honouring the bladders of seals and the Korekore performed regular rituals to the *mhondoro* spirits for rain. The histories of both societies also represent quite different responses to colonialism and to the religion brought by those who invaded their lands.

Despite these and many other fundamental differences, both the Yupiit and Korekore fit into the category Indigenous Religions. Both societies extol the land; that is, they belong to a place; they are localized and kinship-related, although in Zimbabwe locality and kinship are expressed also at regional levels through a history of paramount chiefs. In Alaska, ancestors live in and through their namesakes and have only a vague identity apart from their continued existence in their living descendants. Yet, in both cases, ancestors play fundamental roles in carrying forward their respective traditions by buttressing the authority of social obligations. In addition, both societies emphasize the need for a medium between the alternate world of spirits and ordinary life; in Alaska, this is the shaman (*angulkuq*), and in Zimbabwe the spirit medium (*svikiro*). Although the shaman and the medium operate quite differently and relate to vastly contrasting spirit worlds, both indicate how alternate realities engage with and influence ordinary social existence. In other words, I have tried to show in both cases how the term indigenous applies as belonging to a place, as localized, as kinship-orientated and, finally, as ancestor-related. I have also indicated in what ways both transmit their traditions about postulated non-falsifiable alternate realities authoritatively and in ways that dictate rigidly enforced social rules and boundaries. I have reached these conclusions not on the basis of essentialist presuppositions nor because I am employing a quasi-theological definition of religion, but because I have applied a quite pragmatic and empirical working definition to both cases. This method enables me to distinguish an indigenous religion from other religions and serves more broadly as a useful heuristic device in the comparative study of religions generally.

Chapter 7

Indigenous Religions and the Debate over Primitivism

In the first two chapters of this book, I traced the history of the academic study of Indigenous Religions and noted how the category today has become accepted widely in academic teaching and how it is being employed in university textbooks with increasing frequency. I observed that in many cases the term merely has been substituted for earlier unacceptable usages ranging from 'savage' through 'primitive' to 'primal', implying that those who use it retain notions of philosophical essentialism, which at the very least cannot be supported empirically, and in many cases conceal theological assumptions. In Chapter 3, I sought to rectify these persistent errors by providing a scientific definition of indigenous as localized and kinship-related, which I followed in Chapter 4 by my dual definition of religion as transmitting an authoritative tradition about postulated non-falsifiable alternate realities. In the last two chapters, I have demonstrated how this pragmatic approach to the study of Indigenous Religions can be applied in quite disparate geographical and cultural settings by examining first the significant life cycle rituals of the Yupiit peoples of Alaska, largely as they were practised up to 1930, and then by focusing on the dynamic and adaptive character of Indigenous Religions amongst the Shona-speaking Korekore and Zezuru groups in Zimbabwe. If I have succeeded in demonstrating through these case studies that the category Indigenous Religions can be used in academic circles today without employing earlier forms of theological essentialism, I will have overcome the intellectual hazards created by the 'world religions paradigm'.

In this chapter, I bring my overall argument to a conclusion by contributing to three inter-related debates around the recent revival of Western primitivism. The first, which has been voiced by Armin Geertz, implies that the study of Indigenous Religions entails a preoccupation, similar to that maintained by late nineteenth-century anthropologists, with the exotic and unusual. If this charge were to prove credible, it would mean that my efforts to place Indigenous Religions on the curriculum of academic departments, rather than reflecting progressive thinking, actually would revert to outdated Western notions of superiority bordering on racism. Another version of the primitivism objection derives from the contention expressed by Geertz and Jan Platvoet that the study of Indigenous Religions reflects an 'insider' preoccupation with concerns that are not primarily academic, as evidenced by 'new age' spiritualities like neo-shamanism or, at a different level, by the positive re-evaluation of the term animism advocated by Graham Harvey and some of his associates. A third way that the study of Indigenous Religions is increasingly regarded with suspicion derives from the argument advanced by Aidan Campbell that by emphasizing locality and kinship, indigenous societies are defined strictly in terms of ethnicity, which quite dangerously encourages 'tribal' divisions while at the same time revives the stereotypical image of indigenous peoples as basic or primitive and hence as helpless in the face of global interventions. In the sections that follow, I describe each of these critical objections to the study Indigenous Religions in detail before defending my own position against them point by point.

The 'Primitivism' Debate: Armin Geertz's Critique

The debate about Indigenous Religions as a contemporary form of primitivism has been advanced by Armin Geertz, a specialist in the Hopi peoples of North America and a scholar of religions at Aarhus University in Denmark. As I noted in the Introduction to this book, Geertz (2004: 37–70) wrote a highly significant article entitled 'Can we move beyond primitivism?' for Jacob Olupona's edited volume entitled *Beyond Primitivism*. Geertz's sub-title to his paper is perhaps more important than the main title: 'On recovering the indigenes of indigenous religions in the academic study of religion.' Geertz acknowledges that the term primitivism, although associated negatively with nineteenth-century ideas of cultural evolution and the superiority of Western civilization, also has a positive, but romantic, side where people in Western society look at the 'primitive' as a pure and innocent form of humanity. In religious studies, the noted scholar Mircea Eliade, between 1950 and 1980, promoted a romantic view of what he called 'archaic man' as a legitimate academic category (see Cox, 2006: 183–7), which Geertz associates with 'cultural primitivism' and defines, following Lovejoy and Boas, as 'the belief of men living in a relatively highly evolved and complex cultural condition that a life far simpler and less sophisticated in some or in all respects is a more desirable life' (Geertz, 2004: 38; see also Lovejoy and Boas, 1965). Eliade puts it this way: 'By reactualizing sacred history, by imitating the divine behaviour, man puts and keeps himself close to the gods – that is, in the real and the significant' (Eliade, 1987: 202). According to Geertz, although this defines the primitive in chronological terms, that is, as living in an earlier, more innocent time, its most defining characteristic is that it idealizes the exotic, so that by studying indigenous people today, we are enabled to see what life was like before it was infected by the errors and complexities of modernity. In this sense, the study of indigenous peoples is rooted, according to Geertz (2004: 39), in the '*attraction of the exotic*' (emphasis his).

Geertz then outlines the history of positive and negative forms of primitivism, drawing attention in particular to the impact of Darwinian ideas of biological evolution on concepts of social progress in the West. I have already shown in earlier chapters how the academic study of 'primitive' religions developed against a backdrop of nineteenth century attitudes, and have argued that some of the most outlandish exponents of evolutionary thought even doubted that Africans were human. Geertz emphasizes that in the study of religions, as I noted in the cases of W. H. Ridgeway and J. G. Frazer in Chapter 1, the romantic notion prevailed over the more negative connotations associated with social evolution. What Geertz (2004: 50) calls 'the longings of the Romantic for another time or another place, a distant paradise, or a future utopia' defined many of the central concerns of late nineteenth-century thinkers and formed the basis on which 'the study of religion … flourished'. He adds that such notions remain with us today by motivating much recent interest in the academic study of Indigenous Religions.

Geertz follows this historical survey by attacking the assumptions used to distinguish indigenous from other types of societies, which he claims depend on artificial antitheses constructed by academics. Scholars have emphasized that indigenous cultures are oral as opposed to literary, that they are rural rather than urban, that their way of thinking is dictated by tradition and not by purposive action (Geertz, 2004: 51). After dismissing such polarities between the indigenous and the modern, Geertz claims that the category indigenous actually is vacuous and that its use cannot be justified 'empirically or theoretically' (2004: 51). This is because what scholars mean when they refer to indigenous 'names a category of cultures that do not in fact exist, that do not have characteristics that are not shared by all other cultures and peoples, and that therefore is of little intellectual or analytical advantage' (2004: 51). This can be shown, for example, by noting that small-scale societies exist in urban centres in Europe and that the kinship systems of many people in the West are 'extremely simple in comparison with the highly complex kinship system of the technologically simple Australian Aborigines' (2004: 51). Geertz goes on to suggest that there is no connection between complexity within societies and literacy, as can be demonstrated by 'the highly organized political structures of the Yoruba and the Dahomey' (2004: 51). In other words, the ways that indigenous peoples have been defined in scholarly literature cannot be justified when societies around the world are compared objectively.

This implies that the primary reason for separating out indigenous societies for special attention by academics is ideological or at least value-laden. A sense of worth is assigned to various stages of culture, either in terms of the romantic, who values the idealized notion of the primitive, or the evolutionist, who regards the indigenous as less developed and in need of the benefits offered by higher forms of civilization. Citing Francis L.K. Hsu, former Chair of Anthropology at Northwestern University, Geertz notes that 'the most troublesome meaning of the term "primitive" is connected with various shades of inferiority' (Geertz, 2004: 51; see also Hsu, 1964: 169–78). Hsu largely is referring to those who rate Western values higher than so-called indigenous ones, but the principle of assigning value to cultural acts is the same in both the romantic and evolutionary theories. Rather than describing societies on the basis of scientific evidence, therefore, we are led by Geertz to conclude that the study of Indigenous Religions veils hidden presuppositions, which are neither empirically testable nor philosophically defensible. Rather, they often conceal irrational notions that, when brought into the open, differ little from uninformed prejudices. This becomes clear from a series of questions posed by Hsu:

> Is the custom of sending children to boarding school or to summer camp more or less primitive than that of continuous parental supervision of the children at home? Is a totalitarian system of government more or less primitive than tribal rule or benevolent despotism? Is a religious system based upon monotheism with a history of heresy persecution, witch hunting, and holy crusades more or less primitive than another with a *laissez-faire* attitude toward different creeds and ritual practices?' (cited by Geertz, 2004: 51).

It is clear that Hsu is referring to the old-style Darwinian view of the primitive which social evolutionists have used to assert the superiority of Western culture. Geertz contrasts this with positive forms of contemporary primitivism, or what he calls 'neo-primitivism', which he says comprises a wide range of movements in modern society, including neo-shamanism, the Eliadian tradition in the History of Religions at the University of Chicago, postmodern primitivism expressed in recent art and theatre and feminist movements. He concludes that it is not possible to eradicate such ideas altogether since this 'would involve struggling against massive tides of general cultural values and historical contingencies around the globe' (2004: 61). Of course, the old-style negative view of the primitive largely has been left behind, but the romantic attachment to the primitive remains rooted in Western thinking, thereby perpetuating a distorted notion of indigenous cultures. If we are to overcome neo-primitivism, therefore, it must result from a frontal attack on romantic, idealized characterizations of indigenous societies. This will come, Geertz (2004: 62–3) argues, only through an academic re-commitment to the 'Enlightenment Project', by which he means 'a celebration of what characterizes us as humans, namely critical rationality'. This requires bringing to consciousness the hidden prejudices buried within romantic notions of primitive societies as preserving 'values lost in some mythical past' and by challenging inaccurate or meaningless distinctions between indigenous cultures and the rest of the world (2004: 62).

J.G. Platvoet and the Charge of Primitivism in the Writings of Graham Harvey

Geertz's criticism of neo-primitivism disguised as the study of Indigenous Religions has been advanced by the Dutch scholar of religions, J.G. Platvoet, who accuses Graham Harvey of exemplifying just this current trend in religious studies through his many publications on Indigenous Religions to which I referred in the Introduction to this book. If Platvoet's application of Geertz's argument to Harvey's work is accurate, it serves as a severe indictment against the most prolific contemporary exponent of the study of Indigenous Religions in academic teaching and research. In effect, it would mean that Harvey is guilty on two counts. First, he has embedded a romantic notion of the indigenous into the study of religions, and by so doing has distorted indigenous cultures even more powerfully than have been done by more overt racist notions derived from outdated theories of social Darwinism. Second, he has quite inaccurately imposed distinctions, in an Eliadean fashion, between the indigenous and the non-indigenous by contrasting an indigenous person as 'belonging to a place' with a modern human who in a globalized world suffers from a sense of rootlessness (see Eliade, 1987: 202–5).

Platvoet's comments appear in a review article written for the *Bulletin* of the African Association for the Study of Religions (2004: 47–52), in which he discusses Olupona's *Beyond Primitivism* (2004), and three of Graham Harvey's edited or co-edited books, *Indigenous Religions: A Companion* (2000), *Indigenous Religious Musics* (Ralls-MacLeod and Harvey, 2000) and *Readings in Indigenous Religions* (2002). Platvoet argues that these books, taken together, raise three important issues: (1) to what extent a reflexive methodology aids the study Indigenous Religions; (2) what 'traits' distinguish Indigenous Religions from other religions of the world; (3) the significance of rapid changes in the contemporary world on the persistence and shape of Indigenous Religions. In his discussion of Olupona's volume, Platvoet (2004: 49) calls Geertz's contribution 'the focal article' in the entire book, since it traces the history of 'primitivist concepts in Western scholarship in indigenous religions' and because it demonstrates that primitivism 'continues till this present day'. When he considers Harvey's volumes, Platvoet accuses Harvey (2004: 52) of pursuing 'his own agenda' defined by his 'partisan interest in indigenous religions and modern neo-paganism'. Rather than studying Indigenous Religions in a rational way, following Geertz's call for a re-commitment by academics to the Enlightenment Project, according to Platvoet, Harvey becomes an advocate for indigenous people by promoting 'joyous participation' in their religious activities and by aiding them in their struggles as 'the First Nations of the Fourth World Movement' (2004: 48). It is here that Platvoet reaches his most biting criticism of Harvey by accusing him of exemplifying 'the "new primitivist" approaches which Armin Geertz criticised' (2004: 52).

Taken by themselves, Platvoet's criticisms may sound rather placid, but when they are placed into the context of Geertz's stinging attack on the romantic and unacademic portrayal of Indigenous Religions by neo-primitivist scholars of religion, the depth of his charges against Harvey becomes evident. Indeed, their significance was not missed by Harvey, who replied in the next issue of the *AASR Bulletin* that 'the allegation that my work clearly pushes the new primitivist approaches ... is both insulting and damaging to my work and that of colleagues participating in it' (Harvey, 2004: 38). He denies that the subject matter in any of the books reviewed by Platvoet deals with 'primitive' peoples or their religions. He objects further that neither he nor the contributors to his volumes were concerned to idealize the past, but instead they focused on 'contemporary or recent cultural and religious self-expressions among indigenous people' (2004: 38). Finally, he denies that he is partisan towards contemporary Pagans, despite having written about them. He then switches tactics by confronting Geertz's assumption, which presumably Platvoet also shares, that 'critical rationality' defines the only methodology appropriate to genuine academic research. Harvey counters that such 'Cartesian versions of modernity', rather than being 'globally applicable' are probably nothing more 'than a Western/European tribal view of and approach to the world' (2004: 38). He asserts that his edited books 'demonstrate that similar issues are debated among scholars of North American indigenous religions as among those interested in Oceanic and African indigenous religions' (2004: 38). The positive contributions of his volumes to promoting understanding of indigenous peoples and their religions thus are demeaned by Platvoet's 'unhelpful allegation of primitivism' (2004: 39). If we separate the emotional response of an offended author from the actual allegations against his edited volumes, we find emerging a fundamental philosophical difference between what might be regarded as an empirical, neutral approach to the study of religions, as advocated by Geertz and Platvoet, and one that includes the perspectives of insiders and embraces the self-reflective argument, in the words of David Hufford (1999: 294), that 'observations are all made from somewhere'.

Aidan Campbell: 'Modern Primitivism' and the African as Victim

I find further support for the incisive arguments against the recent interest in the indigenous advanced by Geertz in a book by Aidan Campbell, entitled *Western Primitivism: African Ethnicity*. Campbell's book was published in 1997 by the internationally respected publisher Cassell (now a part of the Continuum group) at a time when he was convener of ethnic studies for the London-based research group Africa Direct. Before analysing his argument in depth, it is important to put Campbell and the organisation with which he is identified into context. Africa Direct, according to SourceWatch, is a 'think-tank with close links to the LM [Living Marxism] Group'.[1] Africa Direct sponsored a conference in 1997 to discuss the genocide in Rwanda, in which, again according to SourceWatch, 'in contrast to mainstream

---

[1] www.sourcewatch.org/index.php?title=LM_group.

thinking, the refusal to recognize that genocide occurred in 1994 was characteristic of the discourse at the conference'.[2] The Living Marxism Group is described by SourceWatch as a 'loose collection of individuals and organizations characterized by an anti-environmentalist, apparently libertarian ideology' that 'opposes all restrictions on business, science and technology, especially biotechnology'. Its members often employ pseudonyms, seemingly to allow them to operate in different settings and to disguise the fact that they belong to 'a relatively small ideological clique'. Aidan Campbell also goes by the name Andrew Clarkson. These associations are not enough for us to dismiss many of Campbell's compelling arguments, but they do indicate why we need to treat his analysis of ethnicity with a certain amount of caution. It is also relevant that SourceWatch is a project of the Center for Media and Democracy, which itself propagates a political perspective aimed at exposing front groups and what it regards as distortions in the media derived from government or corporate sources. The intense interest of such ideologically motivated groups in ethnicity confirms the politically sensitive nature of discussions surrounding the meaning of 'indigenous'.

Campbell argues that the recent positive attitudes towards the 'primitive', prevalent in the West as a whole and exemplified by the spate of Western volunteers working in exotic places for non-governmental organizations (NGOs), reflect a romantic notion that stresses the importance of locality and ethnic origins, but in a way that is wholly consistent with contemporary Western social values and underlying racist notions. Campbell (1997: 17) notes that 'primitivism celebrates weakness and underdevelopment as being more humane than the rugged entrepreneur of the 1980s or the racist thug'. He (1997: 17) adds that the interest in indigeneity in Western society has its roots in primitive art, influenced by Gauguin and Picasso, and in literature following seminal works like Huxley's *Brave New World* and Golding's *The Inheritors*. Campbell regards the latest preoccupation with body art in the form of tattoos and pierced noses as evidence that even 'the most elegant people' in society have embraced the myth of primitivism (1997: 17). The fascination with new age movements and paganism also demonstrates the popular interest in the primitive, since such movements 'are reliant upon the growth of the notion of the secluded self' (1997: 18). They are also closely related to what Campbell calls 'sympathy for nature', based on the primitivist assumption that 'man pollutes but a primitive man pollutes a lot less' (1997: 18). Nonetheless, neo-primitivism can be distinguished from the old-styled notion of 'the noble savage', since technology has become the primary tool of the Western 'neo-primitivist'. Cyber space acts as an invisible network connecting people in ways that stretch conventional notions of body and mind, interpreted by modern neo-shamans as similar to the way the body of the traditional shaman was torn apart and re-assembled. For advocates of contemporary primitivism, Campbell asserts, 'the mechanically reconstructed techno-shaman can offer us guidance' (1997: 20).

In Campbell's view, neo-primitivism has made ethnicity the focal point for the way Westerners relate to and interpret the non-Western world, and, in his case, to African societies. Of course, he argues, 'the primitivist standpoint is based on Western criteria', which means that Africans are always seen first as a member of an ethnic group and then only as possessing other characteristics. For example, 'you meet an African airline pilot: he's a Dinka who can fly planes. You meet an African doctor: she's a Tutsi who can perform heart surgery' (1997: 48). Beneath this way

---

of looking at Africans loom hidden and oftentimes unconscious racist assumptions. 'Whenever you meet an African, you wonder what their ethnic identity is' which simply 'reinforces the prejudice that a person's origins are determinant' (1997: 49). Campbell adds that the media compound such underlying prejudice by presenting Africans as 'diminished or undeveloped individuals' (1997: 49). The great rock concerts, which raised large sums of money for Africa, beginning with Bob Geldof's 'Band Aid' in 1985 right up to the 'Make Poverty History' concerts in 2005, underscore the widespread idea in the West that 'Africans are childlike victims who are at risk from the modern world because they are so unfamiliar with it'. Campbell concludes: 'This perspective presents a completely distorted picture of Africa and Africans (1997: 49).

Campbell makes it clear from the outset that he sees far more serious exponents of neo-primitivism than what he calls 'mavericks like the New Age anti-road protesters and crystal mystics' (1997: 3). Of course, this is quite consistent with the anti-environmentalist positions of the Living Marxism Group. Nonetheless, his main thesis aims at undermining the current fascination with ethnicity, which he associates with a new form of 'tribalism'. He asserts that 'once "ethnic" was a term of abuse … Now the whole world is made up of ethnicities' (1997: 3). He adds: 'More and more academic fields are coming round to relying upon ethnicity and indigenism to provide their underlying explanation of human behaviour' (1997: 4). Campbell's basic argument can be stated in stark, but simple terms: 'As a real and objective phenomenon innate to Africa, my proposition is that ethnicity does not exist' (1997: 6). By ethnicity Campbell is referring to a relationship between the West and Africa based on 'an ideological framework for Africa constructed in the West' (1997: 6). To demonstrate this, he draws attention to the way the West has interpreted ethnicity over the past twenty years. Following the fall of the Soviet Union, ethnicity was regarded as 'a source of conflict' resulting from the disorientation in the West when it lost a coherent enemy against which it could direct its mission and justify 'its activities around the rest of the world' (1997: 6–7). According to Campbell, ethnicity stepped in to fill the void left by communism, but it proved to be a weak substitute, since no ethnic threat could hope to replace a foe like the Soviet Union which had the *real* capacity to destroy the world several times over' (1997: 7) (emphasis his). Of course, Campbell was writing prior to 11 September 2001, after which the 'war on terror' has provided the West with a powerful, if somewhat elusive, opponent against which to direct its ideology. In Campbell's view, when ethnicity failed to provide a coherent enemy for the West, it was transformed into 'a source for celebration rather than fear' (1997: 7), so that now 'everyone can be a member of an ethnic minority' (1997: 3).

Campbell's thesis implies that the recurring focus on ethnicity as an explanatory theory in academic studies, when translated into policies of Western governments and non-governmental organizations, makes neo-primitivism, in its romantic, largely positive sense, innocuous when compared with the potentially dangerous emphasis on ethnicity presently dominating Western discourse on Africa. In recent years, he argues, a view has been promoted widely by NGOs that the only way to solve 'ethnic conflict is to emphasize the local even more' since 'ethnic conflicts negate genuine ethnicity' (1997: 82). Campbell admits that his study 'does not pretend to be a general analysis of ethnicity' but functions as 'an assessment of only one particular form … – modern moral ethnicity', which he associates closely with 'modern primitivism' (1997: 10). His underlying assumption is that today a sense of 'profound despair' has replaced an earlier optimism about advancing the ideals of Western civilization.

The future, as a result, in the minds of ordinary people in the West appears entirely uncertain and even is regarded with a sense of foreboding. The past, likewise, is rejected since 'it is irrevocably associated with the discredited institutions of the establishment'. With past and future both excluded from present thinking, Campbell concludes, 'a cult of primitivism has blossomed in the West that is completely different to traditional notions of primitivism' (1997: 7). By emphasizing humanity's closeness to nature, it seems to mirror traditional primitivism, but differs from it since the modern primitive exercises no control over nature. As we have seen, the entire realm of spirits in traditional societies, which regulated the relationship between the natural world and human communities, could be influenced by specially chosen spirit mediators. In the place of spirits, Campbell contends that modern primitivism has introduced high technology, which on the surface would seem to provide the masses with effective means of influencing external circumstances. Instead, it merely 'enhances the consumption – and therefore the comfort – of passive individuals' (1997: 7). Rather than providing genuine empowerment, modern forms of technology simply help people cope with their 'diminished ability to control their own lives, and therefore introduces a measure of stability into existing society' (1997: 7). Campbell sees in this new form of primitivism numerous contradictions, which are 'smudged over' by the renewed interest in ethnicity as a 'moral' resolution (1997: 7). Moral ethnicity for Campbell responds precisely to the Western preoccupation with the individual, which has contributed to a sense of impotence with respect to the larger world. When ethnicity is defined morally in this sense, therefore, it 'presents the comfort of the diminished individual as the highest virtue that society should aspire to' (1997: 7–8).

Moral ethnicity for Campbell is closely aligned in academic studies to the theory of social construction, defined by Abercrombie, Hill and Turner as 'the process whereby people actively construct their social world rather than have it imposed upon them' (2000: 320). Similarly, Campbell (1997: 189) defines social constructionist theories as entailing 'the notion that individuals can construct their own ethnic identity through interpersonal relationships with each other'. As a primary exponent of this view, he cites Terence Ranger, who argued in his landmark essay 'The Invention of Tradition in Colonial Africa', that 'far from being a single "tribal" identity, most Africans moved in and out of multiple identities, defining themselves at one moment as subject to this chief, at another moment as a member of that cult, at another moment as part of this clan, and yet at another moment as an initiate in that professional guild' (Ranger, 1992: 248; Campbell, 1997: 192). This is why, according to Campbell, Ranger argued that the Rhodesian attempt to recruit 'a bogus layer of loyal chiefs' failed as a political tool and why the people instead turned to spirit-mediums as true representatives of tradition (Campbell, 1997: 193; see also Ranger, 1985: 251). Campbell notes that the idea of cultural flexibility was voiced much earlier than Ranger by the Austrian anthropologist Siegfried Nadel, who in 1942 argued that political structures were rigid and exclusive, but cultural identities 'have fluid boundaries' (Campbell, 1997: 194; see Nadel, 1942: 17–18; For a discussion of Nadel's 'functionalist' anthropology, see Walker, 1970: 6). In Campbell's view, the ethnic flexibility argument reflects just another 'primitivist' perspective, since it portrays Africans as victims of colonialist interference, who otherwise, in their pure condition would possess an inordinately high degree of 'personal malleability and particularism' (1997: 195). This viewpoint fell into disuse in the 1980s but was revived in the 1990s when 'anomy and alienation, risk and chaos, globalization and niche marketing, became the buzz words' (1997: 195). In the end, theories of ethnic flexibility, which inherently deny the identity of stable groups depict Africans as 'passive individuals who can only enter into local relations with other people' (1997: 203). This fits very well with the Western idea of moral ethnicity, which seeks to comfort individuals, but grants them little power to affect the wider society.

The theory of social constructionism, particularly its central thesis that 'all social phenomenon are merely contingent constructions', entails for Campbell a series of disabling contradictions (1997: 203). By 'demystifying' ethnicity, at the same time, it discredits indigeneity. By asserting that ethnicity is fluid and determined locally, it fails to explain how cultural diversity is maintained over time, since logically 'if cultures are compatible, and can flow into each other, then diversity must eventually be abolished' (1997: 204). If this is not the correct conclusion to reach, then there must be 'limits to fluidity', but what are they? The localism associated with social constructionist theories is difficult to reconcile with globalization, unless ethnicity is 'culturally essentialist'. If so, Campbell maintains, such a view cannot be distinguished 'from racial theories of African essentialism' (1997: 204). These inherent contradictions between 'ethnic universality' and 'alleged localism' leave the 'much vaunted fluidity' of social constructionists 'looking rather wooden' (1997: 204). Campbell then asserts that advocates of this theory have attempted to resolve the contradiction by 'mixing identities only at the level of individual discourse' as seen in the 'irrational concept of "the diaspora", which represents 'a backdoor attempt ... to smuggle ethnicity back on to the agenda even after it has been disposed of by ... notions of "hybridity" and the flexibility of identities' (1997: 204).

Campbell's attack on indigeneity is based on his argument that local identities in contemporary Africa are never really local, since they are subject to numerous global influences. Citing a report of '40 experts' who attended a conference on development held in 1989 in Harare, Campbell isolates two of its main conclusions, called in the report 'moral imperatives', as particularly relevant to his argument. The first asserts that development workers 'should be careful not to challenge or undermine local culture' and the second instructs them to 'help create indigenous, societal or other infrastructures for the management of aid' (1997: 102). Campbell insists that, although these 'imperatives' appear ethically sound, in reality they elevate 'parochial' interests, which are depicted as being vulnerable to outside manipulation, thereby perpetrating the idea of the helpless African. That outside interests are at times benevolent is immaterial, since, equally, malevolent influences could be exerted on a people who in either case are regarded as victims. Campbell puts it this way: 'The problem with this Western sponsorship of local identity is that it celebrates the passive subordination of African people to the ethnically shrouded agendas and institutions of the Great Powers and their NGOs' (1997: 103). Campbell adds that by being portrayed as victims, Africans become further disempowered, since they develop a deep cynicism about their own ability to create social organizations to improve their living conditions. Campbell concludes that 'privileging the local' represents a 'primitivist viewpoint' that ignores the fact that 'the local is always a greater source of reaction than the national or the international' since it 'paves the way for rivalries to breed along ethnic lines' (1997: 104). Localism, rather than alleviating ethnic rivalries, actually exacerbates them.

Campbell's arguments, when considered alongside those of Geertz and Platvoet, must be taken seriously in the context of this book. Although in earlier chapters I have criticized what I have called Graham Harvey's essentialist approach to Indigenous Religions, I have accepted part of his definition of indigenous as belonging to a place, that is as being local as opposed to global and thus as being organized along kinship lines with obvious associations to ancestral traditions. In this latter sense, I have emphasized the rural nature of Indigenous Religions, although as Harvey has rightly demonstrated, I have asserted that to belong to a place does not necessarily mean living in that place. Contrary to what Campbell dismisses as the 'irrational concept of "the diaspora"', the migration of rural people to urban centres in Zimbabwe, for example, does not sever their connection to their homesteads and their ancestors, whom they still remember by name. Nonetheless, in my case studies, I have analysed indigenous peoples in Alaska and Zimbabwe by referring to their ethnic identities. I have also stressed the importance of traditional authority in religion, although I have argued that this applies generally, not just to indigenous forms of religion. Many of the charges levelled at Harvey indirectly from Geertz and Campbell, and quite openly by Platvoet, in other words, apply generally to my argument in this book. Certainly, if the academic study of Indigenous Religions represents a return to an exotic, romanticized and idealized picture of 'primitive' societies, then this work and all other volumes on Indigenous Religions distort reality by inserting a subtle but invidious prejudice into what otherwise would appear to constitute legitimate academic studies.

It will be clear, therefore, that the success of my overall aim in this book hinges on my ability to respond to these fundamental criticisms. In the first instance, I will argue that the empirical methodology I have employed throughout this study contrasts sharply with contemporary Western movements that emphasize the exotic nature of 'primitive' religion. In this sense, I contend that Geertz's analysis is directed not against my own theories of Indigenous Religions, but against a particular way indigenous societies have been interpreted to promote the idea of an original, pristine form of humanity. In order to demonstrate this, I examine neo-shamanism, which embodies in most popular literature on the subject, and even in some academic writings, the notion that by re-enacting what traditional shamans purportedly have experienced since time immemorial, the modern 'neo-shaman' participates in an archaic, but universal, form of religious healing. I argue that such contemporary Western movements bear only a superficial resemblance to Indigenous Religions, a point I illustrate by outlining two cases in neo-shamanism derived from my own earlier research. I examine next Graham Harvey's argument in his most recent book, where he defends the academic revival of the term 'animism'. It will be important for me to draw a firm line between my own non-theological, scientific approach and Harvey's stance, which, in my view, while avoiding a neo-primitivist position, reflects almost entirely the standpoint of an animist believer. I then return to Campbell's argument by re-asserting the priority of the local as a defining characteristic of what I mean by indigenous, but without falling into what Campbell calls the error of 'modern primitivism'. Although I find many of his arguments compelling and insightful, I ultimately reject Campbell's position as internally contradictory and as fundamentally biased against localized, indigenous societies.

Characteristics of Neo-Shamanism

Neo-shamanism frequently is associated with a loose conglomeration of movements in the West known as the 'New Age', which Sutcliffe and Bowman describe as a 'codeword in a larger field of religious experimentation' they prefer to call 'alternative spirituality' (2000: 1). Michael York (2004: 308–9) explains that the New Age is notoriously difficult to define because 'it does not conform to traditionally understood forms of religious organization'. He adds that it is just its 'non-institutional nature' that makes it so appealing in the current context of Western consumer society. 'The New Age', he says, 'is a spiritual consumer supermarket that is steadily superseding the appeal of traditional religion in the West through its affirmation and celebration of free spiritual choice.' Piers Vitebsky, who is an anthropologist with a specialization in shamanism in the Russian Far East, argues that the interest in shamanism in the contemporary West has resulted from a series of disillusionments ranging from 'a new hesitancy in Euro-American intellectual colonialism' through a 'loss of confidence in Christianity and the scientific world-view' (Vitebsky, 1995: 150). Wide-ranging movements have followed in the wake of this declining confidence in traditional Western institutions, he says, including the spread of Eastern religions, such as Buddhism, the rise of new forms of paganism, new age religions and the exponential growth of charismatic churches. In this wider context, Vitebsky explains, 'shamanism is seen as a non-institutionalized, undogmatic form of spirituality which offers considerable scope for personal creativity' (1995: 150).

The term neo-shamanism specifically is applied to contemporary Western movements that incorporate traditional shamanic techniques, which the practitioners describe as the most ancient form of religion. In her feature article in Christopher Partridge's edited volume, *New Religions: A Guide*, Elizabeth Puttick (2004: 292) describes neo-shamanism as 'a fast-growing new religion in industrialized countries', the popularity of which she credits in part to the 'antiquity' of traditional shamanism. One of the features of neo-shamanism is just this appeal to an ancient practice, which its adherents claim, in Puttick's words, is shared 'between traditions that could not possibly have had contact for tens of thousands of years, such as the Australian Aborigines and the arctic tribes' (2004: 292). Literature on traditional shamanism is varied, with some scholars emphasizing that particular practices are more typically associated with shamans than others. For example, the sociologist I.M. Lewis has argued that spirit possession in Africa is a form of shamanism, since the medium goes into a trance-like state during which his or her body is taken over by a spirit (1989: 9). Mircea Eliade (1989: 6), by contrast, whose book on shamanism influenced both academic and popular understandings after its publication in English in 1964, insists that the primary characteristic of the shaman involves travelling to the upper and lower worlds with the aid of spirit helpers. Marete Jakobsen (1999: 7–8), who has written about traditional Greenlandic shamans, contends that the most defining trait of a shaman is his or her ability to attract a number of spirits, which are overcome in a series of ordeals and eventually mastered, so that their powers become readily accessible to the shaman.

Despite these different emphases, most scholars agree that, although quite local variations exist, traditional shamans can be identified by four main features: (1) they go through a series of initiations, including ordeals often entailing death, bodily dismemberment and re-constitution of the body, before being accepted by the community as authentic; (2) shamanic powers require the assistance of spirit helpers, sometimes animal spirits or the spirits of unknown creatures, whom shamans control and manipulate; (3) the main technique shamans employ is to induce a trance in a séance, during which they leave their bodies and travel to other worlds; (4) shamans largely act beneficently within their communities in a number of ways, such as healing those who are sick (frequently caused by a malevolent spirit stealing the person's soul which the shaman recovers during otherworldly travels), predicting the weather to aid in hunting or agriculture, diagnosing the causes of misfortune, assigning proper remedies for misfortune or prognosticating more generally about the future.

Although the word, shaman, comes from the Tungus (Siberian) word, *saman*, the root of which ('sa') refers to someone 'who knows' (Jakobsen, 1999: 3), it has been applied widely to refer to any practitioner who satisfies the four criteria I have just listed, ranging widely from Native American 'medicine-men' to those who go into ecstatic trance dances in Malaysia as described by the anthropologist, Raymond Firth (1996: 119–20) and, as I just noted, to spirit mediums in Africa, similar to those I portrayed in the last chapter as being possessed by *mhondoro* spirits or *midzimu* in Zimbabwe. Vitebsky (1995: 132) notes that in the history of religions, particularly since Mircea Eliade wrote his classic book on the topic, the shaman has been regarded as an 'archaic' figure who persists today in numerous contrasting cultures and in the guise of many religious expressions. Vitebsky asserts that it is commonly believed that 'since it is shamans who make the soul-journeys to the realms of supernatural beings, it must be they who gave the world its generally accepted ideas about the cosmos, heaven and hell' (1995: 132). Eliade regarded the shaman as the ideal religious person, the *homo religiosus*, since, as he demonstrated through detailed descriptions of shamanism in central and north Asia (Eliade, 1988: 181-214; see also Eliade, 1987: 53–4; 202), the shaman directly encountered the gods and spirits on behalf of a community by leaving his or her body and travelling to other worlds in states of ecstatic trance.

It is partly due to Eliade's influence that new movements in the West have sprung up, which claim to have tapped into this most ancient of religious practices. Nowadays, individual shamanic specialists are trained in the techniques of ecstasy. They in turn conduct workshops aimed at helping others to go on their own shamanic journeys, usually to experience release either from physical or mental stress, or sometimes from both. As Puttick (2004: 293) notes, 'the majority of Western shamanic teachers have been trained in Core Shamanism', a movement which asserts that a universal collection of shamanic beliefs and practices can be identified and extracted from ancient cultures around the world and taught, beginning with weekend or intensive workshops. One of the leading exponents of this view is Michael Harner, an anthropologist who beginning in the 1950s worked amongst the Jivaro people in Ecuador, and later established the Foundation for Shamanic Studies in California, which has fostered numerous branches around the world (Harvey, 2002b: x). The other leading figure associated with neo-shamanism is the controversial anthropologist Carlos Castaneda (1925–1998), who from the late 1960s to the mid-1970s wrote nine volumes on the Yaqui Indians of South America, the first of which, published in 1968, describes his mystical experiences under the direction of his indigenous teacher, Don Juan Matus (Castaneda, 1968). Although Castaneda's works now are regarded by many academics as fanciful inventions, they continue to provide guidance for techniques used by leaders in neo-shamanic movements he has inspired (Wallis, 2003: 40; Churchill, 2003: 329; Geertz, 2004: 57–8). Both Harner and Castaneda had a powerful cultural effect, in the words of Marete Jakobsen (1999: 159), by making 'shamanism available to Westerners with no background in traditional shamanism' (159).

Since Castaneda's writings largely have been discredited outside his own following, I will describe Harner's version of 'core shamanism', which today plays a central and defining role in neo-shamanic movements internationally. Harner describes shamanism on the website of the Foundation of Shamanic Studies as derived from 'our ancient ancestors' who for 'over tens of thousands of years

... all over the world discovered how to maximize human abilities of mind and spirit for healing and problem-solving'.[3] He calls this a 'remarkable system' whose practitioners are 'especially distinguished by the use of journeys to hidden worlds otherwise mainly known through myth, dream, and near-death experiences'. In *The Way of the Shaman*, Harner (1980; 2003: 41) describes his first experience of shamanic travel, which occurred while he was conducting anthropological research among the Conibo Indians in Peru.[4] After feeling frustration for a lengthy period at the people's recalcitrance at revealing anything about their religion, Harner describes how they convinced him that to really understand their vision of the supernatural he must drink the liquid of the *ayahuasca* plant, which has hallucinogenic effects. Under the force of the drink, he experienced visions of dragon-like beings, heard 'the most beautiful singing I have ever heard in my life' and experienced an intense sensitivity to his own body (2003: 42–3). When he was sure he was about to die, he called out for human help and was administered an antidote, although the visions continued at a lower level of intensity for some time afterwards (2003: 43). A few years later, he returned to South America to the Jivaro among whom he had first worked, but this time 'not just to be an anthropologist, but to learn firsthand how to practice shamanism in the Jivaro way' (2003: 47). Robert Wallis observes that Harner was one among several anthropologists of the 1960s (including Castaneda), who while working, particularly in South America, 'went native' and 'participated in entheogenorientated rituals which enabled first-hand encounters with shamanic realities' (2003: 28).

Following his work with the Conibo and Jivaro, Harner indicates that he studied briefly among Native American groups such as the Wintun and Pomo in California, Coast Salish in Washington State and the Lakota in South Dakota. He learned from them how to employ shamanic techniques without using hallucinogenic drugs. He says that he has been able to apply this knowledge to his work of 'introducing Westerners to the practice of shamanism' (2003: 55). Indeed, to conduct workshops in most Western countries using drugs would be illegal, and thus he needed to find ways to open the shamanic vision to ordinary people using other methods, such as drumming, intense concentration and techniques of auto-suggestion. He was aided in this by studying 'worldwide ethnographic literature on shamanism' from which he was able to discover that common elements can be found in all forms of shamanism around the world (2003: 55). It was from these experiences and studies that he conceived courses in 'core shamanism', which resulted in 1985 in the establishment of his Foundation for Shamanic Studies.

MaryCatherine Burgess, who studied under Harner, has outlined in her PhD thesis seven defining characteristics of what she calls 'cross-cultural shamanism'. These include shamanic vocation and initiation, shamanic cosmology, a shamanic state of consciousness, shamanic soul flight, shamanic spiritual allies, shamanic soul healing and community support (Burgess, 2005: 35–6). She claims that these categories define how shamans everywhere throughout history have undergone similar types of experience. Shamanic vocation often comes to an individual's awareness through illness or other sufferings, but the initiation is almost always confirmed through ordeals, usually involving dismemberment of the body and its renewal (2005: 36). Burgess acknowledges that the precise manner that vocation and initiation are

---

[3]   www.shamanism.org.

[4]   Citations in this section are taken from Harvey's re-print of chapter one of *The Way of the Shaman*, which is entitled, 'Discovering the Way'.

experienced may vary across cultures, but everywhere 'the shaman must in some way(s) die to the life that existed before the call came' (2005: 36). Similarly, across all cultures, shamans share in a universal cosmology, which divides experience into 'three primary cosmic regions: a lower world, … a middle world, often described as the spiritual dimension of the physical earth, and an upper world referred to at all times as the sky'. The shaman travels between these realms 'through a kind of hole, or opening, in the sky or the earth' (2006: 37). All shamans engage in 'soul journey' or flights of ecstasy, in which they travel, usually accompanied by 'spiritual allies', beginning 'at a starting point in ordinary reality' and then ascending or descending into the 'nonordinary realm of "the spirits" to partner with them for information or healing' (2005: 38–9).

In sharp contrast to Burgess, Marete Jakobsen's research on Greenlandic shamans underscores the opposing characteristics between traditional and 'neo' shamans. Jakobsen, who enrolled in courses in core shamanism in Denmark for research purposes, stresses that, unlike traditional shamans, those trained in Harner's courses come as individuals to solve their own personal problems, or sometimes they are health practitioners who want to learn shamanic techniques to improve their own professional skills (1999: 167–76). For this reason, the training often can be accomplished in a very short time and without the kind of ordeals that shamans in indigenous societies were forced to undergo (1999: 162). Most people who attend core shamanic workshops, she adds, are 'urban practitioners' who are not part of a close community', which, of course, varies substantially from the communal nature of traditional indigenous societies (1999: 162). Jakobsen notes that certain practices are taught in all sessions on core shamanism, such as searching for and finding a 'power animal' and travelling to the Lower and Upper Worlds. Yet, she argues, those who participate in such exercises lack a common myth and shared worldview, as would be found within traditional shamanic cultures (199: 188). This often leads to confusion and varying expectations amongst the participants. Within the workshops she attended, Jakobsen observed that the members of the group were taught how to move between two types of reality: 'Ordinary state of Consciousness' and 'Shamanic state of consciousness'. After having mastered this skill, the neophytes could re-experience healing over and over again and thereby maintain a sense of well-being. The aim of Harner's courses in core shamanism for most participants, Jakobsen concludes, is to teach them how to make the transition between Ordinary and Shamanic consciousness (1999: 165). Those who pursue further training often become shamanic practitioners, who help others through the skills they have mastered. Robert Wallis (2003: 50) notes that not all neo-shamans follow the Harner model based on a universal, 'core shamanism', a fact he claims Jakobsen has overlooked. Although many of her criticisms of the urban shaman are correct, he argues, Jakobsen has assumed mistakenly that 'authentic' shamans, such as the Greenlandic *angakkoq*, can be distinguished from 'inauthentic' contemporary shamanic practitioners.

My own concern in this chapter is to determine if neo-shamanic movements, in the first instance, can be regarded as indigenous and, secondly, if by appealing to an ancient tradition and by asserting the authority of a common spiritual heritage, they can be classified as a 'religion'. These are crucial concerns for my topic, since, as we have seen, if Geertz (2004: 54) is correct, all attempts to 'resuscitate the shamanisms of the past' entail a 'willful return to primitivism'. In 2003, I wrote an article which appeared in *Studies in World Christianity* under the title, 'Contemporary Shamanism in Global Contexts: "Religious" Appeals to an Archaic Tradition?' (Cox, 2003: 69–

87). One of the main questions I posed in the article asked if the current upsurge in shamanic groups constitutes a new 'world religion'. To address this, I presented three case studies, two of which were drawn from my own research conducted in 2001 in the United States. At the end of the article, I concluded that neo-shamanic movements should be regarded at the very least as expressions of religion because, following Hervieu-Léger, 'they all make appeals to a postulated, but shared authority derived from common human ancestors transmitted through an archaic chain of memory' (2003: 86). In light of my discussions in this book, I would like to re-visit this conclusion by offering a different interpretation of the two neo-shamanic cases I presented in my earlier article, which I recount here in a much abbreviated form.[5]

Two Cases in Neo-Shamanism

On 25 July 2001, I conducted an interview with a Celtic shaman, Lenny Staerk of Burlington, Vermont, whom I had invited to speak to a class I was teaching on traditional and contemporary shamanism during the summer session 2001 at Dartmouth College in Hanover, New Hampshire. During the interview, I raised a number of issues, including how he became a shaman, what sorts of approaches he uses in his shamanic practices and how he understands the cosmology of Celtic shamanism. During the interview, Lenny, who is a blind man in his mid-forties, explained that even when he was a boy, he sensed the presence of animal spirits surrounding him, although at the time he knew nothing about them. He referred to one incident specifically when an eagle flew over him and seemed to want to communicate with him. Now, since he has become blind, he knows that the eagle represented a different type of vision that would allow him to see from great heights what most people never can see. Lenny explained that when he was in his twenties he experienced numerous personal problems, which he overcame with the aid of courses led by Michael Harner. Later, he was introduced to Celtic shamanism during a workshop led by Tom Cowan, who has written widely on this topic. According to Cowan's web site, Celtic shamanism combines 'universal core shamanism with traditional European spirit lore to create spiritual practices that can heal and enrich one's own life and the lives of others'.[6] In Cowan's well-known book, *Fire in the Head*, which Lenny cited as highly influential in his own training, Cowan (1993: 7) describes his approach as 'a testimony to the survival and durability of the Celtic spirit and its shamanic qualities', which, he asserts, emerge 'in every age' and which 'retain the vestiges of an older, deeper stratum of belief and practice'. During the Cowan workshops, Lenny met his own animal spirits whom he learned to invoke regularly as assistants when healing people who come to him for private consultations.

During the interview, Lenny outlined his understanding of Celtic cosmology, which he said consists of an upper world, a middle world and an underworld, all connected by 'the Great Tree'. A large number and variety of beings can be found in the three worlds, such as animals, birds and strange creatures, which are employed by a shaman to heal, advise and guide people. The shaman draws on different beings within the three worlds to suit the particular needs of the person who comes for spiritual help. The animals of the upper world are healing spirits, which Lenny said,

---

[5]   The more detailed accounts are found in Cox, 2003: 74–82.
[6]   www.riverdrum.com.

aid him in his own healing sessions. Sometimes, he contacts spirits of animals and trees in the middle world, which is our own world, where the shaman is able to see and detect spirits that are invisible to most people. Sometimes, he noted, he has to go to the lower world, which can be dangerous. In the lower world, the shaman encounters sometimes frightening beings, like 'lizard man and dragons' or spirits of the dead. By travelling between the cosmic regions, Lenny explained, the shaman learns how to relate to different types of spirits and how to call on those that promote healing to alleviate the detrimental effects of spirits that cause illness or discomfort within his clients.

During his presentation on shamanism at Dartmouth College, Lenny showed the class his shamanic drum, which was single-headed and was approximately three feet high and one foot in diameter with a cover made from cowhide. He said he had made the drum himself. After addressing the class and answering questions, he then demonstrated how he uses the drum in his private consultations. He indicated that he usually begins by cleansing the room of unwanted spirits. Although he was providing a demonstration, he indicated that he felt the presence of disturbing spirits in the room. He then walked to a far corner by a window, lifted his drum in an upward and downward movement and began beating on it in a distinctive rhythm. He tapped the drum slowly three times, paused, and repeated the same action for two or three minutes. Although Lenny did not explain to the class the significance of these actions, according to John Matthews (1991: 121), in Celtic tradition beating the drum slowly three times indicates that the shaman is communicating with spirits of the underworld whose presence needs to be neutralized. When Lenny finished the drumming, one of the male students in the class stood up and left the room. Lenny told us not to be worried and assured us that the boy would be fine. He then went outside and called for the student, who came to him. The class could see Lenny and the student through a window, talking to each other. We observed the boy reaching out to touch a large tree, which he seemed to be addressing. Later, the student told me that Lenny was teaching him to communicate with the spirit of the tree and not to be afraid of animals that wanted to contact him. The student told me that a squirrel approached him and brushed his head with his tail. Lenny motioned for the class to come outside by the tree. He told us we could talk to it, learn to be friends with the squirrels that climb up it and could draw on the wisdom of the birds that lodge in its branches.

On 9 August 2001 I arranged for the students in the class to participate in a trance dance at the Lightgate Learning Center, located in the Connecticut River valley town of Thetford, Vermont. In its publicity material, Lightgate described the purpose of the Centre as providing 'a gateway to enlightenment for body, mind and spirit'. In addition to the trance dance, regular activities sponsored by the Center included: 'A shamanic journey through soul hunting'; 'meditative stretching'; and 'sacred sound and sacred chant'. The literature described the Trance Dance as replicating a practice that 'has existed for over 40,000 years' and suggested that people 'all over the world, independent of religion and culture', engage in the event 'to get in touch with greater wisdom and mysteries'. The dance would have numerous effects on the participants, including purifying their 'body, mind, soul and feelings'. As such, it 'is one of the oldest healing rituals we know today'. The participants were told that they would experience 'real nature', but they were assured equally that each person's responses to the dance are 'unique' and that 'every event is a new adventure'. The trance dance was led by one of the Lightgate staff members, Rahel Kuhne, who was described as having been 'a passionate Trance Dance presenter since 1994'.

Eight students and I participated in the dance, which took place outside on a lawn behind the Center's house, bordering large grassy fields in a peaceful, rural setting. We sat down on blankets that had been arranged in a square with candles and burning incense in the middle. Soft instrumental music was playing in the background from a quite large, sophisticated sound system with multiple speakers. After introductions were completed, Rahel explained that dancing is an ancient form of getting in touch with one's inner self, with spirits of animals and nature. She emphasized that entering into trance to experience ecstasy was 40,000 years old, as testified by rock paintings all over the world. She indicated that trance dance has great healing power by combining body and spirit in a way that produces a sense of calm and serenity. She told the group that during the dance, we would encounter various animals, some of which, like the snake, might frighten us. We were told that we should not be afraid if this happens, since the snake has healing properties. Rahel assured us that the entire experience is safe and urged us simply to trust the experience and to forget our own ego. We were then taught a breathing technique to help us concentrate and to stimulate the trance. She explained that we should take two deep breaths through the nostrils in quick succession and then exhale through the mouth. In order avoid feeling self-conscious and to prohibit staring at our fellow participants, Rahel gave us scarves to use as blindfolds. She indicated that when the music begins, we should dance in any way that feels comfortable to us. She told us not to worry about bumping into others, since she would be observing the group's movements and would protect us.

The first sound I heard after standing up and putting on my blindfold was the deep resonating sacred Hindu syllable, 'OM'. The sound reverberated over the speakers creating vibrations that I felt throughout my body. After this, various types of music were played, which seemed to represent sounds from various parts of the world. I identified the early tracks as African music, with its typical drum beating and shaking rattles. I moved with the rhythm until the music slowed and sounded more ominous with deeper and slower beating of the drums and animal-like sounds interspersed between the beats. After the music, drum beating and sounds had been going on for what I judged to be around thirty minutes, a deep male voice came over the tape and announced in a slow, sonorous way: 'Trance Dance is 40,000 years old. It has been practised by our ancient ancestors all over the world.' I recall the voice mentioning Australian aborigines, the Yoruba of West Africa, Umbanda, Vodou, Native Americans, Inuit and Siberian shamans. The voice declared, 'They worshipped animals', and then commanded, 'Now, place your feet solidly on the ground and dance as you enter into trance'. This was followed by the sounds of breathing coming over the tape consisting of two quick sniffs and a loud exhaling of breath. The music then began again, comprising variations of Latin American, African and black American melodies. The rhythm would build up to a fast beat and then slow to a pause before resuming. Rattles could be heard in the background to the music and animal sounds detected, including hissing like a snake. Someone began keeping time with the rhythm by clapping, which others in the group emulated. Suddenly, a very serene choral music was played, which was followed on the tape by the noise of children laughing. The final sound repeated the sacred, vibrating 'OM', which many of the participants joined in saying. Then, there was absolute silence. At this point, Rahel invited us to remove our blindfolds and be seated again on the blankets. I looked at my watch and noted that we had been dancing for two hours. Rahel explained that we needed a little time to re-enter the world and gather out thoughts before leaving for home.

The cases of Lenny Staerk, the Celtic shaman, and Rahel Kuhne, a trance dance leader, share a number of points in common as examples of neo-shamanism. Both justify their practices by appeals to ancient traditions. Lenny referred to the archaic conventions of Celtic peoples which, in the words of Tom Cowan (1993: 113), express 'an ancient spiritual view of our relationship with nature, a oneness with the earth, a belief that within the wooded groves and fields live humanlike presences that are in fact divine'. Under Rahel Kuhne's guidance, the participants in the trance dance quite similarly were told that they had united with humanity's indigenous ancestors, who everywhere had entered ecstatic trances, encountered various animal spirits and experienced renewal as a result. Contact with the spirits in both cases, of course, could be frightening or even dangerous, but in the end proved benevolent to human needs. Both Lenny and Rahel also emphasized the priority of individual experience. In Lenny's case, clients came to him individually to be cleansed and healed. This, of course, is not the only, or even the normal way, contemporary shamanic practitioners operate, since often healing occurs in groups. Nonetheless, the experience remains fundamentally personal and individual. Each participant goes on a private journey, discovers his or her power animals and experiences a type of physical or spiritual restoration that is tailored for quite specific individual needs. Similarly, the trance dance, although conducted as a group experience, was described by Rahel as a 'unique' experience for each participant in the event. Although the music, rhythms and background noises were contrived carefully for the intended group effect, each participant was encouraged to encounter the spirits discovered in the trance in order to promote personal well-being. In the end, the postulated ancient traditions appealed to in both cases fit comfortably within Geertz's category of a romanticized ideal of a primitive past, where people are taught to transcend the artificial boundaries and dualisms of modernity to discover the healing properties found by communicating with a diversity of life forms and spirit worlds.

An Indigenous Religion?

On the basis of my earlier definition, to be indigenous requires the presence of three factors: identification with a locality, that is, belonging to a place; an emphasis on kinship relations expressed through localized or regional societies with political systems organized according to lineage; beliefs and rituals focused primarily on ancestor spirits. Neo-shamanism is not restricted to a locality and it incorporates lineage only insofar as it asserts a universal human capacity to replicate what our earliest ancestors are said to have experienced. That neo-shamanism is a global phenomenon, it could be argued, does not discredit it as a truly indigenous form of religion, but simply reflects the fact that all religions function today in the context of world economic and political systems and are linked by vast transnational communication networks. The claim to indigeneity nonetheless depends on an idea that the neo-shaman corresponds to Eliade's ideal 'archaic man' as the prototypical religious person. As such, the global shaman has nothing whatsoever to do with locality, other than on Eliade's terms, as a being who originally emerged on the scene in various societies as people began to lose direct contact with the gods and needed mediators to communicate for them (for Eliade's application of this idea, for example, within the Altaic horse sacrifice, see Eliade, 1989: 184–200; see also Eliade, 1996: 50–52). Although Eliade provided detailed accounts of shamans in different geographical regions, he reduced them all to the same characteristics to support his thesis that the ideal religious person of the past stands in sharp contrast to the modern human, who is overcome by a deep sense of aimlessness due to a loss of orientation towards the sacred (Eliade, 1989: 184; Eliade, 1987: 202–3). Eliade's book on shamanism obtained widespread academic credibility because he so carefully researched his data, even if most of it was second or third-hand. Harner's core shamanism, by contrast, as Jakobsen has shown so convincingly, makes little attempt to do anything other than compile a list of features that are interwoven into easily learned workshops to meet the demands of Western consumer society. The ancestors within core shamanism thus are idealized figures without any social context, other than that of a Western individualistic society and capitalist economy. This is just as true of Lenny Staerk's Celtic shamanism as it is of Harner's core shamanism. Both are invented and have little relationship to concrete social or cultural settings. In this sense, neo-shamanism cannot be regarded as indigenous: it does not belong to a place, its kinship ties are universal and its ancestors are lost in a romantic idea of primitive humanity.

I do not reach this conclusion because neo-shamanic ancestors are shrouded in the far off past, or are spoken about in mythic language. We have seen in the case of the Korekore of Zimbabwe that stories of the founding ancestors likewise are conveyed in myths, some about quasi-historical leaders but others dealing with autochthonous beings. The difference between these figures and the prototypical archaic person derives exactly from the locality that defines an indigenous people. The Korekore trace themselves to Mutota and his descendants. Powerful chthonic beings, like Dzivaguru and his son Karuva, pre-dated the occupation of the land by Mutota's children, and thus their lineage is unknown. Still, they come from the earth; they are of the place; they can be located in the land surrounding the Zambezi River. The great pre-colonial dynasties of Zimbabwe are traced to these early ancestors and are perpetuated today through the ancestors of chiefs, village headmen and family elders. The indigenous people of Zimbabwe, although not autochthonous, therefore, are defined by locality, are organized according to a defined system of lineage and are related ritually to a hierarchy of ancestral spirits, known by name. This is far different from contemporary forms of shamanism which belong everywhere and nowhere, where specific lineage relations matter not at all and where the ancestors are important only because they readily engaged in that most primitive of human experiences, ecstatic trance, now re-discovered and made available as a technique promoting personal growth and individual well-being.

If it is clear that neo-shamanism is not indigenous, on my definition at least, whether or not to classify it as a religion is far more ambiguous. As illustrated in the cases of Lenny Staerk and the trance dance of Rahel Kuhne, neo-shamanism stresses its archaic roots. These appeals to a heritage of belief seem consistent with Hervieu-Léger's definition of religion as a chain of memory, the authority of which adherents claim is obtained from humanity's earliest ancestors. In the case of Lenny Staerk, the appeal to a legitimating Celtic memory, transmitted from generation to generation, corresponds closely to Hervieu-Léger's analysis of religion as based on an authoritative tradition. If we add elements of my own definition, we see that neo-shamanic movements maintain beliefs and postulate experiences about non-falsifiable alternate realities. Neo-shamanism thus fits into a definition of religion, apart from one central factor, that of an identifiable community, if by that phrase we mean a group that is bound together, not only by the same general beliefs and experiences, but by a tradition which is passed on within the community with an overwhelming authority. It is very difficult to conceive weekend workshops, where people gather for short periods of time to achieve personal life goals, in such a way. Often the relationships established in such groups are transitory, and, if they persist, normally are informal and not bound by an authoritative tradition. This is precisely the conclusion Marete Jakobsen (1999: 177) reached following her research on neo-shamanic courses in Denmark:

> Neo-shamanism with its highly individualized method of using spirit-helpers and healing, its non-cult character, its openness of mind to the supernatural experiences of the participants and its link with an archaic past of all cultures and thereby the sense of universality and fellowship between present cultures, its holist approach to Nature and man; all appeal to the members of a society which is seen as highly fragmented and diffuse, secular in its approach to healing, education and social interaction.

On my definition of Indigenous Religions, therefore, neo-shamanism would be excluded, since it is neither indigenous nor a religion. The wave of individualized, self-help movements prevalent in many sectors of contemporary Western society, as a result, bear only superficial resemblances to the subject matter constituting the academic study of Indigenous Religions. As such, courses in universities on Indigenous Religions should not be confused with sociological studies of neo-shamanic groups and their connections to individualism, capitalism and the search for personal fulfilment. These are legitimate academic topics, but they do not constitute what is meant by Indigenous Religions, as I have shown convincingly by my case studies.

Does this mean that Geertz is wrong to accuse advocates of the study of Indigenous Religions of neo-primitivism? Only partially, in so far as he associates the academic study of Indigenous Religions with the aims of neo-shamanic practitioners, like Michael Harner, who, by emphasizing their scholarly credentials, confirm what Geertz sees as a 'trend in the academic world' that thrives 'on primitivistic assumptions and especially on the celebration and romantization of the exotic' (Geertz, 2004: 57). I am in full agreement with Geertz, that the study of neo-shamanism does not 'help us pursue the study of particular religions or even of religion in general' (2004: 59). It is useful for other purposes, particularly for documenting how the history of Western intellectual imperialism has proceeded by studying the 'other' in order, in Geertz's words, 'to address our own spiritual, ideological and religious needs' (2004: 59; see also Carrette and King, 2005: 2–6). By firmly separating Indigenous Religions from neo-shamanism, therefore, I have dislodged one pillar supporting Geertz's argument, but his most powerful contention still needs to be addressed: the study of Indigenous Religions 'leaves little room for living indigenes who do not conform to our stereotypes' (2004: 59). This charge must be considered in the first instance as an indictment of academics who promote the study of Indigenous Religions in order to challenge dominant Western assumptions about the world as undermining an imagined and undisturbed holistic view of nature, and hence of surreptitiously sneaking primitivism back on to the academic agenda. It is clear that Jan Platvoet identifies Graham Harvey as a scholar who has committed just this fundamental error. Although I regard Platvoet's criticism as misplaced, I contend that Harvey, while avoiding primitivism, commits an equally fatal methodological error by pushing the insider position so far that it cannot be separated from a confession of faith.

Harvey: A Theology of Animism

Harvey's latest book, *Animism: Respecting the Living World*, picks up at just the point his earlier works left off, by re-affirming 'that the world is full of persons, only some of whom are human' (2005a: xi). His aim ostensibly is to revive the use of a word that has been discredited largely due to a host of academics, beginning with the likes of Frazer, Tylor and Durkheim, who have disparaged indigenous worldviews as being unable to distinguish between animate and inanimate objects. These negative descriptions of animism, resulting from 'colonialist ideology' have clouded 'academic engagement with people and their lived realities' (2005a: 3). What Harvey calls the 'new animism' refers to a term of 'self-designation among some indigenous and nature-venerating religionists' (2005a: 3), which has been re-discovered by many contemporary academics, such as Irving Hallowell, Terri Smith, Ken Morrison and Nurit Bird-David. Harvey says the 're-visitation of the term' by such scholars employs a critical analysis that fundamentally challenges the old notions of animism which were based on theories of 'modernism, intellectualism and evolutionism' that depicted indigenous practices as 'foolishly erroneous' (2005a: 20). Bird-David, in particular, is cited approvingly by Harvey for contrasting 'animist discourse' with 'dualistic dichotomies' particularly by confronting the hegemonic power of 'Cartesian objectivism' within traditional Western academic methodologies (2005a: 21; see also, Bird-David, 2002: 73–105).

In his preface to the book, Harvey defines his own methodology as research based on dialogue or 'conversation'. The old animism resulted from the work of scholars who were 'certain about "objectivity"', an approach which today has been replaced by 'words like dialogue, reflexivity and reactivity' (2005a: xv)'. Contemporary scholars, in other words, are explicit about their aims, methods and practices and thus regard their research as entailing 'conversation, respect and relationship' (2005a: xv). Harvey notes that dialogue is undertaken not only with human communities, but, following Hallowell, also with 'other-than-human persons' who 'are members of indigenous communities' (2005a: xvi). Clearly, this incorporates the perspectives of indigenous peoples, who relate to and engage with a wide number of living forces, which, following Harvey's understanding of conversation, must be included in such a dialogical approach. Harvey suggests that this requires academics 'to attend to the ways in which wisdom might be sought in conversation with all sorts of persons' (2005a: xvi). Harvey's own word for this reciprocal relationship with the communities he is researching is 'guesthood', which entails a 'radical version of dialogue' by celebrating an 'academic presence among, and full participation with, our hosts' (2005a: xvi).

In my view, this approach cannot be called 'primitivism', since it is based on a long-established methodology in the study of religions that privileges the perspectives of insiders. It takes the phenomenological notion of 'empathy' a step further than classical phenomenologists such as Gerardus van der Leeuw or Ninian Smart intended, by involving the researcher's own worldview quite transparently in a conversation among equals, including the researcher and the researched community (see Cox, 2006: 118–26; 160–62). This approach is quite consistent with new trends in religious studies scholarship, as has been shown by recent works, such as those of Gavin Flood, who has employed the theories of the Russian linguistic philosopher, Mikhail Bakhtin, to advance the phenomenology of religion beyond its traditional aim to uncover objectivity to one that finds meaning in the context of narrative and relationship (see Flood, 1999: 150–68). Harvey's approach, however, does raise the persistent problem associated with phenomenology that by giving priority to the perspective of believers, the scholar goes beyond engaging in dialogue for academic purposes and instead becomes an advocate for the beliefs and practices of religious communities. If this is done unreflectively, it becomes evangelism. If it entails analysis and critical reflection, it is indistinguishable from theology.

In Graham Harvey's case, the boundary between what might be called 'animist theology' and the academic study of Indigenous Religions is virtually unrecognizable. His work is fully academic; it employs critical skills and scholarly reflection. Nonetheless, it is clear that he is a believer; he is an animist. His research is undertaken to promote the animist cause in opposition to what he regards as the distortion of reality foisted on the world by dualistic thinking, which severs mind from matter and distinguishes not only organic from inorganic substances, but sees personhood as resident only within humans. This has encouraged colonial attitudes of superiority, has fostered disrespect for different worldviews (at least those that are classified as unscientific) and has placed the planet on the verge of environmental catastrophe. These are entirely defensible positions, but, in my view, they are confessional, and hence theological, in the broadest sense of the term. They come from inside a tradition; they reflect a stance that replicates the same goals, for example, as those writing from within Christian dogmatic theology, including the branch known as apologetics, where the faith is defended against its detractors.

We see this position outlined clearly in Harvey's preface to his book, where he defines 'animisms' as 'theories, discourses and practices of relationship, of living well, of realising more fully what it means to be a person, and a human person, in the company of other persons, not all of whom are human but all of whom are worthy of respect' (2005a: xvii). One could interpret this as purely descriptive language, but quite obviously it is value-laden by approving of the animist 'theories, discourses and practices' it is describing. This becomes evident by the central argument of his book, which Harvey says 'hinges on the question of what a person is' (2005a: xvii). In conventional usage, he notes, a person is contrasted with an object. 'Persons may be spoken *with*. Objects ... are usually spoken *about*' (2005a: xvii) (emphasis his). Persons characteristically are 'volitional, relational, cultural and social beings', who have the capacity to exercise judgement and to make decisions freely. This sounds quite straightforward and even common sense, until Harvey asserts that some persons look like objects and some objects behave like persons. He explains: 'Neither material form nor spiritual or mental faculties are definitive (except in the "old animism" where they are *the* problem)' (2005a: xvii) (emphasis his). He observes there is little distinction between Christians who affirm that persons extend beyond humans, for example, to angels, and the wider use of personhood in animism in which it is possible to speak of 'rock persons' or 'tree persons'. Harvey is right, from a theological point of view. Christian theologians affirm not only the personhood of angels or demons, but of God, and debate the meaning of the one deity in three 'persons' (2005a: xviii). I have argued that scholars of religion regard all such theological statements as claims about 'postulated non-falsifiable alternate realities'. They are affirmed by believers, but not by the scholar of religions, unless the scholar is a theologian. This is not restricted to Christianity, but to any confession, including adherents within Indigenous Religions.

Not only is Harvey writing as an animist theologian, but he adopts also the role of an animist social activist, much in the same way that Christians have developed theologies of liberation or feminism. By depicting animism as a much maligned theory and as a worldview held widely among the most oppressed peoples of the world, Harvey takes up the cause of righting the wrongs perpetrated by a hegemonic Western ideology. He writes: 'animists live a theory of personhood and selfhood that radically challenges the dominant point of view which is that of modernity' (2005a: xviii). It does so by asserting that 'intelligence, rationality, consciousness, volition, agency, language and desire … are shared by humans with all other kinds of persons' (2005a: xviii). This view, if widely recognized, would inject a radically alternative perspective into 'a variety of debates that will be of interest to a host of heirs, prisoners, customers, clients and scholars of Western worldviews' by positing 'a different relationship between mind and matter, consciousness and physicality, culture and nature than that enshrined in Cartesian dualism' (2005a: xviii).

In these statements, Harvey is not reverting to a form of primitivism, where he idealizes a pristine form of ancient humanity. He is providing a rationale for a view of the world that he believes would produce positive effects not just for the human condition, but for the whole of life. If it became widely accepted, animist theories would counteract a wide variety of evils, from the random destruction caused by warfare to the attack on the environment derived in part from a worldview that fails to recognize personhood in nature. In this sense, Platvoet is wrong to associate Harvey with Geertz's attack on advocates of 'neo-primitivism'. On the contrary, Harvey epitomizes a scholarly approach that places 'living indigenes' at the centre of research. He may do so from his own prior commitment to a particular worldview, but this is true of every scholar. The problem does not arise because Harvey incorporates an insider's point of view into his analysis, but because he is unequivocally an insider. Harvey is not a neo-primitivist, and hence by implication a reverse racist, but he is an animist theologian. It is this perspective which I have rejected categorically in this book as entirely inconsistent with the role of a scholar of Indigenous Religions. I contend that it is possible to remain committed fully to what Geertz calls the critical rationality inherent in the Enlightenment Project while still approaching indigenous peoples dialogically with respect, transparency and an openness to new theoretical perspectives. My view asserts that research proceeds academically only by employing an empirical, scientifically testable (or falsifiable) methodology that prohibits endorsing the perspectives of the people the scholar studies. 'Going native' produces practitioners, like Castaneda and Harner in an obvious way, but, at a more sophisticated level, is indistinguishable from Harvey's theological animism, or, for that matter, from any other confessional approach.

Re-asserting the Local as Indigenous: A Response to Aidan Campbell

Numerous themes recur throughout Aidan Campbell's book on African primitivism that appear consistent with the position advocated by Armin Geertz. Both Campbell and Geertz regard primitivism as an invention that reflects the current cultural situation emerging out of Western consumer society rather than accurately representing the concerns of indigenous peoples. The Western emphasis on individualism has distorted the true picture of traditional forms of life in indigenous societies by reconfiguring them according to the tenets of 'modern' or 'neo-primitivism', which have been contrived largely to meet the personal crises endemic throughout Western society. In this regard, both Campbell and Geertz understand the 'new age' responses, as epitomized in movements like neo-shamanism, as exemplars of this new form of Western primitivism. Their arguments echo those of Hervieu-Léger that the new wave of individualistic self-help movements in the West do not meet the criteria for 'religion', but represent responses of people to an increasingly atomized society. Their position also supports my analysis of the way the capitalist solution to the land settlement in Alaska illustrates, on the one hand, the hegemonic and unified power of the free market, but on the other fundamentally contradicts an indigenous sense of community by transforming traditional understandings of the land into privately owned shares in corporations. In Campbell's words, 'the volatile market ... organizes social relations in a capitalist society', but while it organizes, it also 'disturbs'; while it 'integrates', it also 'atomizes' (1997: 205).

It is at this point, however, that my agreement with Campbell ends. His denial of ethnicity entails a direct assault on localization, which he sees as another form of Western exploitation, foisted in this case by the objects of his most venomous attack, NGO workers. Campbell contends that by emphasizing the importance of local traditions, notably expressed in primitive cultural forms, African self-determination is thwarted. The result is an undue emphasis on what he calls 'long defunct cultures' which has the effect of discouraging 'future social experimentation' as 'risky' and hence as something to 'be avoided' (1997: 227). Along with the renewed interest in the indigenous by NGOs, Campbell's targets include academics who, due to their anti-essentialist bias, believe that 'a world made up of multiplying identities ... expresses creativity and makes for the best possible world' (1997: 206). He condemns the cultural relativism inherent in such views, and accuses its advocates of fostering primitivism by depicting 'ethnic communities as morally appropriate because they stand next to nature' (1997: 207). They do this not for altruistic reasons, but, in the first place, 'to excuse the West from having to explain why it has failed to modernize Africa, and second, to excuse the West from having to explain why it has lost faith in the ability of its own system to deliver decent living standards' (1997: 207).

On closer analysis, it soon becomes apparent that Campbell's arguments contain within them numerous disturbing contradictions. For example, he contends that Africans have been portrayed by advocates of 'modern primitivism' as victims of outside influences, either benevolent and malevolent, but at the same time he castigates the West for not exercising its influence to ensure a better way of life in Africa. He condemns social constructionist theories for their emphasis on the role of Africans in developing their own local self-identities while at the same time claiming that the same theories render them impotent to initiate social change. When indigenous people affirm the values inherent in their own traditions, he claims that ethnic divisions are exacerbated making hatred and violence more, rather than less, likely, while, in a muddle of fuzzy thinking, he denies the real existence of ethnic identities. He condemns generalized and inaccurate characterizations of African societies, but demeans academics for refusing to employ essentialist reductions to classify indigenous peoples. Finally, he misses altogether the primary aims of academic research by confusing them with value-laden propositions, probably because his own objective is ideological and hence polemical.

My initial response to Campbell, and indeed indirectly to Harvey, is to re-state the purpose of scholarly research. All academic interpretations are constructions from the outside. In the human sciences, researchers generally employ methods that incorporate the perspectives of those they are studying, but because scholarly research follows strict guidelines, the researcher cannot avoid imposing a way of proceeding that follows the rules of a long-established critical tradition. In this sense, it is impossible to avoid the charge that academic research possesses inherent limitations, which cannot be violated if the research is to remain thoroughly academic. Even in light of the contemporary awareness that objectivity is never truly objective and that neutrality is impossible to achieve, the academic follows strict procedures to ensure that any research findings can be tested and potentially falsified. This means that scholarly studies always impose culturally-determined assumptions on the objects of research. In other words, I am arguing that empirical research represents a cultural approach that has been developed largely in the West and that its results must satisfy the rigid standards imposed by an academic culture. The academic thus does not approach any study primarily for altruistic reasons, as both Harvey and Campbell imply, apart from a self-defined commitment to the value of expanding knowledge and understanding. To define indigenous as local and kinship-based, therefore, carries no 'value' other than one that seeks to clarify the parameters within which the study takes place. My opposition to essentialist theories and my assertion that for too long kinship-based groups have been excluded from the study of religions, are not moral complaints, but ones based on a prior assumption that scholarly research must always proceed in a self-critical way and with a view to scientific accuracy.

So-called tribal or ethnic designations for indigenous peoples clearly have been constructed from the outside. I have already drawn attention to the fact that the word 'Shona' was not a self-designated term employed by the majority of the indigenous people in Zimbabwe, but may have been developed by colonial authorities for their own purposes, or may even have been employed by the Ndebele as a derogatory descriptor for the people they had conquered. Even more localized names, such as Korekore or Zezuru, were not used in a self-contained way to indicate a people living largely in one location (Beach, 1980: x–xi; Mutswairo, 1996: 1; Bourdillon, 1987: 16–17). The Inuit are somewhat different, since this and related words, such as Yupiit, as we have seen, translate in local languages as 'the real people' and refer to the way communities understood themselves. Nonetheless, it is unlikely that they thought of themselves as a distinct people who could be contrasted with other ethnic groups. The language used in the academic study of indigenous peoples thus admittedly is contrived to serve scholarly purposes. That such designations now have been largely accepted by indigenous peoples themselves reflects the changing relations of such groups with other communities and the wider world. Within academic studies today, to use these designations for a variety of indigenous peoples is practical, and indeed necessary, to describe and analyse cultural patterns that characterize peoples living in specific locations.

This approach can only be regarded as dangerous if the assumptions beneath such academic designations are not made explicit. By admitting that they are constructions with political implications, the scholar makes it clear that ethnic labels are always to some degree artificial and that potentially they can be misconstrued in precarious and oppressive ways, as Terence Ranger has so aptly demonstrated (1992: 247–62). Yet, for purposes of academic credibility, there is no alternative, other than refusing to discuss local situations or to revert to the discredited assumptions of essentialism. No doubt, Ranger's insistence is correct that boundaries between peoples always have been fluid, or at least less static than colonial administrators found convenient. His view, however, does not invalidate the need to define particular groups or to outline their specific religious beliefs and practices. Ranger's aim after all is not to dispute that African traditions existed, but to show that when African customs were codified by colonial authorities, 'a new and unchanging body of tradition had been created' (1992: 251). I have already demonstrated in the case of Zimbabwe that what Ranger calls 'a concept of immemorial "African Traditional Religion"' (1992: 252), or in other circles might be labelled academic reification (Smith, 1964: 50–74), wrongly portrays Indigenous Religions as static, unchanging and stuck in the past.

This observation, however, entails a very different point from my own insistence that by emphasizing the local nature of such studies, academics are less prone to make sweeping generalizations and much more likely to restrict their conclusions to quite testable observations.

In the context of contemporary multi-cultural Britain, the Muslim scholar Tariq Modood, who is the founding Director of the Centre for the Study of Ethnicity and Citizenship at the University of Bristol, has added a different perspective on ethnicity by arguing for what he calls 'public ethnicity', which is based on the notion that equality means 'not having to hide or apologize for one's origins, family or community' (2004: 247). Modood's call for tolerance within a multi-cultural society may suggest in Campbell's words that 'ethnicity … can now mean almost anything' (1997: 207), but tolerance (as opposed to cultural relativism) provides the foundation for what Modood (2004: 248) describes as 'the right to have one's "difference" (minority ethnicity, etc.) recognized and supported in the public *and* private spheres' (emphasis his). Modood's aim is to analyse how Muslim communities relate to processes of assimilation in contemporary Britain, but central to his argument is the inherent right of ethnic minorities to retain their particular cultural identities while at the same time broadening 'the public symbols' of the dominant national culture (2004: 248). This, of course, leads to a different discussion from mine, but in so far as Modood analyses relationships between local cultural identity in national and global contexts, it bears directly on Campbell's critique of ethnicity. In the framework of my own presentation of Indigenous Religions, it also supports my emphasis on the importance of local, kinship relations, even if these have always been internally dynamic and have been altered under external historical forces, most recently by colonial influences and the processes of globalization.

For these reasons, I think Campbell is wrong when he criticizes academic studies that focus on locality and 'indigenism' (1997: 89). He is equally wrong if his objection to the idea of ethnicity is that it has been conceived in the West in order to define a particular type of relationship between the West and the non-Western world. In itself, this is inevitable in so far as academic approaches derive from Western constructs and largely carry forward the Enlightenment principles of critical rationality, as noted by Geertz. Of course, it is entirely legitimate to question the type of relationship the West promotes towards African peoples, or towards other ethnic groups, as Modood has shown so clearly. In this light, Campbell's attempt to discredit social constructionist theories as purely individualistic remains unconvincing. Ranger, for example, is not reducing all social processes to atomized acts of individual self-determination when he notes that allegiances and identities in traditional societies have been fluctuating, nor is this Harvey's intent, for that matter, when he stresses the fluidity of 'belonging to a place' in contemporary diaspora studies. In the end, Campbell's negative attitude towards local cultures explains the primary motivation beneath his charge that those who privilege indigeneity promote modern forms of primitivism. At the conclusion of his book, this attitude becomes clear when he denigrates indigenous cultures in a quite prejudicial way by referring to them as 'backward' and socially retrogressive (1997: 212).

Concluding Comments

In this chapter, I have shown that the academic study of Indigenous Religions is not vulnerable to the insightful critiques articulated so forcefully by Armin Geertz, whose objects of censure in part are the neo-shamanists, who for reasons entirely divorced from the interests of indigenous peoples, contrive practices, putatively obtained from traditional shamanism, to address largely personal problems in line with a proliferating number of alternative Western therapies. It is in this sense that Geertz somewhat paradoxically cites with approval the comment of Barbara Meyerhoff, an anthropologist who collaborated with Carlos Castaneda, that 'it is the obligation of the lettered to make written records of the lore of the unlettered simply a record – not a mirror of ourselves or our needs and fantasies' (Geertz, 2004: 59). The study of the religions of indigenous peoples as I have presented it, of course, involves more than making a 'record', because it includes analysis and critical reflection, but at the very least it aims at a scientific study quite antithetical to the ends of 'neo-primitivism'. This is precisely why I have argued that neo-shamanism neither fits as indigenous nor as a religion, and equally why I have rejected Graham Harvey's attack on the critical rationality inherent in the Enlightenment project as an expression of Harvey's own version of 'theological animism'. I have also maintained that the charges levelled by Aidan Campbell at the concepts I have advocated are at best misdirected, since they derive from Campbell's prior ideological assumptions which promote intrinsically biased attitudes towards local, indigenous cultures. I am content, therefore, after reviewing the central critique of primitivism in this chapter by Geertz and Campbell, and by indicating precisely why the study of Indigenous Religions should not be confused either with neo-shamanism or animist theology, to let my prior analyses stand as evidence that the study of Indigenous Religions defines a legitimate academic category that is fully justified as field of study in university courses in Religious Studies.

A Practical Conclusion

I have justified the study of Indigenous Religions in this book on a number of grounds. On the most basic level, I have contended that it defines a crucial scholarly category by incorporating a wide spectrum of human activities that otherwise would be ignored in academic research. I have also contended that without some way of classifying the religions of indigenous societies, a highly significant number of the world's population would be omitted from research in religious studies, although such societies might be covered from the perspectives of other disciplines, such as anthropology or sociology. My argument asserts that scholars of religion, who conventionally study the 'world religions', have every academic right, and even an intellectual duty, to pay attention to the religious beliefs and practices of indigenous peoples. I have sought to clarify why this is so by defining indigenous and religion in particular ways, and by exemplifying these through my case studies. In the process, I have sought to dismantle the essentialist assumptions inherent in the world religions paradigm, and the ways the study of Indigenous Religions in recent publications have been incorporated into that paradigm. I have also challenged many of the presuppositions of the pioneers in the study of Indigenous Religions, like E.G. Parrinder and Andrew Walls, although I have supported fully their innovative contributions to the field, including the visionary taught master's course Walls and Harold Turner introduced in the University of Aberdeen in 1976 on 'Religion in Primal Societies'.

If I have succeeded in presenting a credible case for including Indigenous Religions in the curricula of religious studies undergraduate and postgraduate degrees, it is only fair that I should offer some direction as to how this track of study might be implemented. This, of course, is a practical issue, but it reverts back to the beginning of this book, when I suggested that there are as many indigenous religions in the world as there are indigenous societies. If my contention that indigenous is defined by locality and kinship is correct, the study of the religions of such societies would include a limitless number of potential topics. Conversely, if religion is defined as the authoritative transmission of the traditions, beliefs and experiences of identifiable communities about postulated non-falsifiable alternate realities, the course could appear overly concerned with institutions and thus favour a sociological approach. Finally, such a study would lack integrity if it did not pay attention to globalizing forces, which have produced a quite complex arrangement of new and/or syncretic religious expressions that in many cases have transformed, disrupted or even displaced traditional localized, kinship-based religions. It would seem necessary to include this aspect in a course on Indigenous Religions, but it would need to be accomplished without transgressing the definitional boundaries I have imposed on this field of study.

With these complex considerations in mind, I would suggest that an undergraduate Honours programme devoted to the study of Indigenous Religions in every case should adopt a tri-partite structure. In the first instance, a section of the course needs to be devoted to methodological issues, much as I have done in this book, by engaging in discussions about the problematic nature of Indigenous Religions and placing these alongside issues of limitation and definition. Different disciplinary approaches also need to be considered, including the relationship between the study of Indigenous Religions in departments of religious studies and similar research undertaken in other departments in the social and human sciences, such as anthropology, sociology and history. Both theoretical and practical issues should be explored in courses on methodology, such as, among others, debates about primitivism, insider/outsider perspectives, field methods, self-reflexivity and the authenticity of 'new age' as an Indigenous Religion. The phenomenology of religion, and the related approaches it has spawned, such as Gavin Flood's narrative theory and Graham Harvey's notion of 'guesthood', need to be considered, not just as theories, but as practical options guiding actual field studies. A full third of the course should be devoted to examining methodological issues in the study of Indigenous Religions.

Another third of the curriculum should comprise studies in particular Indigenous Religions, if staff composition makes such an option feasible. It is obvious that not every area of the world can be covered in the curriculum, but there need to be enough lecturers in a department who possess sufficient expertise to offer a variety of case studies in specific Indigenous Religions. This corresponds to what I have done in this book when I considered the Indigenous Religions of the Yupiit of Alaska and the Korekore of Zimbabwe. The case studies should be presented as useful for comparative purposes in order that the study of Indigenous Religions can be shown to contribute more generally to critical reflection within religious studies regarding the selection of appropriate comparative categories. Specific cases, nonetheless, need to be analysed always in sharp contrast to the theological tendency of scholars working in the Eliadean tradition who identify a universal essence, called 'religion', which they then allege transposes itself into innumerable manifestations in time and space.

Finally, the interaction between Indigenous Religions and various globalizing forces should constitute another section of the study. Courses could be constructed, for example, on African Initiated Churches, from the perspective of Indigenous Religions. New Religious Movements in indigenous societies might also be included, covering such topics as cargo cults in Melanesia, the African-Caribbean movement called Santeria, Candomblé in Brazil or the Native American Church. In addition, courses which focus on how one practice in an Indigenous Religion has produced new expressions could be studied, as, for example, how Christian pilgrimages to traditional mountain shrines in Korea have influenced and been influenced by indigenous shamanism, or how various indigenous traditions in Asia have been fused with Hindu or Buddhist movements. The actual content of sections covering case studies in Indigenous Religions and New Indigenous Religious Movements depends practically on the specializations of staff in a department, but always the focus needs to be maintained on Indigenous Religions and not transferred subtly to studies in new age or contemporary Western religious innovations.

An Honours programme on Indigenous Religions would need sufficient courses at pre-Honours level to make a specialization in a department credible. For this reason, a basic introduction to methodologies in the study of religions, which normally forms part of any religious studies degree, should feed into the Indigenous Religions specialization. Within first and/or second year courses in religious studies, a section introducing the methodological problems associated with Indigenous Religions, a limited case study or studies and some reference to the dynamic nature of Indigenous

Religions should be included. I have already indicated that departments of religious studies need to think of creative ways to transform the traditional world religions paradigm into more academically credible, non-essentialist approaches. Clearly, I have not rejected a geographical approach in this book, but I have insisted that the very broad treatment of vast regions of the world, as has been done in numerous texts, oversimplifies religion and tends to reinforce traditional world religions approaches by ignoring local differences. This problem is not easily overcome, particularly at introductory levels. Thematic courses might provide useful alternatives, for example, by studying social contexts from religious perspectives, such as might be indicated in courses on comparative religious influences on contemporary political structures, or by examining types of religious practitioners in different settings, or by looking at religious activities comparatively, such as sacrificial rites. If such topics could be integrated into an introductory course alongside studies in methodology, the academic study of religions, including Indigenous Religions, could be moved away from its association with reified and essentialized notions of the religions of the world by studying religious practices and groupings in specific social and cultural contexts.

Taught postgraduate courses offer greater scope for specialization than undergraduate degrees and at a greater depth, but the same elements need to be included in both: methodologies, studies in specific Indigenous Religions and dynamic processes amongst indigenous societies. Depending on the length of a postgraduate course, an element of fieldwork would be useful, but this needs to be weighed against practical considerations, including language limitations. The postgraduate thesis, even in taught master's courses, often plays a significant part in the overall programme, and this would in many cases be aided by field research. The thesis, in any case, should address methodological issues, both theoretical and practical, that relate specifically to the study of Indigenous Religions, and it should provide the student with an opportunity to write about religion in at least one indigenous society, even if this is obtained by consulting the field descriptions of other researchers.

Clearly, because so many universities around the world follow different academic procedures and employ varying curricular styles and methods of assessment, it is not possible for me here to provide anything more than the general guidelines I have indicated as requisite for implementing studies in Indigenous Religions. I would underscore that the three elements in the programme I have identified, methodologies, studies in specific Indigenous Religions and dynamic processes, although essential, can be combined in numerous inventive ways depending on local circumstances and staff proficiency. In the end, the integrity of any academic programme in this field must be constrained by its focus on 'indigenous' and 'religion', but the permutations around these terms should not be unduly restricted nor bound by outdated models. Obviously, if my arguments in this book prevail, it will mean that the development of new curricula in Indigenous Religions will confront scholars of religion with a series of methodological challenges, not the least of which involves translating theories practically into specific course offerings in ways that eventually could revolutionize the way we think of, and hence study, religion itself.

Bibliography

Abercrombie, Nicholas, Hill, Stephen and Turner, Bryan S. 2000. *The Penguin Dictionary of Sociology*. 4th ed. London: Penguin Books Ltd.

Abimbola, Wande. 1991. 'The Place of African Traditional Religion in Contemporary Africa: The Yoruba Example', in Jacob K. Olupona (ed.). *African Traditional Religions in Contemporary Society*. St. Paul, Minnesota: Paragon House.

Alexander, Jocelyn. 2003. '"Squatters"', Veterans and the State in Zimbabwe' in A. Hammar, B. Raftopoulos and S. Jensen (eds). *Zimbabwe's Unfinished Business. Rethinking Land, State and Nation in the Context of Crisis*. Harare: Weaver Press, 83–117.

Anderson, H. Dewey and Eells, Walter Crosby. 1935. *Alaska Natives. A Survey of Their Sociological and Educational Status*. Stanford University, California: Stanford University Press and London: Humphrey Milford, Oxford University Press.

Anttonen, Veikko. 2005. 'Norse Shamanism', in C. Partridge (gen. ed.). *The New Lion Handbook. The World's Religions* (3rd edition, revised and expanded). Oxford: Lion Hudson, 124–5.

Archer, John Clark. 1938. *Faiths Men Live By*. New York: Thomas Nelson and Sons.

Barnhard, Alan and Kenrick, Justin. 2001. 'Preface', in A. Barnhard and J. Kenrick (eds), *Africa's Indigenous Peoples: 'First Peoples' or 'Marginalized Minorities'?* Centre of African Studies: University of Edinburgh, vii–xv.

Baylis, Philippa. 1988. *An Introduction to Primal Religions*. Edinburgh: Traditional Cosmology Society.

Beach, D.N. 1980. *The Shona and Zimbabwe 900–1850. An Outline of Shona History*. Gweru, Zimbabwe: Mambo Press.

Berens, Denis (ed.). 1988. *A Concise Encyclopedia of Zimbabwe*. Gweru, Zimbabwe: Mambo Press.

Berger, Thomas R. 1985. *Village Journey. The Report of the Alaska Native Review Commission*. New York: Hill and Wang.

Bergland, Axel-Ivar. 2005. 'The Zulu', in C. Partridge (gen. ed.). *The New Lion Handbook. The World's Religions* (3rd edition, revised and expanded). Oxford: Lion Hudson, 132–33.

Berner, Ulrich. 2004. 'Africa and the Origin of the Science of Religion. Max Müller (1823–1900) and James George Frazer (1854–1941) on African Religions', in F. Ludwig and A. Adogame (eds). *European Traditions in the Study of Religion in Africa*. Wiesbadan: Harrassowitz Verlag, 141–49.

Bhebe, Ngwabi and Ranger, Terence. 1995. 'Introduction' in N. Bhebe and T. Ranger (eds). *Society in Zimbabwe's Liberation War. Volume Two*. Harare: University of Zimbabwe Publications, London: James Currey, Portsmouth: Heinemann, 6–34.

Binsbergen, Wim van. 2003. *Intercultural Encounters. African and Anthropological Lessons towards a Philosophy of Interculturality*. Münster: Lit Verlag.

Bird-David, Nurit. 2002. '"Animism"' Revisited: Personhood, Environment, and Relational Epistemology', G. Harvey (ed.). *Readings in Indigenous Religions*. London: Continuum, 73–105.

Boal, Barbara. 2005. 'Indigenous Religions in Asia', in C. Partridge (gen. ed.). *The New Lion Handbook. The World's Religions* (3rd edition, revised and expanded). Oxford: Lion Hudson, 104–7.

Bouquet, A.C. 1950 (3rd ed.). *Comparative Religion*. Harmondsworth: Penguin Books.

Bourdillon, Michael F.C. 1997 3rd ed. *The Shona Peoples. An Ethnography of the Contemporary Shona, with Special Reference to their Religion*. Gweru, Zimbabwe: Mambo Press.

Bowie, Fiona. 2000. *The Anthropology of Religion: An Introduction*. Oxford: Blackwell Publishers.

Bowie, Fiona. 2005a. 'The Anthropology of Religion', in Christopher Partridge (gen. ed.), *The New Lion Handbook: The World's Religions*. Oxford: Lion Hudson, 19, 22.

Bowie, Fiona, 2005b. 'The Bangwa', in C. Partridge (gen. ed.). *The New Lion Handbook. The World's Religions* (3rd edition, revised and expanded). Oxford: Lion Hudson, 131.

Bruce, Steve. 2002. *God is Dead. Secularization in the West*. Oxford: Blackwell Publishing.

Burch, Ernest S., Jr. 1998. *The Iñupiaq Eskimo Nations of Northwest Alaska*. Fairbanks: University of Alaska Press.

Burgess, MaryCatherine. 2005. *Contemporary Shamanic Practice in Scotland: A New Paradigm of Spirituality and Religion*. Unpublished PhD thesis, University of Edinburgh.

Burke, T. Patrick. 1996. *The Major Religions. An Introduction with Texts*. Oxford and Cambridge: Blackwell Publishers.

Campbell, Aidan. 1997. *Western Primitivism: African Ethnicity. A Study in Cultural Relations*. London and Washington: Cassell.

Carrette, Jeremy. 2005. 'Critical Theory and Religion', in Christopher Partridge (gen. ed.). *The New Lion Handbook: The World's Religions*. Oxford: Lion Hudson, 28–31.

Carrette, Jeremy and King, Richard. 2005. *Selling Spirituality. The Silent Takeover of Religion*. London and New York: Routledge.

Case, David. S. and Voluck, David A. 1984, 2nd ed. *Alaska Natives and American Laws*. Fairbanks: University of Alaska Press.

Castaneda, Carlos. 1968. *The Teachings of Don Juan: A Yaqui Way of Knowledge*. Berkeley, California: University of California Press.

Cave, Sydney. 1929. *Christianity and Some Living Religions of the East*. London: Duckworth.

Chidester, David. 1996. *Savage Systems: Colonialism and Comparative Religion in Southern Africa.*

Chigwedere, A.S. 1980. *From Mutapa to Rhodes 1000–1890 A.D.* London: Macmillan.

Chiura, Tichawona. 1991. *Mutiusinazita Religious Cult in Marondera District, Zimbabwe.* Unpublished MA thesis, Department of Religious Studies, Classics and Philosophy, University of Zimbabwe.

Chryssides, George D. 1999. *Exploring New Religions.* London: Cassell.

Churchill, Ward. 2003. 'Spiritual Hucksterism. The Rise of the Plastic Medicine Men', in G. Harvey (ed.). *Shamanism: A Reader.* London and New York: Routledge, 324–33.

Clarke, Peter. 1997. 'Primal Religions' in Chris Richards, *The Illustrated Encyclopedia of World Religions.* Shaftesbury, Dorset, Rockport Massachusetts and Melbourne, Victoria: Element Books Limited, 14–23.

Cowan, Tom. 1993. *Fire in the Head. Shamanism and the Celtic Spirit.* San Francisco: Harper and Row.

Coward, Harold (ed.). 1997. *Life after Death in World Religions.* Maryknoll, New York: Orbis Books.

Cox, James L. 1991. *The Impact of Christian Missions on Indigenous Cultures. The 'Real People' and the Unreal Gospel.* Lewiston, New York: Edwin Mellen.

Cox, James L. 1995. 'Ancestors, the Sacred and God: Reflections on the Meaning of the Sacred in Zimbabwean Death Rituals', *Religion* 25 (4): 339–55.

Cox, James L. 1996a. 'The Classification "Primal Religions" as a Non-empirical, Christian Theological Construct', *Studies in World Christianity: The Edinburgh Review of Theology and Religion* 2 (1), 55–76.

Cox, James L. 1996b. 'Methodological Considerations Relevant to the Truth of African Traditional Religions', in Jan Platvoet, James Cox and Jacob Olupona (eds). *The Study of Religions in Africa: Past, Present and Prospects.* Cambridge: Roots and Branches, 155–71.

Cox, James L. 1998a. *Rational Ancestors: Scientific Rationality and African Indigenous Religions.* Cardiff: Cardiff Academic Press.

Cox, James L. 1998b. 'Religious Typologies and the Postmodern Critique', *Method and Theory in the Study of Religion*, 10: 244–62.

Cox, James L. 1999. 'Intuiting Religion: A Case for Preliminary Definitions', in J.G. Platvoet and A.L. Molendijk (eds). *The Pragmatics of Defining Religion: Contexts, Concepts and Contests.* Leiden: Brill, 267–84.

Cox, James L. 2000a. 'Spirit Mediums in Zimbabwe: Religious Experience in and on behalf of the Community', *Studies in World Christianity. The Edinburgh Review of Theology and Religion* 6 (2), 190–207.

Cox, James L. 2000b. 'Characteristics of African Indigenous Religions in Contemporary Zimbabwe', in G. Harvey (ed.). *Indigenous Religions: A Companion.* London and New York: Cassell, 230–42.

Cox, James L. 2003. 'Contemporary Shamanism in Global Contexts: "Religious" Appeals to an Archaic Tradition?', *Studies in World Christianity: The Edinburgh Review of Theology and Religion,* 9 (1): 69–87.

Cox, James L. 2004a. 'Afterword. Separating Religion from the "Sacred": Methodological Agnosticism and the Future of Religious Studies', in S. Sutcliffe (ed.). *Religion: Empirical Studies*. Aldershot: Ashgate, 259–64.

Cox, James L. 2004b. 'From Africa to Africa: The Significance of Approaches to the Study of African Religions at Aberdeen and Edinburgh Universities from 1970 to 1998', in F. Ludwig and A. Adogame (eds). *European Traditions in the Study of Religion in Africa*. Wiesbaden: Harrassowitz Verlag, 255–64.

Cox, James L. 2005a. 'The Land Crisis in Zimbabwe: A Case of Religious Intolerance?' *Fieldwork in Religion* 1 (1), 35–48.

Cox, James L. 2005b. 'Inuit', in C. Partridge (gen. ed). *The New Lion Handbook. The World's Religions* (3rd edition, revised and expanded). Oxford: Lion Hudson, 123–25.

Cox, James L. 2005c. 'African Indigenous Religions', in C. Partridge (gen. ed). *The New Lion Handbook. The World's Religions* (3rd edition, revised and expanded). Oxford: Lion Hudson, 126–30.

Cox, James L. 2006. *A Guide to the Study of Religion: Key Figures, Formative Influences and Subsequent Debates*. London and New York: Continuum.

Cox, James L. and Sutcliffe, Steven J. 2006. 'Religious Studies in Scotland: A Persistent Tension with Divinity', *Religion* 36: 1–28.

Daneel, M.L. 1970. *God of the Matopos Hills. An Essay on the Mwari Cult in Rhodesia*. The Hague and Paris: Mouton.

Daneel, M.L. 1998. 'Mwari the Liberator: Oracular Intervention in Zimbabwe's Quest for the "Lost Lands"', in James L. Cox (ed.). *Rites of Passage in Contemporary Africa*. Cardiff: Cardiff Academic Press, 94–125.

Danquah, J.B. 1944. *The Akan Doctrine of God*. London: Lutterworth Press.

Dawson, Andrew. 2005. 'South American Indigenous Religions', in C. Partridge (gen. ed.). *The New Lion Handbook. The World's Religions* (3rd edition, revised and expanded). Oxford: Lion Hudson, 114–19.

Drebert, Ferdinand. 1959. *Alaska Missionary. A Testimony to God's Faithfulness, and to the Power of the Gospel*. Bethlehem, Pennsylvania: The Moravian Book Shop.

Dupré, Wilhelm. 1975. *Religion in Primitive Cultures*. The Hague: Mouton.

Eliade, Mircea. 1967. *From Primitives to Zen: A Thematic Sourcebook of the History of Religions*. London: Collins.

Eliade, Mircea. 1987 [1957]. *The Sacred and the Profane. The Nature of Religion*. San Diego, New York and London: Harcourt.

Eliade, Mircea. 1989 [1964]. *Shamanism. Archaic Techniques of Ecstasy*. London: Arkana Penguin Books.

Eliade, Mircea. 1996 [1958]. *Patterns in Comparative Religion*. Lincoln and London: University of Nebraska Press.

Eliade, Mircea and Ioan P. Couliano, with Hillary S. Wiesner (eds). 2000. *The HarperCollins Concise Guide to World Religions*. New York: HarperCollins.

Evans-Pritchard, E.E. 1937. *Witchcraft, Oracles and Magic among the Azande*. Oxford: Clarendon Press.

Fienup-Riordan, Ann. 1990. *Eskimo Essays. Yup'ik Lives and How We See Them*. New Brunswick, New Jersey and London: Rutgers University Press.

Fienup-Riordan, Ann. 1994. *Boundaries and Passages. Rule and Ritual in Yup'ik Eskimo Oral Tradition*. Norman and London: University of Oklahoma Press.

Fienup-Riordan (ed.). 1996. *Agayuliyararput. Kegginaqut, Kangiit-llu. Our Way of Making Prayer. Yup'ik Masks and the Stories They Tell* (transcribed and translated by Marie Meade). Seattle and London: Anchorage Museum of History and Art in association with the University of Washington.

Fienup-Riordan, Ann. 2000. *Hunting Tradition in a Changing World. Yup'ik Lives in Alaska Today*. New Brunswick, New Jersey and London: Rutgers University Press.

Firth, Raymond. 1967. *Tikopia Ritual and Belief*. London: George Allen and Unwin.

Firth, Raymond. 1996. *Religion: A Humanist Interpretation*. London and New York: Routledge.

Fisher, Mary Pat. 1997. *Living Religions. An Encyclopedia of the World's Faiths*. London and New York: I.B. Tauris Publishers.

Fisher, Mary Pat. 1999. *Religion in the Twenty-first Century*. London: Routledge.

Fitzgerald, Timothy. 2000. *The Ideology of Religious Studies*. New York and Oxford: Oxford University Press.

Flint, Robert. 1882. *Christianity in Relation to Other Religions* (Faiths of the World Lecture 12). Edinburgh and London: W. Blackwood and Sons.

Flood, Gavin. 1999. *Beyond Phenomenology. Rethinking the Study of Religion*. London and New York: Cassell.

Forde, Daryll. 1950. 'Double Descent among the Yakö', in A.R. Radcliffe-Brown and D. Forde (eds). *African Systems of Kinship and Marriage*. London, New York and Toronto: Oxford University Press (published for the International African Institute), 285–332.

Fortes, Meyer. 1945. *The Dynamics of Clanship among the Tallensi*. London: published for the International African Institute by Oxford University Press.

Forward, Martin. 1998. *A Bag of Needments. Geoffrey Parrinder and the Study of Religion*. Bern: Peter Lang.

Fowler, Jeaneane and others (ed.). 1997. *World Religions: An Introduction for Students*. Brighton: Sussex Academic Press.

Frazer, James G. 1963 [1922]. *The Golden Bough. A Study in Magic and Religion. I Volume, Abridged Edition*. New York: Macmillan Publishing Company.

Garbett, Kingsley. 1977. 'Disparate Regional Cults and a Unitary Field in Zimbabwe', in R.P. Werbner. *Regional Cults*. London, New York and San Francisco: Academic Press, 55–92.

Geertz, Armin W. 2004. 'Can We Move Beyond Primitivism? On Recovering the Indigenes of Indigenous Religions in the Academic Study of Religions', in J.K. Olupona (ed.), *Beyond Primitivism. Indigenous Religious Traditions and Modernity*. New York and London: Routledge, 37–70.

Gelfand, Michael. 1979. *Growing Up in Shona Society. From Birth to Marriage*. Gweru, Zimbabwe: Mambo Press.

Ginnelly, Emma. 2005. 'An Analysis of the Signifier Indigenous'. Unpublished MSc Dissertation, submitted to the School of Divinity, University of Edinburgh.

Giulianotti, Richard and Gerrard, Michael. 2001. 'Cruel Britannia? Glasgow Rangers, Scotland and "Hot" Football Rivalries', in G. Armstrong and R. Giulianotti (eds). *Fear and Loathing in World Football*. Oxford: Berg, 23–42.

Giulianotti, Richard and Robertson, Roland. 2006. 'Glocalization, Globalization and Migration: The Case of Scottish Football Supporters in North America'. *International Sociology* 21 (3), 171–98.

Hallowell, A. Irving. 1960. 'Ojibwa Ontology, Behaviour, and World View', Stanley Diamond (ed.). *Culture in History: Essays in Honor of Paul Radin*. New York: Columbia University Press. Reprinted in Graham Harvey (ed.). 2002. *Readings in Indigenous Religions*. London and New York: Continuum, 17–49.

Hamilton, Malcolm. 2005. 'The Sociology of Religion', in Christopher Partridge (gen. ed.), *The New Lion Handbook: The World's Religions*. Oxford: Lion Hudson, 23–5.

Hammar, Amanda and Raftopoulos, Brian. 2003. 'Zimbabwe's Unfinished Business: Rethinking Land, State and Nation', in A. Hammar, B. Raftopoulos and S. Jensen (eds). *Zimbabwe's Unfinished Business. Rethinking Land, State and Nation in the Context of Crisis*. Harare: Weaver Press, 1–47.

Harner, Michael. 1980. *The Way of the Shaman: A Guide to Power and Healing*. San Francisco: Harper and Row.

Harner, Michael. 2003. 'Discovering the Way', in G. Harvey (ed.). *Shamanism: A Reader*. London and New York: Routledge, 41–56.

Harold-Barry, David. 2004. 'One Country, "Two Nations", No Dialogue', in David Harold-Barry (ed.). *Zimbabwe: The Past is the Future*. Harare: Weaver Press, 249–60.

Harvey, Graham. 1997. *Listening People, Speaking Earth: Contemporary Paganism*. London: C. Hurst and Co.

Harvey, Graham. 2000. 'Introduction' in G. Harvey (ed.). *Indigenous Religions: A Companion*. London and New York: Cassell, 1–19.

Harvey, Graham (ed.). 2002a. *Readings in Indigenous Religions*. London: Continuum.

Harvey, Graham (ed.). 2002b. *Shamanism: A Reader*. London: Routledge.

Harvey, Graham. 2004. 'Response to a Review in AASR Bulletin 21', *AASR Bulletin* 22: 38–9.

Harvey, Graham. 2005a. *Animism: Respecting the Living World*. London: C. Hurst and Co.

Harvey, Graham. 2005b. 'Understanding Indigenous Religions', in C. Partridge (gen. ed.). *The New Lion Handbook. The World's Religions* (3rd edition, revised and expanded). Oxford: Lion Hudson, 100–104.

Harvey, Graham and Thompson Jr, Charles D. 2005. 'Introduction' in G. Harvey and C.D. Thompson Jr (eds). *Indigenous Diasporas and Dislocations*. Aldershot and Burlington: Ashgate, 1–12.

Hastings, Adrian. 1986. 'AWF as Editor', in J. Thrower (ed.). *Essays in Religious Studies for Andrew Walls*. Aberdeen: University of Aberdeen, Department of Religious Studies, 5–9.

Hastings, Adrian. 2004. 'African Christian Studies, 1967–1999: Reflections of an Editor', in F. Ludwig and A. Adogame. *European Traditions in the Study of Religion in Africa*. Wiesbaden: Harrassowitz Verlag, 265–74.

Hervieu-Léger, Danièle. 1993. 'Present-Day Emotional Renewals. The End of Secularization or the End of Religion?', in W.H. Swatos, Jr. (ed.). *A Future for Religion? New Paradigms for Social Analysis*. Newbury Park, California, London and New Delhi: Sage Publications, 129–48.

Hervieu-Léger, Danièle. 1999. 'Religion as Memory: Reference to Tradition and the Constitution of a Heritage of Belief in Modern Societies', in J.G. Platvoet and A.L. Molendijk (eds). *The Pragmatics of Defining Religion. Contexts, Concepts and Contests*. Leiden: Brill, 73–92.

Hervieu-Léger, Danièle. 2000. *Religion as a Chain of Memory* (translated by Simon Lee). Cambridge: Polity Press.

Hervieu-Léger, Danièle. 2001. 'The Twofold Limit of the Notion of Secularization', in L. Woodhead (ed.). *Peter Berger and the Study of Religion*. London and New York: Routledge, 112–25.

Hick, John. 1984. 'Religious Pluralism', in F. Whaling (ed.). *The World's Religious Traditions. Current Perspectives in Religious Studies*. Edinburgh: T. and T. Clark., 145–64.

Hinnells, John R. (ed.). 1998. *A New Handbook of Living Religions*. Harmondsworth: Penguin Books.

Hsu, Francis L.K. 1964. 'Rethinking the Concept "Primitive"'. *Current Anthropology* (5), 169–78.

Hufford, David J. 1999. 'The Scholarly Voice and the Personal Voice: Reflexivity in Belief Studies', in R. McCutcheon (ed.). *The Insider/Outsider Problem in the Study of Religion*. London and New York: Cassell, 294–310.

Hume, Lynne. 2005. 'Australian Aboriginal Religion', in C. Partridge (gen. ed.). *The New Lion Handbook. The World's Religions* (3rd edition, revised and expanded). Oxford: Lion Hudson, 110–12.

Hume, Richard Ernest. 1924. *The World's Living Religions: An Historical Sketch*. New York: Scribners.

Idowu, E. Bolaji. 1962. *Olódùmarè. God in Yorùbá Belief*. London: Longmans.

Idowu, E. Bolaji. 1973. *African Traditional Religion: A Definition*.

Jakobsen, Marete Demant. 1999. *Shamanism. Traditional and Contemporary Approaches to the Mastery of Spirits and Healing*. Oxford and New York: Berghahn Books.

Jensen, Jeppe Sinding. 2003. 'Social Facts, Metaphysics and Rationality in the Study of Religion as a Human Science', in J.S. Jensen and L.H. Martin (eds). *Rationality and the Science of Religion*. London and New York: Routledge, 117–35.

Kaplan, Flora Edouwaye S. 2000. 'Some thoughts on Ideology, Beliefs, and Sacred Kingship among the Edo (Benin) People of Nigeria', in J. Olupona (ed.). *African Spirituality. Forms, Meanings, and Expressions*. New York: The Crossroad Publishing Company, 114–51.

Keen, Rosemary. 2005. 'Church Missionary Society Archive: Editorial Introduction'. Adam Matthew Publications: http://adam-matthewpublications.co.uk/digital_ guides.

Kellett, E.E. 1948 [1933]. *A Short History of Religions*. London: Victor Gollancz Ltd.

Kippenberg, Hans G. 2003. 'Rationality in Studying Historical Religions', in J.S. Jensen and L.H. Martin (eds). *Rationality and the Science of Religion*. London and New York: Routledge, 157–66.

Kuper, Hilda. 1947. *An African Aristocracy: Rank among the Swazi*. London: Published for the International African Institute by Oxford University Press.

Lambert, Yves. 1999. 'Religion in Modernity as a New Axial Age: Secularization or New Religious Forms?' *Sociology of Religion* 60 (3): 303–32.

Lan, David. 1985. *Guns and Rain. Guerrillas and Spirit Mediums in Zimbabwe*. London: James Currey and Berkeley and Los Angeles: University of California Press.

Langdon, Steve J. 2002. *The Native People of Alaska. Traditional Living in Northern Land* (4th ed.). Anchorage: Graphics.

Leeuw, van der, Gerardus. 1938. *Religion in Essence and Manifestation. A Study in Phenomenology* (translated by J.E. Turner). London: George Allen and Unwin).

Lewis, I.M. 1989, 2nd ed. *Ecstatic Religion. A Study of Shamanism and Spirit Possession*. London and New York: Routledge.

Loeliger, Carl. 'Melanesia', in C. Partridge (gen. ed.). *The New Lion Handbook. The World's Religions* (3rd edition, revised and expanded). Oxford: Lion Hudson, 113–14.

Long, Charles H. 2004. 'A Postcolonial Meaning of Religion: Some Reflections from the Indigenous World', in J.K. Olupona (ed.), *Beyond Primitivism. Indigenous Religious Traditions and Modernity*. New York and London: Routledge, 89–98.

Lovejoy, Arthur and Boas, George. 1965 [1935]. *Primitivism and Related Ideas in Antiquity*. New York: Octagon Books.

Ludwig, Frieder and Adogame, Afe (eds). 2004. *European Traditions in the Study of Religion in Africa*. Wiesbaden: Harrassowitz Verlag.

Mbiti, John S. 1969. *African Religions and Philosophy*. London: Heinemann.

McCutcheon, Russell T. 2005. 'Understanding Religion', in Christopher Partridge (gen. ed.), *The New Lion Handbook: The World's Religions*. Oxford: Lion Hudson, 10–13.

McLoughlin, Seán. 2003. *World Religions: A Source Book*. London: Flame Tree Publishing.

Masunungure, Eldred. 2004. 'Travails of Opposition Politics in Zimbabwe since Independence', in David Harold-Barry (ed.). *Zimbabwe: The Past is the Future*. Harare: Weaver Press, 147–92.

Masuzawa, Tomoko. 2005. *The Invention of World Religions Or, How European Universalism was Preserved in the Language of Pluralism*. Chicago and London: The University of Chicago Press.

Matthews, John. 1991. *The Celtic Shaman: A Handbook*. Shaftsbury, Dorset: Element Books.

Mbiti, John S. 1969. *African Religions and Philosophy*. London: Heinemann.

Mbiti, John S. 1970. *Concepts of God in Africa*. London: SPCK.

Mbiti, John S. 1975. *Introduction to African Religion*. London, Ibadan, Nairobi: Heinemann.

Mitchell, Donald Craig. 2001. *Take My Land. Take My Life. The Story of Congress's Historic Settlement of Alaska Native Land Claims, 1960–1971*. Fairbanks: University of Alaska Press.

Molendijk, Arie L. 1999. 'In Defence of Pragmatism', in J.G. Platvoet and A.L. Molendijk (eds). *The Pragmatics of Defining Religion. Contexts, Concepts and Contests*. Leiden: Brill, 3–19.

Moore, Sally Falk. 1993. 'Changing Perspectives on a Changing Africa', in R.H. Bates, V.Y. Mudimbe and J. O'Barr. *Africa and the Disciplines. The Contributions of Research in Africa to the Social Sciences and Humanities*. Chicago and London: University of Chicago Press, 3–57.

Morgan Peggy and Clive Lawton (eds). *Ethical Issues in Six Religious Traditions*. Edinburgh: Edinburgh University Press.

Morris, Brian. 1987. *Anthropological Studies of Religion: An Introduction*. Cambridge: Cambridge University Press.

Mutswairo, Solomon. 1996. 'Who Is Mbire?', in S. Mutswairo, E. Chiwome, N.E. Mberi, A. Masasire and M. Furusa (eds). *Introduction to Shona Culture*. Eiffel Flats, Zimbabwe: Juta Zimbabwe (Pvt) Limited, 16–39.

Nadel, Siegfried F. 1942. *A Black Byzantium: The Kingdom of Nupe in Nigeria*. Oxford: Oxford University Press.

Newberry, J.W.E. 2005. 'Native North Americans', in C. Partridge (gen. ed). *The New Lion Handbook. The World's Religions* (3rd edition, revised and expanded). Oxford: Lion Hudson, 120–22.

The New Lion Handbook: The World's Religions. 2005. 'Timeline of the World's Religions', in Christopher Partridge (gen. ed.), *The New Lion Handbook: The World's Religions*. Oxford: Lion Hudson, 36–7.

The New Lion Handbook: The World's Religions. 2005. 'The World Religions: Map', in Christopher Partridge (gen. ed.), *The New Lion Handbook: The World's Religions*. Oxford: Lion Hudson, 34–5.

Nigosian, S.A. 1994 (2nd ed.). *World Faiths*. New York: St. Martin's Press.

Noss, David S. and Noss, John B. 1990 (8th ed.). *A History of the Worlds Religions*. New York: Macmillan.

Noss, John B. 1963 [1949]. *Man's Religions*. New York and London: Macmillan.

Nthoi, Leslie S. 1998. 'Wosana Rite of Passage: Reflections on the Initiation of Wosana in the Cult of Mwali in Zimbabwe', in James L. Cox (ed.). *Rites of Passage in Contemporary Africa*. Cardiff: Cardiff Academic Press, 63–93.

Nthoi, Leslie S. 2006. *Contesting Sacred Space: A Pilgrimage Study of the Mwali Cult of Southern Africa*. Trenton, N.J.: Africa World Press.

Olupona, Jacob K. (ed.). 2000. *African Spirituality: Forms, Meanings and Expressions*. New York: Crossroad.

Olupona, Jacob K. 2004. 'Introduction', in J.K. Olupona (ed.), *Beyond Primitivism. Indigenous Religious Traditions and Modernity*. New York and London: Routledge, 1–19.

Oquilluk, William. 1981. *People of Kauwerak. Legends of the Northern Eskimo*. Anchorage: Alaska Pacific University Press.

Oswalt, Wendell H. 1963. *Mission of Change in Alaska. Eskimos and Moravians on the Kuskokwim*. San Marino, California: The Huntington Library.

Oswalt, Wendell H. 1967. *Alaskan Eskimos*. San Francisco: Chandler Publishing Company.

Oswalt, Wendell H. 1999. *Eskimos and Explorers* (2nd ed.). Lincoln and London: University of Nebraska Press.

Otto, Rudolf. 1926. *The Idea of the Holy: An Inquiry into the Non Rational Factor in the Idea of the Divine* (translated by John W. Harvey). London: Humphrey Milford and Oxford University Press.

Palmer, Robin. 1990. 'Land reform in Zimbabwe, 1980–1990', *African Affairs* 89 (355), 163–81.

Pals, Daniel L. 2006. *Eight Theories of Religion, 2nd ed.* New York and Oxford: Oxford University Press.

Parrinder, Geoffrey. 1949. *West African Religion: Illustrated from the Beliefs and Practices of the Yoruba, Ewe, Akan and Kindred Peoples*. London: Epworth.

Parrinder, Geoffrey. 1954. *African Traditional Religion*. London: Hutchinson House.

Parrinder, Geoffrey, 1961. *West African Religion. A Study of the Beliefs and Practices of Akan, Ewe, Yoruba, Ibo, and Kindred Peoples*. (2nd edition, completely rewritten, revised and Enlarged). London: The Epworth Press.

Parrinder, Geoffrey. 1962. *Comparative Religion*. London: George Allen and Unwin Ltd.

Parrinder, Geoffrey. 1964. *The World's Living Religions*. London: Pan Books Ltd.

Parrinder, Geoffrey. 1965. *Jesus in the Qur'an*. London: Faber and Faber.

Parrinder, Geoffrey. 1996 [1980]. *Sexual Morality in the World's Religions*. Oxford: One World.

Partridge, Christopher (ed.). 2004. *New Religions: A Guide. New Religious Movements, Sects and Alternative Spiritualities*. New York: Oxford University Press.

Partridge, Christopher. 2005a. 'Preface to the Third Edition', in Christopher Partridge (gen. ed.), *The New Lion Handbook: The World's Religions*. Oxford: Lion Hudson, 9.

Partridge, Christopher. 2005b. 'Phenomenology and the Study of Religion', in Christopher Partridge (gen. ed.), *The New Lion Handbook: The World's Religions*. Oxford: Lion Hudson, 14–18.

Penelhum, Terence. 1997. 'Christianity' in Harold Coward (ed.). *Life after Death in World Religions*. Maryknoll, New York: Orbis Books, 31–47.

Platvoet, Jan G. 1992. 'African Traditional Religions in the Religious History of Humankind', in G. ter Haar, A. Moyo and S.J. Nondo (eds). *African Traditional Religions in Religious Education. A Resource Book with Special Reference to Zimbabwe*. Utrecht: Utrecht University, 11–28. Reprinted 1993, *Journal for the Study of Religion* 6 (2): 29–48.

Platvoet, Jan G. 1996a. 'The Religions of Africa in their Historical Order', in J. Platvoet, J. Cox and J. Olupona (eds). *The Study of Religions in Africa: Past, Present and Prospects*. Cambridge: Roots and Branches, 46–102.

Platvoet, Jan G. 1996b. 'From Object to Subject. A History of the Study of the Religions of Africa', in J. Platvoet, J. Cox and J. Olupona (eds). *The Study of*

Religions in Africa: Past, Present and Prospects. Cambridge: Roots and Branches, 105–38.

Platvoet, Jan G. 2004. 'Beyond "Primitivism": "Indigenous Religions"'. *AASR Bulletin* (21), 47–52.

Popper, Karl L. 1959 [1935]. *The Logic of Scientific Discovery*. New York: Basic Books.

Puttick, Elizabeth. 2004. 'Shamanism', in C. Partridge (ed.). *New Religions: A Guide. New Religious Movements, Sects and Alternative Spiritualities*. Oxford: Oxford University Press, 292–3.

Pyysiäinen, Ilkka. 2003. *How Religion Works. Towards a New Cognitive Science of Religion*. Leiden: Brill.

Raftopoulos, Brian. 2003. 'The State in Crisis: Authoritarian Nationalism, Selective Citizenship and Distortions of Democracy in Zimbabwe', in A. Hammar, B. Raftopoulos and S. Jensen (eds). *Zimbabwe's Unfinished Business. Rethinking Land, State and Nation in the Context of Crisis*. Harare: Weaver Press, 217–42.

Raftopoulos, Brian. 2004. 'Current Politics in Zimbabwe: Confronting the Crisis', in David Harold-Barry (ed.). *Zimbabwe: The Past is the Future*. Harare: Weaver Press, 1–18.

Ralls-MacLeod, Karen and Harvey, Graham. 2000. 'Introduction' in K. Ralls-MacLeod and G. Harvey (eds). *Indigenous Religious Musics*. Aldershot and Burlington: Ashgate, 1–21.

Rambachan, Anantanand. 1997. 'Hinduism' in Harold Coward (ed.). *Life after Death in World Religions*. Maryknoll, New York: Orbis Books, 66–86.

Ranger, Terence. 1985. *Peasant Consciousness and Guerrilla War in Zimbabwe: A Comparative Study*. London: James Currey.

Ranger, Terence. 1992. 'The Invention of Tradition in Colonial Africa', in E. Hobsbawm and T. Ranger (eds). *The Invention of Tradition*. Cambridge: Cambridge University Press (Canto Edition), 211–62.

Ranger, Terence. 1999. *Voices from the Rocks: Nature, Culture and History in the Matopos Hills of Zimbabwe*. Bloomington, Indiana: Indiana University Press and Oxford: James Currey.

Rattray, R.S. 1923. *Ashanti*. Oxford: Clarendon Press.

Richards, Chris. 1997. 'Introduction' in Chris Richards,. (gen, ed,), *The Illustrated Encyclopedia of World Religions*. Shaftesbury, Dorset, Rockport Massachusetts and Melbourne, Victoria: Element Books Limited, 6–13.

Ridgeway, William Henry. 1868. *Striving Together for the Faith of the Gospel*. London: Groomsbridge.

Ridgeway, William Henry [W.H.R.]. 1869. 'The Natural History of Man – Africa'. *The Church Missionary Intelligencer*, New Series (5): 53–60.

Rule, Joan. 2005. 'The Foe of Papua New Guinea', in C. Partridge (gen. ed). *The New Lion Handbook. The World's Religions* (3rd edition, revised and expanded). Oxford: Lion Hudson, 108–109.

Samkange, Stanlake. 1968. *Origins of Rhodesia*. London: Heinemann.

Sharpe, Eric J. 1986. *Comparative Religion: A History*, 2nd ed. London: Duckworth.

Shorter, Aylward. 1975. *Prayer in the Religious Traditions of Africa*. Nairobi: Oxford University Press.

Smart, Ninian. 1977. *The Religious Experience of Mankind*. Glasgow: Collins Fount Paperbacks.

Smart, Ninian. 1999. *World Philosophies*. London and New York: Routledge.

Smith, Edwin W. 1936. *African Beliefs and Christian Faith*. London: The United Society for Christian Literature.

Smith, Edwin W. (ed.). 1950. *African Ideas of God: A Symposium*. London: Edinburgh House Press.

Smith, Huston. 1965. *The Religions of Man*. New York: Harper and Row Perennial Library (first published 1958, New York: Harper and Row Publishers).

Smith, Jonathan Z. 1978. *Map is Not Territory. Studies in the History of Religions*. Leiden: E.J. Brill.

Smith, Wilfred Cantwell. 1964. *The Meaning and End of Religion. A New Approach to the Religious Traditions of Mankind*. New York: Mentor Books.

Smith, Wilfred Cantwell. 1998. *Patterns of Faith around the World*. Oxford: Oneworld Publications (first published 1962 as *The Faith of Other Men*, New York: Mentor Books).

Smith, William Robertson. 1889. *Lectures on the Religion of the Semites*. Edinburgh: Adam and Charles Black.

Söderblom, Nathan. 1933. *The Living God: Basal Forms of Personal Religion*. London: Oxford University Press.

Spierenburg, Marja J. 2004. *Strangers, Spirits, and Land Reforms. Conflicts about Land in Dande, Northern Zimbabwe*. Leiden and Boston: Brill.

Spiegelberg, Frederick. 1956. *Living Religions of the World*. Englewood Cliffs, New Jersey: Prentice-Hall.

Sutcliffe, Steven and Bowman, Marion. 2000. 'Introduction' in S. Sutcliffe and M. Bowman (eds). *Beyond New Age. Exploring Alternative Spirituality*. Edinburgh: Edinburgh University Press, 1–13.

Taylor, John B. 1976. *Primal World Views. Christian Dialogue with Traditional Thought Forms*. Ibadan: Daystar Press.

Tempels, Placide. 1959 [1945]. *Bantu Philosophy* (translated from the French version, *La Philosophie Bantou* by C. King). Paris: Presence Africaine.

Thornberry, Patrick. 2001. 'Indigenous Peoples in International Law: Definition, Claims, Process', in A. Barnhard and J. Kenrick (eds), *Africa's Indigenous Peoples: 'First Peoples' or 'Marginalized Minorities'?* Centre of African Studies: University of Edinburgh, 79–94.

Tiele, C.P. 1973 [1897]. 'Extracts from *Elements of the Science of Religion*' in J. Waardenburg, *Classical Approaches to the Study of Religion: Aims, Methods and Theories of Research. I. Introduction and Anthology*. The Hague and Paris: Mouton, 96–104.

Trigg, Roger. 2003. 'Rationality, Social Science and Religion', in J.S. Jensen and L.H. Martin (eds). *Rationality and the Science of Religion*. London and New York: Routledge, 99–116.

Turner, Harold. 1971. *Living Tribal Religions*. London: Ward Lock Educational.

Turner, Harold. 1986. 'Andrew Walls as Scholar', in J. Thrower (ed.). *Essays in Religious Studies for Andrew Walls*. Aberdeen: University of Aberdeen, Department of Religious Studies, 1–4.

Turner, John W. 1998. *Continent Ablaze. The Insurgency Wars in Africa 1960 to the Present*. London: Arms and Armour Press (Cassell).

Tylor, Edward B. 1871. *Primitive Culture: Researches into the Development of Mythology, Religion, Art, and Custom* (2 vols.). London: J. Murray.

Vitebsky, Piers. 1995. *The Shaman. Voyages of the Soul: Trance, Ecstasy and Healing from Siberia to the Amazon*. London: Duncan Baird Publishers.

Vogt, Carl. 1864. *Lectures on Man: His Place in Creation, and the History of Earth* (edited by James Hunt). London: Longman, Green, Longman, Roberts.

Walker, Jr, Deward E. 1970. *The Systems of North American Witchcraft and Sorcery*. Moscow, Idaho: University of Idaho Press.

Wallis, Robert J. 2003. *Shamans/Neo-Shamans: Contested Ecstasies, Alternative Archaeologies, and Contemporary Pagans*. London and New York: Routledge.

Walls, Andrew F. 1980. 'A Bag of Needments for the Road: Geoffrey Parrinder and the Study of Religions in Britain'. *Religion* 10: 141–50.

Walls, Andrew F. 1983. 'Centre for the Study of Christianity in the Non-Western World, University of Aberdeen, Scotland, *British Association for the History of Religions Bulletin* 39: 10–11.

Walls, Andrew F. 1987. 'Primal Religious Traditions in Today's World', in F. Whaling (ed.). *Religion in Today's World. The Religious Situation of the World from 1945 to the Present Day*. Edinburgh: T. and T. Clark, pp. 250–78.

Walls, Andrew F. 1988. 'Foreword', in P. Bayliss. *An Introduction to Primal Religions*. Edinburgh: Traditional Cosmology Society, v.

Walls, Andrew F. 2004. 'Geoffrey Parrinder (*1910) and the Study of Religion in West Africa', in F. Ludwig and A. Adogame (eds). *European Traditions in the Study of Religion in Africa*. Wiesbaden: Harrassowitz Verlag, pp. 207–15.

Ward, Kevin. 2000. 'Introduction', in K. Ward and B. Stanley (eds). *The Church Mission Society and World Christianity, 1799–1999*. Grand Rapids, Michigan and Cambridge: William B. Eerdmans Publishing Company and Richmond, Surrey: Curzon Press Ltd., 1–12.

Watts, Fraser. 2005. 'The Psychology of Religion', in Christopher Partridge (gen. ed.), *The New Lion Handbook: The World's Religions*. Oxford: Lion Hudson, 26–8.

Werbner, Richard P. 1977. 'Continuity and Policy in Southern Africa's High God Cult', in R.P. Werbner (ed.). *Regional Cults*. London, New York and San Francisco: Academic Press, 179–218.

Westermann, Diedrich. 1937. *Africa and Christianity*. London: Oxford University Press.

Whaling, Frank. 1996. 'Religious Studies', in D.F. Wright and G.D. Badcock (eds). *Disruption to Diversity. Edinburgh Divinity – 1846–1996*. Edinburgh: T. and T. Clark, 151–65.

Whaling, Frank. 1999. 'Theological Approaches', in P. Connolly (ed.). *Approaches to the Study of Religion*. London and New York: Continuum.

Wood, J.G. 1868. *The Natural History of Man: Africa*. London: George Routledge and Sons.

Wood, J.G. 1874–1880. *The Natural History of Man; Being an Account of the Manners and Customs of the Uncivilized Races of Man, Volumes I and II*. London and New York: George Routledge and Sons.

Wright, David F. 1993. 'New College, Edinburgh', in N.M. de S. Cameron (ed.). *Dictionary of Scottish Church History and Theology*. Edinburgh: T. and T. Clark, 624.

Woodhead, Linda and others (ed.). 2002. *Religions in the Modern World: Traditions and Transformations*. London and New York: Routledge.

York, Michael. 2004. 'New Age Traditions', in C. Partridge (ed.). *New Religions: A Guide. New Religious Movements, Sects and Alternative Spiritualities*. Oxford: Oxford University Press, 308–12.

Index